CLAUDE SIMON

CLAUDE SIMON

NARRATIVITIES WITHOUT NARRATIVE

MÁRIA MINICH BREWER

University of Nebraska Press   Lincoln & London

© 1995 by the University of Nebraska Press
All rights reserved
Manufactured in the United States of America
The paper in this book meets the minimum requirements
of American National Standard for Information Sciences—Permanence
of Paper for Printed Library Materials, ANSI Z39.48-1984.
Library of Congress Cataloging in Publication Data
Brewer, Mária Minich, 1944–
Claude Simon: narrativities without narrative / Mária Minich Brewer.
p. cm. Includes bibliographical references and index.
ISBN 0-8032-1261-5
1. Simon, Claude—Technique. 2. Narration (Rhetoric) I. Title.
PQ2637.I547Z58 1995 843'.914—dc20 94-30413 CIP

For D. C. B. M. L. K.

Contents

Acknowledgments, ix
Introduction, xi
Narratives of the "End of Ideology," xx
(Re)Turns of Narrative, xxiii
Like a Narrative: Myth, History, and Genre in the Aftermath, 1
Narrativities of Order and Disorder, 1
Myth versus . . . , 10
Recasting Oedipus, 14
Refiguring Narrative and Cultural Legacies, 31
Narratives of Legacy, 32
Legacies of Narratives, 45
Times of Narrative Legacies, 66
Parody in Postmodernity: Replication and Cultural Critique, 73
Parody of Narrative, 83
Parody in Revolution, 88
General and Particular Mobilizations: Gender, War, and Narrative, 113
Women and the War Machine, 119
From Particular to General Mobilizations, 130
Remarks on an Aesthetic of Disaster, 137
Notes, 149
Bibliography, 163
Index, 179

Acknowledgments

To those who have helped to bring this project to fruition, I express my sincere thanks. I am deeply grateful to Daniel Brewer, my first reader, whose generosity and agility of spirit have been of inestimable importance to this book. My heartfelt thanks go to Maria Paganini and Eileen Sivert at the University of Minnesota for combining intellectual support with feeling and humor. I thank Timothy Murray, Elizabeth Guthrie, Jane Newman, John Smith, and Winifred Woodhull, whose friendship and sense of dialogue have been of so much value. Ross Chambers and Renée Hubert have been exceptionally generous. In my graduate years, at the State University of New York at Buffalo and Yale University, I was fortunate to have had as teachers many challenging and gifted people, among whom I thank Olga Bernal for inspiring me early on to work in critical thought and experimental writing. I appreciate Claude Simon's kind interest when I began this project. Some of the ideas in this study were first presented in the context of seminars, so I want to thank the students at the University of Minnesota for their participation. I am pleased to acknowledge grants and leaves from the University of Minnesota that have allowed me time for research and writing.

I thank the publishers who have given permission to use material previously published as articles, parts of which appear here in a revised form. "An Energetics of Reading: The Intertextual in Claude Simon," *The Romanic Review* 73, no. 4 (Nov. 1982): 485–504; "Recasting

Oedipus: Narrative and the Discourse of Myth in Claude Simon," *Stanford French Review* 9, no. 3 (Winter 1985): 415–34; "Narrative Fission: Event, History, and Writing in *Les Géorgiques*," *Michigan Romance Studies* 6 (1986): 25–39, Department of Romance Languages of the University of Michigan; and "Parodies, répliques, écritures" and "Histoires complémentaires: quêtes symboliques et syntaxes réinventées," *La Revue des Sciences Humaines* 220 (1990): 157–71, 180–83.

Introduction

No this is not a disentanglement from, but a progressive knotting into.
—THOMAS PYNCHON

This book's objective is to elaborate the notion of "narrativities without Narrative" as a condition for understanding the cultural formations and critical interventions of contemporary writing. It is devoted, unapologetically, to a single author, yet the questions raised in its readings involve the status of narrative in a variety of present-day literary and cultural formations. My readings pursue the intersections between the narrative elements of literature and of material and symbolic culture, history, and technology. They address the ways in which postmodern narrative mediates an unsettling, back-and-forth movement that shifts between general, universalizing concepts of narrative order and the particular formations of relationships and events. Focused on the work of one of the most inventive and challenging French novelists of the second half of the century, the 1985 Nobel laureate Claude Simon, this study reevaluates the force and potential of the narrative paradigm for cultural and critical understanding by considering the workings of narrativity in his writing.

Simon's work has been the object of many fine, sustained readings, which have variously interpreted it as being phenomenological, modernist, elemental, formalist, realist, new novelist, deconstructive, and so on. It has also provided the point of contact for intense debate between, on the one hand, proponents of formal understandings of fiction generated from within language and, on the other, those stressing the importance of representation, history, and visibility.[1] Critics often discuss either the narrator-identified novels (from *Le Vent* to *Histoire* and *Les Géorgiques* to *L'Acacia*) or those in which such a focus is not individualized (the last third of *La Bataille de Pharsale, Orion aveugle, Les Corps conducteurs, Triptyque, Leçon de choses, La Chevelure de Bérénice, L'Invitation*). Yet the divergence between these two readings, which is symptomatic of a more widespread uncertainty as to the relationships between history and textuality, needs to be reevaluated. Taking a cue from Celia Britton's reading of the contradictory desire for representation and textuality in Simon, Fredric Jameson has recently reframed the historical and the formal novels by referring them both to the postmodern.[2] To account for the alternation between the personal, modernist, Faulknerian texts and the impersonal, postmodernist ones, Jameson takes the latter as the common model for Simon's distance from both aesthetics, which are reproduced in the form of pastiche and bravura imitation.[3] Both aspects, however, need to be read in a less dualistic framework, one that does not finally restore the opposition between content (personal) and form (impersonal), representation and textuality, and then dialectically resolve their difference to the benefit of formal reproduction alone. By exploring the narrativities of Simon's work, I seek to avoid reducing it to any one of these aesthetic orders.

This book is not intended as another general theory of narrative, whose totalizations, exclusions, and ideological aims are progressively dismantled in Simon's writing. In my readings I trace the turning of narrative into figure and figure into narrative. Indeed, reading figures of narrativity constitutes a particularly effective form of resistance to universalizing narratives in literature, social communication, and theory. It provides insight into the symbolic and material formation of historical, social, and cultural situations. At the same time, however, my analyses do not continue along the well-traveled antinarrative path opened up by Jean Ricardou's formal notion of fiction generated by language alone. Simon's own insistence on privileging "word for word" textuality held in the "present of writing" certainly has encouraged critics to pursue the linguistic and semantic relays in his work.[4] Nonetheless, although the analyses in this book also privilege intensive readings of Simon's writing, they do so with a goal different from analyses focused on its microtextual properties. Skillful as these are in providing a description of textual configurations, they do not consider the question of narrative or narrativity to be significant in the formal relationships they describe. These accounts thus risk reproducing some of the dominant narrative orders that organize ideology.

Simon's writing shows narrative orders to be precisely those that enact cultural repression in the service of power, habit, and ideological and technological mobilization. Rejecting the "logic of narrative" as being didactic, arbitrary, and ideologically deceptive, Simon explores the dynamic possibilities of description realized through the metaphorical nature of language, its knots and crossroads of meanings.[5] He never dismisses narrative order as being "merely" a matter of formal conventions, nor does he underestimate its pervasiveness and powers. On the contrary, he identifies narrative as a powerful agent of some of the most violent events to which an individual in twentieth-century history, society, and culture is subject: those of dogmatism, terror, and ideology. His understanding of narrative, which he also calls "instituted meaning," is thus by no means a formal one; narrative for him is a general order and the order of the general that permeates all discourse, language, and representation. His essay *La Corde raide* critiques narrative representation as distorting phenomena and experience, giving them an order or form they do not possess. Increasingly, this critique leads in his fiction to a series of encounters with narrative representation in its most general and particular articulations. In the aftermath of war, Simon's writing returns to the detail and the trace, from the fragments of which he invents a new function for the narrative figure.

Simon has described the situation after World War II and Auschwitz as one in which art, ideology, and humanism were no longer possible. He notes a widespread return to the "primordial, to the elementary, to matter, and to things."[6] In postwar visual art, for instance, he remarks a pervasive "dropping of the gaze and the narrowing of the visual field." Such art, based on not the "deceptiveness of *trompe l'oeil*, but collages and constructions," "exists only to show its constituent parts." Speaking of his writing as the return to the "ground" or the "elementary," Simon has provided formulations of keen interest for the question of narrativities without narrative. He refers, for example, to "the progressive disappearance of the fictive, which leaves only a narrow margin of maneuver. I only try," he says, "as best as possible, to tell stories and memories, to describe things, images." His idea is to return to things: "reprendre les choses en enlevant leurs noms propres" ("take things back by removing their proper names").[7] These statements seem to confirm what critics take to be Simon's desire to attain formal, linguistic credibility by eliminating moralizing and ideological fables from writing. In fact, however, they demonstrate that his writing resists the narrative orders deployed in fiction's abstract concepts and proper names by locating itself within a new understanding of the conditions, means, and ends of narrative practices as such.

I argue in this book that the critique of narrative in Simon's writing is founded on particular figures of sociality, material and symbolic culture, and history. His remarkable commitment not only to description but to describing the particular as a figure with virtual narrativity is what makes his work especially valuable for understanding some of the protean forms and effects of contemporary narrative. His work on the narrativity of these figures constitutes a linking agent or hinge that turns writing to its occasions, to its cultural legacies, for instance, in myth, history, parodic replication, visibility, sexuality, the conditions of war, and technology.

Social and historical changes have lent new urgency to the need to grasp cultural narratives in their material, symbolic, and ideological dimensions. Narrative paradigms cannot adequately be grasped within the limits described by the formal sequence of the signifying chain defined exclusively in narratological or logical terms. Some of the difficulties lie in the fact that both narrative and narrativity are often presumed to have an atemporal and universal narrative order or horizon. In the wake of structuralist narratology, the concept of narrative is modeled on a transcendental or rational order that is applied to the internal properties of narrative in terms of concepts such as logic, causality, sequence, and deep structure. On closer scrutiny, however, even the most general narrative order turns out to be modeled on a specific, historically defined aesthetic of narrative.

Some recent theories of narrative have used the term *narrativity* in a variety of ways. Philip Sturgess takes up the following ones: as an immanent story structure based on Greimas's structural model (Shlomith Rimmon-Kenan), as the property of the reader's construction (Robert Scholes), as a property that exists in different degrees in narrative events and minimal stories (Gerald Prince), as the way real events are classifiable as a narrative (Hayden White), and as the putting into sequence of discrete units (Keith Cohen).[8] Sturgess relates narrativity to the Marxist notion of self-contradiction in narratives (Pierre Macherey, Terry Eagleton) as well as to the deconstructive one of double narrative logic or self-deconstruction (Paul de Man, J. Hillis Miller). I will seek to integrate the term both with issues of reading at the textual and figural levels and with the broader narrative paradigms of social construction. (I take up deconstruction and the narrative hermeneutics of history later in this introduction.) Sturgess discusses microtextual elaboration, but the narrativity he extrapolates from it is a singular internal logic of narrative based on a higher-level causality, which I find difficult to locate in postmodern and contemporary writing.[9] Prince's idea that narrativity exists in different degrees in narrative events and minimal stories is interesting because it leads us to take up the question of the limits and diversity of narrativity. D. A. Miller's phenomenological notion of the narratable as a horizon of shifting terms is of importance as well,[10] but because these terms are fixed neither historically nor conceptually, they are unavailable for understanding the type of narrative interplay between text and reference that I pursue. The significance of reading and writing in issues of narrativity cannot be overestimated, but reading is a process not only of unification but of dispersal as well. In this connection Teresa de Lauretis makes what I find to be useful distinctions between *narrative* and *narrativity*. In her poetics of gendered subjects, the object is not "narrative but narrativity." "Narrative theory," she writes, "is no longer nor primarily intent on establishing a logic, a grammar, or a formal rhetoric of narrative; what it seeks to understand is the nature of the structuring and destructuring, even destructive, processes involved in textual and semiotic production."[11] She distinguishes in this way between "narrative (i.e., the growth and flowing of plot into story across the narrative layering of events, actantial functions, and discursive registers) . . . and narrativity (the effective functioning of narrative on and with the reader/ spectator to produce a subject of reading or a subject of vision.)"[12]

Narrativity as I understand it cannot be abstracted from the situated character of writing and reading, which itself cannot be separated from a process of working on the language of detail and figure. Narrativity is protean in its metamophoses, in its ability to slip in and out of general oppositional terms such as inside/outside, logical/illogical, aesthetic/cognitive, textuality/referentiality, figural/literal, general/particular, fictive/nonfictive, literary/nonliterary. Because these are figural, paradigmatic concepts as well as narrative, syntagmatic ones, however, they are actualized both in figures of narrativity and in the narrativity of figures.

As I elaborate it, the narrativity of figures in Simon's writing works to turn texts to their contexts. In the same movement, it accounts for the narrative effects of signifying practices at work in these contexts. Narrative figurality presumes that sense construction, reading, and writing involve making virtual connections between discrete details and that these connections, rather than being governed by conventional narrative order, are engaged in making and unmaking sense without finality. To realize the critical potential of narrativity, it must be defined not a priori but as it emerges in its displaced and multiple figures. There is no way of limiting a figure to a rhetorical trope without that limitation already suggesting a narrative and social construct. Conversely, there is also no limiting of narrative to a formal structure without that structure turning into a figure in which a broader cultural narrativity is always to be read. Once a figure is read narratively, it cannot be reduced either to the formalism of language as play or to the metafictional view of the text's self-theorization. The full potential of a figural reading of narrativity, as well as a narrative reading of figurality, has yet to be explored. Attempts to reduce their relationship to a formal logic misread, I believe, the inventions of postmodern writing and reading. How may these new formations be acknowledged without reducing them to dominant or discredited narrative orders (ideology)? By reading the figures of narrativity and the narrativity of figures, it becomes possible to chart the ways in which fiction identifies the narrative modes at work in cultural texts and contexts and reinvents them in its writing. Paradoxically, then, narrative modalities themselves, such as figure, detail, and positionality in discourse, provide the concepts making possible a critique of narrative from sociocultural, psychoanalytic, and historical perspectives. The notion of narrativity without Narrative helps to make explicit the resistances that literary texts can offer to the hegemonic aims of today's master narratives, including those of general theory, the supposed dominance of decontextualized images (simulacra), phallogocentrism, mobilization, and power. To be able to identify the heterogeneous elements involved in texts' resistances, we need to address more directly the range and diversity of narrative questions that are potentially at issue in figures of narrative.

The legacies of cultural narratives in Simon are neither simple nor limited; they encompass residual and resurgent narratives, which seem at times to contradict his defense of a "formal" aesthetics of language at the expense of its social and political dimensions. Some readers identify phallocentric and misogynist representations of women. For instance, Jean Duffy's compendium of quotes on women in his novels shows the pervasiveness of stereotypical images of them as sex-object, child, animal, and even food, sexist images that perpetuate tiresome oppositions such as that between the good mother and the sexy, available artist's model.[13] She notes the absence of dynamic and self-possessed women whose identities exist outside their dependence on male characters. When women are given agency in history, land management, or commerce (Marie in *L'Herbe,* Batti in *Les Géorgiques,* and the antique dealer in *Histoire*), they are masculinized or described as sexless or celibate. She correctly notes that whereas such images may refer to particular narrators' obsessions in the "personal" novels, in the "impersonal" ones, without the mediation of the individual narrator, they are read as the author's opinions. She also mentions that men's bodies are described as dispassionately and pornographically as women's. Simon's writing and these observations raise certain questions. Can it be said that he reproduces gender stereotypes without providing a way of situating and judging them? Or does he identify them as specific modes and tactics of ideologically motivated discourse? Finally, even granting that he *does* situate them, is that in itself sufficient to offset their negative effects on and for women and men? In the course of this book I argue that Simon's work on the cultural figuration of women, the details and social narratives by which they are constituted, has been extraordinarily underestimated. In fact, the understanding of women comes from his attentive scripting of the details of their lives, bodies, and artifacts, details that are shown to belong to the forces of patriarchy, war, economy, and history.

The counterexample of Alain Robbe-Grillet is depressingly instructive. Despite the antihumanist and antinarrative program he set forth in his essays and novels, the latter may be read more critically from the point of view of their narrativity. What, for instance, is being told through Robbe-Grillet's "vacant" subject position in *Le Voyeur* and *La Jalousie*, his discontinuous descriptions, his shifts in time? It is the narrative of cultural simulacra and the aesthetic "freedom" to subjugate women in a space of formal reproduction. His replication of narrative stereotypes indicates that although he may explicitly "subvert" traditional narrative categories such as subjectivity, anthropomorphism, and realist representation, this does not mean that narrative issues have been done away with. On the contrary, his writing deploys a different, more oblique narrativity of sexual oppression: nonaccountability for and indifference to sexual violence and murder. Critics have justified Robbe-Grillet's recycling of pornographic images by arguing that a narrative frame that systematically disrupts the illusion of the real provides a critical distance from them. They claim that he intended to display, and thereby subvert, the ready-made images of sexual fantasy pervading consumer society. Yet issues of gender relations and the aestheticization of women's sexuality cannot be resolved within formal and fictional terms alone.[14] In other words, the recycling of cultural simulacra in contemporary fiction needs to be treated with regard to their narrative legacies.

The analysis of cultural legacies at the level of their figures of narrativity promises to cast light onto questions of violence and gender, of sexist ideologies and their critique. It has the potential to intervene by blocking the process whereby the marginalizing of women and racial and economic others is reproduced. As the methods of psychoanalytic, feminist, poststructural, and cultural critique show, the "constructivist" aspects of the social bond emerge in the very language and images that describe the subject's position in social discourses and representations.

Narrative paradigms and their cultural legacies are all-important for understanding a text's figuration of relationships to others, environments, time, objects, events, and actions. In sum, fiction tells us much about the multiple and heterogeneous discursive and figural elements that construct realities. In my readings I take the "constructivist" argument beyond that of describing themes or authorial motivation to focus on the specific figures of writing that narrativize cultural legacies. I question whether the rejection of "narrative representation" in Simon (and postmodern writing) is sufficient for understanding what is possibly the more radical dismantling and refiguring of narrative in his or any writing. This dismantling results not in an abandoning of narratives but in an exploration of their most constitutive features. Such a reading of narrativities without narrative can tell us the most about the processes of reproducing and inventing cultural narratives both explicitly and implicitly, consciously and unconsciously, in writing and culture.

In much experimental writing today, traditional narrative representation is thematized as suspect and often appears in forms that are negative and parodic. In addition, critics' repeated references to the terms *antinarrative* or *nonnarrative* reveal the degree to which narrative is believed to be in retreat, devalorized in favor of the notion of languages, discourses, and texts. Narrative representation has symbolized what avant-garde writers reject: the mimetic representation of reality, narrative omniscience, identity, ideological thesis, the logic of causality, teleology, and truth. It has been taken as the umbrella concept through which the transcendental subject unifies notions of causality, plot, space, and time—in short, historical representation. Narrative, however, is far from being a field of reference that we can claim to have moved beyond once and for all. In a sense, the crises of the postmodern, including those of subjectivity, agency, historical teleology, and truth, all imply at some level a symbolic, if not a hermeneutic, understanding of the idea of narrative representation. Yet the persistent narrativity in contemporary literature assumes forms so radically altered that they elude analyses that take narrative to be determined by one model alone, the anachronistic model of the universal subject's self-presence in the unity of space, time, and teleology.

Narratives of the "End of Ideology"

What are some of the issues involved in rethinking narrative terms? Narrative appears to function in a paradoxical way at the present time, when belief has waned in any encompassing, universal narrative of knowledge, history, and subjectivity.[15] The decline of master narratives calls into question the continued value of narrative as an epistemological model and mode of cognition.[16] As master narratives become denaturalized, they lose their role as an integral, irrefragable part of thinking, perceiving, and being. They are seen instead as *ways* of thinking, perceiving, and being. Formerly a general horizon of possibility framing representation, narrative becomes an object of analysis whose particular rules, functions, and instances must be charted. This remapping and the transformation of the narrative paradigm since World War II are among the most challenging issues of postmodernism.

What is called theory's antihistorical impulse is closely related to a widespread desire following the war for the "end of ideology." Insofar as ideology is transmitted through discursive modes, the discourses ordering them were identified as suspect forms of ideological representation.[17] The relationships between military, political, and intellectual history are assuredly much too complex to be treated in mimetic terms alone. Marked by the legacies of war *and* its discourses, the postwar "era of suspicion" (Nathalie Sarraute) is characterized also by the appearance of formalism, structuralism, and semiotics. These models implied that by returning to the very conditions of possibility of signification (to its organizing systems and governing structures), one might neutralize the social and political thought that had programmed war, genocide, nuclear death, and the cold war. The famous disappearance of the humanist concept of "man," announced by Theodor Adorno and taken up by Michel Foucault, distributes "man" among sciences and disciplines as an object of inquiry and confirms the concept's atomization in the face of this century's successive and continuing atrocities.

It is in the postwar context that narrative representation wanes as a naturalized model of intelligibility and that intense scrutiny is given to its modes, genres, and functioning. Borrowing from structural linguistics and anthropology, narratology produced two different definitions of narrative, one instrumental, the other anthropological. The instrumental definition of narrative describes it as a set of specific conventions, codes, and techniques that tells a story.[18] Narratology's other definition is anthropological, that of the life story, as drawn by Roland Barthes's universalizing compass: "Carried by articulated language, spoken or written, fixed moving images, gestures, and the ordered mixture of all these substances; narrative is present in myth, legend, fable, tale, novella, epic, history, tragedy, drama, comedy, mime, painting . . . stained glass windows, cinema, comics, news item, conversation. . . . Caring nothing for the division between good and bad literature, narrative is international, transhistorical, transcultural: it is simply there, like life itself."[19] Yet Barthes also establishes a narrative immanence separate from other social, ideological, and economic systems; he ends by dividing narrative from world, temporal logic from history, form from context, and words from things.

Even the most restrained, instrumental definition of the structural logic of plot, causality, point of view, and subject of utterance already fully entails an anthropological notion of narrative in culture and institutions, but some of the difficulties in treating narrative are also the source of its critical potential. Whenever attempts are made to limit narrative to the formal properties of communication (sender/receiver, time, and plot), it becomes generalized on a symbolic level by the very terms that would contain it. The interplay and tension between these two tendencies in narrative analysis need to be explored more thoroughly rather than dismissed as the insufficiency of either one theory or the other (instrumental or anthropological, communicative or symbolic). The notion of narrative in both implies a discursive and situational understanding of questions of beginnings and endings, causality, subjectivity, and temporality. An example lies in Ferdinand de Saussure's structural linguistics, which is significant because of its influence on the study of narrative. For Saussure, the nature of the sign is arbitrary, but that arbitrariness functions only at the level of *langue*, the grammar of language. As *parole*, the sign is drawn into the realm of problems of motivation, such as those involving the subject of enunciation, positionality in discourse, figurality, and so on. Although the structural study inspired by Saussure shifted analysis to levels at which social, historical, and ideological forces supposedly did not intervene, except insofar as they were filtered by the grids of systems, the opposite was the case. The so-called retreat from ideology in the study of structural systems in anthropology, semiology, and literary theory was in fact involved in reproducing a broad range of social, political, and historical narratives.[20]

Read in the context of structural-formal analyses, the content of "cold-war" fiction was believed to have migrated into form, locating itself especially in the self-reflexive turn of modern writing. This, at least, was one of the literary versions of structuralism's linguistic turn. "New novel" experimentation provided impetus for text-oriented analyses and, later, reader-oriented ones (reception aesthetics, reader response). Thought to take writing and fictionality as their subject and content, these novels were read in terms of their modes of textuality, autotextuality, and intertextuality. Critics especially sought out devices they called antimimetic and antinarrative, whose demystifying strategies were designed to free the novel from the tenets of realism and its modes of representation. In France the idea of narrative was often used interchangeably with a Balzacian "realism" that avant-garde writing was intent on undoing. Criticism's methods and those of the literary text it analyzed at times appeared to replicate each other, with theory and practice becoming two distinct genres of a common formalism. Such "specular" theories devalorize aspects of novels that are too thematic, subjective, expressionist, and representational. Ironically though, what critics dismissed as the "intrusions" of representation and referentiality are in effect precisely the sites where one can locate the social, political, and historical dimensions of language, writing, and interpretation. Frequently offered as *the* defining character of postmodern fiction, the notions of self-representation, self-reflexivity, and autotelism are simply not adequate for the real challenges posed by fiction today. Operating with no regard for the constitution of social and symbolic representations, or rather, narrowing them by means of a formal definition, reflexive metafiction and its theory no longer have any cultural field in which to exercise their much-vaunted critique of narrative representation.

Both the theory and practice of the novel must be reevaluated from the point of view of their narrativities. For example, the work of Samuel Beckett, with its reduction of space, time, character, fiction, and language, engages the very limits of "voice" and narrative intelligibility in general. Writers such as Sarraute, Claude Ollier, and Robert Pinget also need to be reconsidered. In Marguerite Duras's case, feminist and Lacanian approaches to violence and desire in her novels raise many unresolved issues concerning her replication of particular cultural narrativities. Like Beckett and Duras, Michel Tournier is seldom mentioned in discussions of new novel experimentation, yet he articulates the pervasive and perverse narrativities at work in Europe's social, sexual, and historical representations. As interest grows in new writing that cannot be grasped only in the terms of narrative paradigms that are the legacy of Western representation, reading needs to become more attentive to the specificities of different narrativities. The new writing of differences within and without, in greater Europe and the Americas, Africa, Asia, and the Caribbean, requires that we not crudely reduce these differences to familiar Western narrative paradigms. Nor can we skeptically claim that it is possible to speak only from within these paradigms. Instead, readings that emphasize figures of narrativity use the displacing tactics of the particular to dislodge general narrative orders when these function as coercive instruments in the service of power and mystification. In its figures narrativity thus becomes a means to negotiate new relations between the particular and the general, identities and differences, self and others, men and women, narrative and its "others." Pointing up the specificities of context and the intersections of differences, narrativity is a signifying process that splits against itself, questioning its own tendency to emulate the dogmatisms of narrative in general as well as the limits of closed particularisms. By unfolding the figures of narrativity, reading may elaborate more fully the concrete situations in which diverse and powerful discourses arise. Narrativity's critical edge is maintained as it moves between its specific, figural instances and the contexts of narrative genres.[21]

(Re)Turns of Narrative

Because we have no idea what a culture would be in which the meaning of "telling" was no longer known—PAUL RICOEUR

The permutations of narrative paradigms in contemporary writing need to be considered in relation to two opposing tendencies in postmodernity: either to abandon narrative in favor of so-called nonnarrative models or to generalize it as a global metaphor for cognition or representation.[22] In the first instance narrative is jettisoned as an unusable past inherited from the Enlightenment and the nineteenth century. Yet to discard it, as some postmodern theorists do, is to miss the changes that its forms, functions, and significance have undergone in modern history and thought. At most, critics who would dismiss narrative as excess baggage concede that the narrative paradigm is still present, recycled as the empty forms and simulacra of narrative. It cannot be so readily discarded, however, because of the need to account for narrativities in the making and their continuing significance in signifying practices. These are indispensable for understanding the postmodern precisely because they focus critical discourses on the modes of presentation and the conditions of production, destination, and reception of texts and discourses. Narrativity raises the issue of the relationships between discourses and powers and how different histories come into contact or conflict with one another. If one of the defining characteristics of the postmodern is the heterogeneous coexistence of a number of different, incompatible, and fragmented narratives, then the narrativities of those narratives still need to be explored. The object, though, is not to produce a general narrative (the narrative of canonical narratives) whose universal aims remain continuous and complicit with other forms of intellectual and economic domination.[23] Analyzing a text's narrativity engages readers in the specific, concrete terms and conditions of communication. Such an analysis does not adopt a metanarrative position exterior to its object because it relies on the particular figures that actualize it. Although stories may well be universal, as Roland Barthes claimed, their specific conditions and modes of destination, reception, and reference are not. Attention to the figures of narrativity reveals, and itself involves, practices of resistance to universalizing discourses in general.

The rejection of the narrative paradigm—except as simulacra or the emptying of forms, which Barthes identified as the condition for instituting mythological or ideological discourse—enfolds a number of questions. What narrative legacies are possible in the age of technology and of mechanical reproduction? How are they constituted? What do they tell? When the postmodern is thought to be governed by total accommodation with the reproduction of culture's simulacra, as it is in Jean Baudrillard's idea of generalized simulacra and in Jameson's mapping of the postmodern logic of capitalism, does narrative merely represent a rear-guard action? Is it the last stand of a nostalgic return to the subject, identity, truth, and history? This study argues that it is not. Significantly, in attempts to minimize the power of narrative order, description comes to occupy the place of narrative, becoming the scene on which the society of the spectacle and its simulacra are obstensibly free to perform unfettered by the narrativized past.

Georg Lukács, writing in 1936, seems to anticipate the terms of current debates when he ascribes to different periods in history the dominance of either experiencing or observing, the priority of either narration or description.[24] For Lukács the dehumanization of social life is tied to the descriptive method itself which he identifies as the inevitable product of capitalism (127). Setting up a dialectic between description and narration, he states axiomatically that "description contemporizes everything. Narration recounts the past" (130). Whereas narrative relates objects and their function to concrete human experience, description constructs an illusory present in which "the spatial 'present' confers a temporal 'present' on men and objects" (130). Lukács identifies the waning of epic signification in the post-1848 ideological crisis, which is exemplified by naturalist fiction's formal methods. The novel's disintegration into "disconnected and autonomous details" (136) is a "kaleidoscopic chaos" where "lifeless, fetishized objects are whisked about in an amorphous atmosphere" (133). Roundly condemning the plurality of disconnected perspectives over which the author has no comprehensive vision, Lukács regrets the passing of the contract between subject, history, and aesthetic order. Description is at once an effect and a further cause of the loss of both epic and artistic significance, whereas narrative guarantees and legitimates both historical and aesthetic order. Lukács's paradigm is observation versus involvement, disorder versus order, object versus subject, present versus past, aesthetic pseudo-order versus epic order of historical and social contradictions, alienation versus integrated social struggles. The terms, though certainly not the valorizations, of these oppositions remain much the same in current debates on the significance of description or narration for postmodern fiction and theory.

Taking into account the importance of description in postmodern fiction,[25] certain literary theorists have argued against the ways in which it may be subsumed by narrative structures, logics, and grammars. For Philippe Hamon, "there is always some narrative in description and vice versa," with narrative and description in constant interaction in reading. Hence, narratological and structural approaches err in making the deep structure of narrative independent of its "semiotic manifestations and its stylistic investments."[26] He locates in description the text's presuppositions, the place where it engages with a society's encyclopedic knowledge or its archives: "description . . . the text's memory, is always more or less 'memorandum' or 'memento'" (45, my translation). In experimental writing, description disengages readers from the story or plot and brings them back to the text's materiality, reengaging them in a lexical "apprenticeship" (264–65). Paradoxically, so as to prevent description's subordination to narrative, Hamon invokes concepts that arguably have their own narrativity (structure of utterance, destination-reception, "apprenticeship," "memory") and serve to bring that of description into focus.[27] For Gérard Genette, however, description has an irreducible narrative finality and remains the auxilliary of narrative.[28] Because he argues that modern literature has, in a reflexive turn, moved away from representation, he takes even the priority it gives to description to be an aspect of narrative. Description is narrativized, in other words, in the act and temporality of writing.[29]

Deconstructive readings intervene pertinently in the postmodern debates centering on the privilege of description over narration. Jacques Derrida raises questions of origin and telos, destination in general, the logic of writing as supplement, and the parergonal logic of frames where the inside is located on the outside and vice versa. A more literary deconstruction would seek to undo the opposition between descriptive and narrative modes, between the metonymic contiguities of the syntagmatic chain and the metaphorical identities of the paradigmatic, between allegory and symbol.[30] "Narrative is the allegorizing along a temporal line of this perpetual displacement from immediacy."[31] The distinction between narrative and description in literary texts is deconstructed in the supplementary logic governing that opposition itself; description is always bordered and exceeded by narrative, and narrative is always bordered and exceeded by description. In American deconstruction, the tension between them is displaced onto the constative and the performative, onto the terms, that is, of J. L. Austin's speech act theory. It appears as the distinction between what the text states in a constative or descriptive mode and what its figural language *does* in a performative or narrative mode.[32] The result is that deconstruction privileges the performative as a register of narrative agency embedded in the rhetoric of the text.

To the extent that deconstruction investigates narrative "elements in the very rhetoric of historical, philosophical, and psychoanalytic texts," it has been thought to contribute to a "poetics of narrative fiction" rather than to undermine it.[33] It uncovers narrative in nonnarrative texts, and fictionality in nonfiction texts, and hence does away with "narrative fiction" as a separate category. But Derrida in fact undermines a positive narrative poetics by considering the implicit divisive laws governing the law of genre. "It is precisely a principle of contamination, a law of impurity, a parasitical economy. In the code of set theories, if I may use it at least figuratively, I would speak of a sort of participation without belonging—a taking part in without being part of, without having membership in a set. The trait that marks membership [*appartenance*] inevitably divides, the boundary of the set comes to form, by invagination, an internal pocket larger than the whole."[34] What he names the (re)mark of *appartenance* (part-icipation) is constitutive of art, literature, and poetry. The paradox of an aesthetic corpus is that the supplementary and distinctive trait defining it as art or narrative ("novel," "poetry," etc.), which is a mark of its inclusion, does not itself belong to any genre or class of texts.

Deconstructive readings work against structuralism's and phenomenology's formal tendency to situate writing and textuality on an atemporal, present *scene*. Yet deconstruction is itself deemed to be ahistorical, more concerned with tracing the continuities of metaphysical thought (a transcendental master narrative if ever there were one) than with historical, cultural, and social discontinuities and change. When deconstructive critics focus on the operations of specific literary texts, they make part of their very practice the negotiation between general and particular that all literary theory (and communication) presupposes but does not necessarily problematize. They extrapolate an understanding of the laws governing contextual realities from the laws inherent in linguistic and rhetorical modes. J. Hillis Miller argues that such realities are generated from within the rhetorical situation of reading itself: "If there is to be such a thing as an ethical moment in the act of reading, teaching, or writing about literature, it must be sui generis, something individual and particular, itself a source of political and cognitive acts, not subordinated to them. . . . There must be an influx of performative power from the linguistic transactions involved in the act of reading into the realms of knowledge, politics, and history."[35]

Thus, it is not that literary deconstruction is unconcerned with the social, political, and cultural domains but rather that it miniaturizes them by containing them within the drama of performative versus constative language, the narrative versus descriptive rhetoric of texts. Its procedures reveal skepticism as to the possibility of knowing cultural and historical forces except insofar as they are transformed into, and function according to, deconstructive terms.[36] In other words, the encounters between different cultural narrativities do not enter the sphere of deconstruction except to the extent that they are already rendered deconstructible. The project of undoing metaphysical oppositions has proved valuable for the detection and critique of Eurocentrism, phallogocentrism, and other such master narratives. Nevertheless, a too narrowly conceived literary deconstruction does not sufficiently allow the powerful and diverse cultural forces involved in discursive transactions, social communication, and the politics of positionality to enter its language. The impassiveness of its discourse locates tension not in social interactions but in the controlled logic of the aporia and the indeterminacy of meaning. This logic will always have the last word as long as it is generated from within literary paradigms alone. The logic governing the opposition between general and particular, narrative and description, ensures their deconstruction—before they can be inflected by cultural narrativities. Thus, the exploration of narrativities without Narrative has deconstructive moments or movements, but these do not have deconstructive ends because cultural narrrativities cannot be described according to the terms of any singular law of narrative, even a deconstructing double or aporetic logic.

In general, "descriptive" models of criticism, stressing function, performance, and technique, do not in fact escape narrative determinations. Some of these theories' most insightful moments in fact occur when they detect implicit cultural narratives in the very procedures of both fiction and theory. Yet because theory may well be "mobilized" by the objects and issues it attempts to describe at a distance from itself, it also reproduces the determinations and conditions of an immanent and transcendent technological horizon.[37] This mobilization is at stake, for instance, in the project of mapping the apparatus of the simulacrum currently underway in image and media studies. It also raises important questions concerning the relevance of narrative for postmodernity. In cultural and media studies antinarrative or pronarrative debates are actually about something else, namely, the relevance of a narrative understanding in the technological culture and society of the postmodern age. The most inventive works in postmodern literature and theory tell precisely of the tangents between the narrative and the technological, which they reinvent without merely reproducing. We need to conceive of ways to speak about the figures of narrativity involved in this encounter to understand their local and global effects. In sum, narrative culture today opens onto the interrelation of technology and narrativity, epistemology and aesthetics—in short, the field of the general and the particular.[38]

If one tendency in postmodernity is to abandon narrative in favor of nonnarrative models, a second is to generalize narrative paradigms in a variety of fields, a practice that accounts for the interdisciplinary return of narrative. Although it reduces narrative functions to a "grammar" of stories, structural narratology is an important precursor on which later interdisciplinary extensions of narrative are modeled. Reference to the narrative model serves to link interdisciplinary work in a variety of domains (epistemology, history, literature, hermeneutics, feminist and gender studies, psychoanalysis, semiotics, film, and postcolonial studies). Whether this common reference signals a new narrative hegemony hinges on how narrative is used and to what ends. In interdisciplinary domains the narrative model reveals the functioning of "literary" elements that otherwise could not be appreciated: fictionality, discursive enunciation, positionality, permutations in narrative, and figurality. Through this turn to the narrative model, various disciplines reflexively make reference to their own discursive condition in a field of conflicting cultural and social forces. In a sense, the phenomenon of interdisciplinarity itself may be one of the most revealing symptoms of the powerful encounter between narrativistic and technological representations in our time.

Paul Ricoeur's work on the underlying hermeneutic of narrative and history intervenes pertinently in this encounter. Narrative emplotment, or *mise en intrigue,* is the experience of time that mediates between event and history/story.[39] Narrative is not used here as a loose analogy for articulating cognition and language; rather, it is the hermeneutic means whereby a temporal model of experience and a narrative structure are used to interpret each other.[40] What for deconstruction would be a problematic, infinite regression of origins is for Ricoeur the opportunity to accord to experience an "inchoative narrative," the transcendental horizon of "the as yet untold stories of our lives that constitute the pre-history, the background, the living imbrication from which the told story emerges" (1:75–76). Significantly, the story's emergence relies on the subject, whose thought is at work in any narrative configuration. Resisting the limitation of narrative to genre, technique, or atemporal logic, Ricoeur's hermeneutic is founded on the subject's experience of time and on the notion of human action, intention, and identity. Narrativizing the subject's experience of time and making the narrative phenomenological, as Ricoeur does, serve to ground both experience and narrative in something other than text, linguistic structure, or semiotic system. Skeptical of announcements proclaiming the death of narrative paradigms, Ricoeur detects such paradigms in the most antinarrative conceptions. The evolution of modern literature has brought it "to blur the limits between genres, and to contest the very principle of *order* that is at the root of the idea of plot" (2:7), but he insists that there always remains in literature a formal principle of configuration which for him is the concept of *mise en intrigue,* that is, the synthesis of the heterogeneous.

In the light of Ricoeur's narrative hermeneutics of time, experience, and fiction, the narrative underpinnings of a variety of interdisciplinary epistemologies become evident. In this sense Ricoeur's work is not only important for philosophy, history, and literature, but also essential as a contribution to thinking about and articulating the experience of the particular and a general *epistēmē*. It is an aesthetic theory located in the powerful nexus of the narrativistic and the technological as the coexistent horizons of our time. A narrative hermeneutics modeled on Ricoeur's work will seek to limit the rationalizing power of the technological as it emerges in formal, spatial, and descriptive models. Moreover, Ricoeur's insistence that narrative (and not the society of the simulacrum) still emplots relationships between subjects and their communities gives a measure of his contribution to a diversified but not relativistic or particularistic theory of culture. His project of considering both history and fiction in terms of their shared narrativity relies on their "assignment to an individual or a community of a specific identity that we can call their narrative identity" (3:246). It is the cultural dimensions of the communal and individual participation in forms of "narrative identity" that still need to be pursued, both in Ricoeur and elsewhere.

In interdisciplinary encounters such as those between hermeneutics, fiction, and history in Ricoeur, it is important to gauge the power of generalization derived from each of the domains involved and how their differences are constantly negotiated. Recent literary and film theories, for instance, reinscribe narrative poetics in terms of one or more disciplines (e.g., philosophy, psychoanalysis, gender and cultural theory). Interestingly, they are linked by the model of a particular narrative aesthetic that usually remains implicit (e.g., modernist, postmodernist, culturalist). Their claims to specificity as well as generality may be recognized and evaluated by examining the underlying narrativity of different theories.

In de Lauretis's work the discourses of semiotics, psychoanalysis, and feminism provide a dynamic, process-oriented view of narrative signification as a "work(ing) of the codes, a production of meaning which involves the subject in a social field."[41] In narrative theory, despite the shift from structure to process, she finds, on the one hand, that the subject in narrative theory is still predominantly dehistoricized and the narrative process universalized and, on the other, that certain influential critical theories are "anti-narrative programs promoting *jouissance* (Kristeva, Barthes), libidinal dispersal (Lyotard), unbounded *différance* (Derrida), or the undifferentiated affectivity of a free subject free of identification and (self-)representation (Deleuze)" (114). My discussion of deconstruction and postmodern theory shows that the narrativity of these theories needs to be reassessed. I agree with de Lauretis, however, that the task in rethinking narrative theory is to "locate the relation of narrative and desire where it takes place, where that relation is materially inscribed—in a field of textual practices" (106). The need is indeed for a "materially, historically, and experientially constituted subject, a subject engendered, we might say, precisely by the process of its engagement in the narrative genres" (106). It is feminist theory as a reflection grounded in experience and practice that provides de Lauretis with the crucial link between psychoanalysis and semiotics, making them both more responsive to the material and symbolic dimensions of social practices. In the current shift away from the generalizing tendency of theory, the conjuncture of literature, psychoanalysis, and cultural semiosis will continue to be of prime importance, especially if these also consider social relations and their representations. The cultural relations weaving the social fabric may be read, I propose, as the replication or reinvention of specific residual and emergent narrativities.

The process of rethinking narrative is crucially positioned between a general theory and the specific instances of narrative. By placing emphasis on narrative and the figures of narrativity in (Simon's) texts, my study intends to open up the possibilities of new readings that privilege the displacing tactics of the particular at the expense of the general narrative order when the latter functions as a coercive law of ideological mythification (Barthes). Narrativity, in its emergent figurality, may be able to realize new ethical relationships between male and female subjects, between Europe, the West, and its "others." Because its condition of emergence relies on its being linked at the same time to specific figures and global narratives, narrativity points up the specificity of context and the experience of difference. It is a term that splits against itself, questioning its tendency to become dogmatic, universalist, and hegemonic, as well as its tendency to remain enclosed in formal paradigms. Narrativity is the concrete situation of a general narrative. It is also the means whereby narrative's most general terms (subject, time, space, plot, and telos) engage reading in the specific instances and conditions of cultural narrativities. The critical edge of narrativity is maintained precisely by our ability as readers to make explicit the interdependence between narrativity as an emerging law of genre and narrativity as contextualized, figural instances. Taking narrativity as a nontotalizable concept or frame, neither immanent nor transcendent, I do not seek in this book any metanarrative position of exteriority with respect to my object of study, Simon's writing. Nor can the analyses proposed here be contained solely by the particular inflections of a closed corpus of writing. Narrativity, as I find it to be at work in Simon's writing and in my own formulations, is not a transcendental horizon, nor can it be elaborated outside powerful historical, social, and cultural realities. Through its focus on a twentieth-century European writer, this study seeks to elaborate the workings of narrative differences. In Simon's novels the work of refiguring narrativity becomes a linking agent that both discriminates and rejoins myth and history, simulacrum and ideology, image and writing, men's and women's narrative situations, and the conditions of war, technology, and peace.

A considerable number of emerging narratives continue to elude the overview of the master narratives of general theory: the turn to local conditions, genre, milieu, specificity, and cultural, social, and sexual differences. Such particularization is for the most part uncharted (but is it unchartable?) by general theory, symptomatic of the breaking up of "empires" not only in world politics but in critical theory as well. The theory of the postmodern, it seems, has been at once prophetic and deluded. The work of Jean-François Lyotard on the "waning of masternarratives" announced the breaking up of the ideological monopolies of totalitarian systems; that of Foucault on the "waning of the subject" and the reality of "micro-technologies of power" mapped the heterogeneous topoi of the postmodern. Yet postmodern thought may also have miscalculated the force with which the conflicting legacies of traditional identities would return in the wake of, and as a reaction to, the collapse of political and economic empires. Postmodern theory was perhaps too hasty in announcing the end of the master narratives of emancipation in the name of nationalism, identity, and territory. It may also have assumed too readily that just because they are plural, decentered, and diverse, all truly "postmodern" micronarratives of the avant-garde would be free of the legacies and problems of master narratives. Narratives, like cultures, never simply disappear unless they are extinguished, and even when Western culture is supposedly in an antinarrativist moment, as it now is, the denial of narrative priority may itself function as a powerful agent of a dispersive narrativity. Such dispersive narrativity is always susceptible to being mobilized into new totalizing narrative orders. It is important to attempt to understand what the cultural legacies of existing and emerging narratives are and how they configure and are reconfigured by changing social, political, and economic realities. Narratives are not merely reflections of social reality; they do not simply imitate what is already there. But that is not to deny their capacity to refer to the real. On the contrary, the workings of narratives bring to the fore foundational questions involving the reciprocal relationships between words and things, representations and cultures. Narrative modalities alone cannot reconcile text and world, and I am not suggesting that the distinction between language and the real can be overcome simply by using narrative (or narrativity) as the mediating master term. As my readings of Simon propose, problems of narrativity neither deny nor resolve the tension between language and its capacity to refer to the real. These questions, as old as thinking itself, cannot be overcome or resolved. "Reading narrativity," however, provides a specific way of framing them that situates them as discourse and writing in relation to history, social practices, and cultural formations.

Questions of narrative therefore engage issues such as the emergence of new discursive formations and the survival, mutation, and reemergence of older, cultural ones. The latter reappear with a tremendous force in the drive to create community and cohesion in the sharing of stories, values, beliefs, goods, capital, and affect. Such spectral returns of narrative identities may be characterized by extreme forms of xenophobia, anti-Semitism, and misogyny. Narrative is at stake in deadly conflicts and struggles on a local and global scale for identities, nationalities, capital, and image, as much as it is involved in the construction of enabling communal symbols and values. The reading of symbolic cultural narrativities can provide insight into the differences and tangents between these forms of narrative resurgence. It allows us to gauge the persistence of discursive and representational modes in the legacies carried by cultural formations and historical conflicts. Clearly, these are issues too large to be fully dealt with here, issues that go beyond my present aim, which is to reevaluate the legacies of narrative in Claude Simon. They are, however, inescapably present throughout, tracing their own narrativities in my readings.

In postmodernism, I propose, narrativity is both an effective and essential term for negotiating the tension between the particular and the general. Its ability to encompass the tangents of particular discursive situations and figures makes it a valuable means of critical intervention in a number of crucial debates concerning the cultural construction of reciprocities and differences. What the narrativities of cultural formations tell us is that to understand the powerful effects of representation, history, and culture, we need to return to the "ground" of their figural and discursive constitution. In short, we must continue to learn to read their material and symbolic legacies, their narrativities without Narrative.

CLAUDE SIMON

1

Like a Narrative: Myth, History, and Genre in the Aftermath

Narrativities of Order and Disorder

In discussions on the waning of master narratives in the technological age, the narrativization of events continues to raise questions that are not about to go away.[1] Lyotard comments on the multiplicity of "petits récits inconvenants" ("small improper narratives") that arise as a refusal of the canonical narratives of state and capital. These canonical narratives are concerned not with signification or interpretation but with a narrative pragmatics, which is the "ensemble des rapports très compliqués qu'il y a entre celui qui raconte et ce dont il parle, celui qui raconte et celui qui l'écoute, et ce dernier et l'histoire dont parle le premier" ("set of very complicated relationships between the teller and what he speaks of, the teller and the listener, and between the latter and the story told by the former").[2] Discourse programmed by the political assigns these relationships in such a way as to foreclose movement between narrative posts or positions. An effective response to such uses disrupts narrative positions by permuting them, by shifting the positions of sender, receiver, and referent: "Destroy narrative monopolies . . . take away from the narrator the privilege he accords himself. Valorize the no lesser power in listening, on the side of the narratee, and also in the execution, on the side of the narrated."[3] Thus, the sender may occupy the position of the receiver, the receiver that of the sender or the referent, and the referent that of the sender or the receiver. This permutational stratagem does not simply engage a multiplicity of micronarratives continually being adjusted to local conditions by the need for a consensus, which is how a relativist pragmatics would explain it.[4] Indeed, what might appear to be a leveling or relativizing of narratives in the postmodern is in fact a rethinking of narrative's capacity to dismantle, block, and resist master narratives. For Lyotard, genres are incommensurable since there exists no general discourse or totalizing genre that might be invoked as a universal judgment, for each genre has its own "interest," and the "force" of a sentence must be judged with reference to the rules of a particular genre. Nevertheless, linkages and passages between phrases or genres must be forged so as to make possible the presentation of the unpresentable that cannot (yet) be signified.[5] This chapter explores the linkages between genres in Simon's writing and the constitutive role of the fragment with respect to narrative order in myth as well as history.

Narrative in *Le Vent* (*The Wind*) derives as much from the listener as from the speaker, the narrator as the narratee, the writer as the reader, the situation as the story, the genre as the events. Its rather conventional story of inheritance, crime, love, and death is recounted in a discontinuous and fragmentary form. This novel takes up the question of mythmaking and its relation to narrative knowledge in ways that shed light on Simon's later, more radical experimentation. It thematizes problems of knowing as a question of telling, and we find innumerable "theories" of narrative invoked to explain events vaguely perceived and escaping understanding. Like the essays of *La Corde raide* (The tightrope), this novel has been read as Simon's commentary on his own work, and its metafictional passages have been lifted out of their fictional context. Yet the modes of telling presented in such passages also pervade the text's writing and figures whose narrativity emerges in a permutational reading of its genres and narrative positions.

Interpreters have focused on the narrator, who, despite his lack of knowledge, is the main source of the narrative. Comparing *Le Vent* to *L'Herbe* (*The Grass*), Gérard Roubichou comments on the former's references to the narrative process, which relies on the convention of a narrator or writer's presence; he prefers the latter, which stages instead the productivity of writing, language, and narration on the textual level.[6] The distinction made here between a hermeneutics focused on a narrator's presence and a textuality focused on the productivity of writing is a recurrent one in interpretations of Simon. It underlies as well divisions of his work into the modernist, personal novels and the postmodern, impersonal ones. Much of *Le Vent*'s tension lies in the interplay between the narrator's attempt to produce a conventional narrative order and the actual discontinuity of his account.[7] Focusing on the narrator's staging of events ("and I seemed to see him," "I could reconstitute it," "you would have to try and represent it") that presents the story as spectacle, Robert Burden takes his discourse to indicate his mystified reliance on a realist model of representation. The narrator's "position," however, may be considered as the "posting" of a narrative genre among other genres, a post that is itself permuted with those of receivers and frames of reference.

In this sense *Le Vent* raises the question not of narrative perspectivism or relativism but of how we read and produce the narrativities of discourse. Such a notion of narrativities without narrative becomes indispensable for grasping the symbolic configurations of myth, history, representability, and community in the postmodern context. Simon's work can be appreciated when his inventiveness is not limited to a closed textuality but acknowledged to engage the broader issues of narrativity and figurality involved in individual and cultural experience, perception, ideology, and history.

The problem of figure and narrativity is signified through the title, *Le Vent*.[8] The wind stands in tension with the subtitle, "tentative de restitution d'un retable baroque" ("attempted restoration of a baroque altar piece"). The title links and opposes the wind—an unstable, shifting element perceived only in its effects on leaves, detritus, papers, and people—to a narrative project, referred to as the restoration of a votive artwork. The ambiguity of the title cannot, however, be reduced to an opposition between nature and culture, between a physical phenomenon and an aesthetic (narrative) project. The wind figures both an element of and in movement and a similarly dispersive narrative project. Such an aesthetic of restoration is presented, then, as a secondary reconstruction performed on a baroque retable in fragments. *Le Vent*'s full manuscript title is "tentative de restitution d'un retable baroque d'après les restes trouvés dans une chapelle en ruines" ("attempted restoration of a baroque altar piece based on the remainders found in a chapel in ruins").⁹ Its ambiguity lies in the way the wind's sense drifts between a dispersive natural force and a narrative project of restoring disseminated remainders in a space itself in ruins. The tension arises here between a singular order of restoration, modeled perhaps on the romantic narrative of reconstructing ruins, and another narrative figured by the wind's dispersive movement.

This tension is echoed in the novel's epigraph from Paul Valéry: "Deux dangers ne cessent de menacer le monde: l'ordre et le désordre" ("Two dangers ceaselessly threaten the world: order and disorder"). The dualism of order and disorder cannot be taken to be determining, since each must be seen in terms of the specific danger it poses. The threat they pose emerges when the difference claimed to distinguish them is undermined. Just as the wind and the narrative project of restoration cannot simply be opposed to each other, so also order and disorder in general cannot be opposed. Since Valéry's pronouncement was written after World War I, and the novel was written in the shadow of the next, his words may be read as referring not so much to abstract, universalizing concepts of order and disorder as to a constantly recurring and dangerous (dis)order in history. The dangers referred to are also those of narratives that, by appropriating the discourse of difference, seek by force to determine the difference between order and disorder. The object of such narratives of order is to impose one order by eliminating what they claim to be disorder.

In the opening lines the work of citation (restoration, altar piece, baroque, epigraph) begun in the title and epigraph continues in the quotation marks that open the direct speech of someone pronouncing a verdict:

> "An idiot, that's all. Nothing but a fool, an imbecile. And everything you could say or suppose or try to deduce or explain only confirms what everyone could see at first glance anyway: just an idiot, plain and simple. Except they let this one walk around loose and talk to people and sign papers and set off catastrophes. Because apparently doctors classify men like him as harmless. . . ." (9, modified)

The town notary speaks not as an individual subject but from a position of discursive legitimacy that he claims the community, the "everyone" for whom he speaks, bestows on him. Someone speaks to the narrator pronouncing an unequivocal judgment in the name of a law that conflicts with the judgment of other "specialists." What or who decides a person's right to be free or not, to communicate or not, to sign documents or not, to cause catastrophes or not? Simon's writing focuses less on Montès, the person being judged, than on how authority for one classifying power (what can be seen in an instant) is being claimed over others (told, deduced, explained). The lawyer denies the narrativity of his own gaze by presenting it as instantaneous, atemporal, and nonnarrative knowledge. The assertion of the power to classify that denies narrativity does not begin here, however. Valéry's epigraph may be read in terms of the tension between order and disorder, the (narrative) danger of each resting on the classification that determines their difference. Both title and epigraph interpret the lawyer's speech and are in turn interpreted by it.

The citational opening and its aesthetic of reconstruction point up how taxonomic authority proceeds by appropriating the particular events of Montès's story. The narrator, presented as a receiver rather than a sender of stories, reflects on his own and others' retelling of the events, thereby questioning any one version's authority:

> the story, or what he imagined, having, . . . like everybody else, like the heroes of those events, only that fragmentary, incomplete knowledge consisting of an accretion of sudden images (and those only partially apprehended by the sense of sight) or an accumulation of words (themselves poorly grasped) or a welter of generally ill-defined sensations, and everything—words, images, sensations—vague, full of gaps, blanks that the imagination and an approximative logic tried to remedy by a series of risky deductions—risky though not necessarily false: because either everything is only chance and then the thousand and one versions, the thousand and one appearances of a story are also a story, or rather are and constitute *the* story. (10)

This idea of plural versions bears a striking resemblance to Claude Lévi-Strauss's structuralist definition of myth: "There is not one true version of which all others are but copies or distortions. Every version belongs to the myth."[10] Fragmentary perceptions of events and their many versions are opposed to the lawyer's claim to the authority of a singular (non)narrative order. Narrative reconstruction "is a little like trying to stick together the scattered, incomplete debris of a broken mirror, clumsily struggling to readjust the pieces, getting only an incoherent, ridiculous, idiotic result" (10, modified). In this way, the totalizing ambitions of (non)narrative discourse are questioned, and the condition of narrative as fragmentary, plural, and dispersive emerges. A return to the wind's "reading-effects" provides a way to grasp the narrativities involved.

Overall, the novel contains two conflicting figurations of time and order. On the one hand, there exists the temporal model of rationality, causality, and continuity that the narrator detects in the structure of tragedy. This narrative order as resolution appears in the text on a figural level as the irremediable pull and irreversible flow of blood, water, and time toward death and closure. On the other, there exists a narrativity whose temporality, modeled on the wind of the novel's title, is discontinuous, reversible, and aleatory: "time alternately telescoping, immobilizing, or dilating." Time is not threadlike, "a one-dimensional duration along which the event-knots—the past, the present, the future—followed one another without conflict," but "a sort of clotted magma" (171–72). In other words, the novel recapitulates and transforms time in Greek tragedy by splitting its figures.[11] Chronos, a principle of universal order, is displaced by another figure of immortal time, Typhon, the wind of the novel's title. In the final pages the narrator attempts to resolve the difference between the two figurations by restoring them to a single narrative order: "everything beginning all over again, indestructible, even the wind itself beginning again" (254). The final sentence, however, which describes in allegorical terms the wind's eternal return, makes dialectical resolution between order and disorder illusory and denies them any finality: "its strength unimpeded, purposeless, doomed to exhaust itself endlessly, without hope of an end, wailing its long nightly complaint as if it were sorry for itself, envying the sleeping men, transitory and perishable creatures, envying them their possibility of forgetfulness, of peace: the privilege of dying" (254). The figure of the wind, with its "sarabandes de papiers, de feuilles et de détritus" ("the saraband of papers, leaves, and whirling rubbish"), constitutes not only an allegory of time but a metaphor for the narrative dimension of writing and reading. The wind's movement links the elements in the town's global description, a parodic substitute for the "bird's-eye view" of traditional narrative omniscience. As an element of aleatory movement, instability, reversibility, and discontinuity, the wind insinuates itself into characters' voices, their gestures, and the movement of events and time. In short, they come to be figured by the wind, which is itself a figuration of narrative.

Montès has a "troubling" effect on events, the capacity of spreading about him "ce trouble, ce chaos, cette confusion, sa façon non seulement de se mouvoir mais de vous entraîner avec lui" (148) ("this confusion, this chaos, this disturbance, not only his way of moving but of dragging others with him" [156]). The youthful restlessness of Montès's niece Cécile is described as sudden changes of direction, her laughter is characterized as "troubled waters," and her rage (against what may be read as patriarchy) is called "anger without a definite object, directed at once against everything and nothing." Maurice, "one of those bits of debris that all wars leave behind," violently mixes into his racist discourse "Greek tragedy, vague innuendoes, and references to his father the General" (142). The wind is not only an external phenomenon, for its sound and fury (pace Shakespeare and Faulkner) inhabit the discourses of the townspeople, haunting their consciousness: "groaning and raging, not outdoors but somehow inside your own head: voices emptied of meaning, full only of noise and, so it seemed, dust" (241, modified). The narrator states that he himself is drawn by Montès, "dragged on in spite of" himself, into a chaotic world: "time extending like a gray wall with neither beginning nor end, patched with old, peeling posters, their torn edges fluttering in the wind, . . . fragments of texts with neither beginning nor end, no continuity, juxtaposed, self-contradictory" (156). The narrator is also, in this figure, precipitated into a problematic narrativity that is a fitting emblem for time and text in postmodernity. The wind figures this writing not as a formal linguistic productivity but as a dimension of writing's narrativity. The gaps and discontinuities between "fragments of texts with neither beginning nor end" cover and disclose yet other incomplete fragments of texts.

8 *Like a Narrative*

In general, what occupies the spaces between narrative gaps and discontinuities? May those spaces themselves be read as narratives, discourses, or genres? Is there any interpretive position from which the multiplicity of fragments may be hierarchized, its narrative bits and pieces ordered? The significance of these questions can be gauged by considering the notorious blank page in Robbe-Grillet's *Le Voyeur*. This page at once designates and dissimulates Mathias's torture, rape, and murder of "Violette" and materializes the text's complicity in his getting away with them. In other words, discontinuity in Robbe-Grillet gives onto the monomyth of sexual domination in a sadopornographic genre. In Simon the hiatus between fragments renders a plurality of conflicting narratives that his writing does not eliminate and instead explores to the full. A gap on one level at once reveals and conceals another narrative, with its own forms of continuity and discontinuity. Simon's cultural narrative, therefore, cannot be blocked at a formal description of intertextually related fragments. It provides reading with figures of the narrative dimensions of specific cultural texts that constitute these texts' conditions of possibility.

Comparisons of Montès's perceptions with various kinds of conventional narrative order can be better grasped if we take the discontinuities and myopia of his perceptions to evoke a postmodern narrativity. Montès's psychic disorder cannot be contained by the notion of character, for his chaotic reality is linked to types of (dis)order imposed by the discursive and narrative function of language. He is more than a character modeled on *The Idiot*'s Prince Myshkin—or rather, both Dostoyevski's and Simon's novels exemplify (differently) Mikhail Bakhtin's understanding of the modern novel's dialogism as offering an image of language and, on occasion, the dialogism of "stupidity."[12] What Bakhtin calls the "hermeneutics of the everyday" are the "forms of transmission of the other's discourse outside of the novel" (157–58). The novel identifies in these "the formal particularities of the transmission and representation of authoritarian speech" (162). In the dialogism of "stupidity" (the idiot), the novel shows a polemical lack of understanding of others' discourse, of languages that are formalized, canonical, and mystifying because of the names they apply to things and events—language that is, for instance, poetic, pedantic, religious, political, and juridical

(215). The novel stages the world of social conventions by singularizing them in the trope of stupidity. The incomprehension of instituted languages teaches writing and reading "to discover and to construct representations of social languages" (216, my translation). In Bakhtin's sociopoetics it is the novel's capacity to singularize social languages that makes it most apt to be a critical microcosm of "plurilinguisticality" (223) in culture.

Defined thus with reference to narration, social languages, and syntax, Montès's "disorder" finally engages the text's writing as a whole. The narrator situates the figure of Montès with respect to different genres (art, literature, tragedy, comedy, myth), discovering as he does so that the fundamental narrativities of these genres are related to those of social languages. Montès is *like* a narrative, by which I do not mean that the text, in its disorder, simply mirrors his thought. Rather, the contradictions and gaps in his perceptions of things become generalized to the narrative as a whole:

> that incoherence, that brutal, apparently absurd juxtaposition of sensations, faces, words, actions. Like a story with the syntax—subject, predicate, object—missing from every sentence. Like what any newspaper article becomes . . . when your eyes happen to notice the torn page wrapped around a bunch of leeks, and then, by the magic of a few, truncated, incomplete lines, life recovers its arrogant independence, becomes again that disordered abundance without beginning or end or order, the words fresh again, freed of syntax, that stale arrangement, that all-purpose cement the copy editor pours out like a sauce, a sticky *béchamel* to bind, to glue together somehow so as to make them tasty the ephemeral and disparate fragments of something as indigestible as a stick of dynamite or a handful of ground glass. (184)

In the everyday consumption of violence and madness, the narrativity of syntax in fact disarms them as an explosive "real," making them available to the community's indifference. In this extraordinary passage the narrator moves from Montès's phenomenological grasp of the world to a comparison with a "nonsyntactical" narrative, and then to fragments of newsprint whose words retain some of the real danger and violence dissimulated by a narrative syntax of cause and effect. Significantly, Montès's discourse of the detail appears here as an early version of what will become generalized as Simon's aesthetic of the detail, the particular, and description: "with his meticulous attention to detail, to the insignificant" (107). Narrativity is figured in different and unexpected contexts, its effects are multiple and heterogeneous.

Simon's writing seeks to connect the event or story fragment to its narrative enunciations, conditions, and contexts. In this way it provides an understanding of an important distinction between the "postmodern" fragment, which is always accompanied by these frames of reference, and the "mythic" fragment, which supposedly gives unmediated access to the world. Simon links mythic fragments, which pervade his novels, to their narrative situations, relating these as well to the historical problematic of two dangers: order and disorder. In the breech left by discredited narrative orders (the disorder of ideological orders), his writing shows a community's "mythic" ordering of fragments, translating them into fables of mythic significance. In the process, his work intimates that historical reasons exist for our suspicion of mythic coherence and unity. Following a general discussion of myth, my reading will focus on the communal (re)production of myth as discourse and figure.

Myth versus . . .

To read the discrete and pervasive reinscriptions of myth in Simon is to discover that the mythical is linked inseparably to narrative experimentation and constitutes an important aspect of his refusal of traditional narrative. Myth is never simply there, however, nor is it ever there simply. As in much contemporary writing, the reading of myth in Simon needs to pass through diverse relays of narrative, discourse, and figure. Fragmented, split off from a singular narrative horizon, myth no longer works as archetypal theme or structure but is diffused in figures' narrativity.

When interpretation describes the mythical in literary texts, it first offers a definition of myth *as such*, without any account of its intricate involvement with literary writing. Separating these two orders of narrative, however, presupposes that myth and literature can be opposed to each other. The phrase "myth and . . ." has the effect of signifying "myth versus . . ." and generates certain traditional oppositions—of myth, for instance, to history, fiction, modernity, and truth. Indeed, the recurrent critique of myth in Western history is itself part of another history, that of the systematic devalorization and reduction of the mythical when it is brought into confrontation with the philosophical, scientific, and rational.[13]

In his "Petite lettre sur les mythes," Valéry offers some insight into contemporary reevaluations of myth. Rather than assign myth to a stable term in a simple opposition to reason, logic, or civilization, Valéry considers myth's value to be the generalized figure it provides of the working of the concept itself. Each concept is doubled by myth; that is, the concept exists also in the mode of mythical thought. Therefore, according to Valéry, to speak of myth in conceptual discourse is still to mythify, to fabricate once again the "myth of myth to respond to the caprice of myth." He rephrases biblical origins as "in the beginning was the Fable," performatively linking the notion of origin and truth to the mythical as narrative. Fable itself recounts the origin as difference:

> C'est une sorte de loi absolue que partout, en tous lieux, à toute période de la civilisation, dans toute croyance, au moyen de quelle discipline que ce soit, et sous tous les rapports,—le faux supporte le vrai, le vrai se donne le faux pour ancêtre, pour cause, pour auteur, pour origine et pour *fin,* sans exception ni remède—et le vrai engendre ce faux dont il exige d'être soi-même engendré.[14]
> [It is a sort of absolute law that everywhere, in all places, in every period of civilization, in every belief, by means of every discipline, and in all respects, falsehood supports truth, truth takes falsehood as its ancestor, cause, author, origin, and *end,* without exception or remedy, and truth engenders the falsehood from which it insists on being engendered. (My translation)]

Valéry poses falsehood (fable or myth) as that which truth engenders, which grows out or develops historically from falsehood as its negative and forgotten origin. (This argument recalls postmodern theories such as those of Derrida, Jacques Lacan, and Luce Irigaray, in which original truth or conceptual unity is split.) In Valéry's terms, myth would be the

Ur-narrative through which the concept of difference itself is recounted. He detects in the play of fable and truth a specific narrative dimension of ancestry, causality, authorship, origin, and end. According to Lévi-Strauss, myths of origin mark the progress from nature to culture; that is, they define a process of differentiation from undifferentiation.[15] But Valéry might add that myths' narratives of generation undo the dualistic and hierarchical opposition between nature and culture, truth and fable, myth and history. In postmodern epistemology, Lyotard would argue, all narrative is devalorized as being mythic when scientific knowledge (technology) attempts to denarrativize its own procedures.[16]

Whenever myth is opposed to speech as reason, to the *logos* of philosophy, it loses its epistemological legitimacy. It survives, but on the margins of the narratives of truth and knowledge. Structurally, it is their necessary but intractable Other. Thus, while it is tempting to treat myth as a further instance of what Western thought seeks to exclude, myth cannot simply be rehabilitated and recuperated as a desired Other of the rationalist tradition. When myth is taken to be a "vaguely defined force or power . . . presented as an autonomous life-giving force with no fixed structure or form,"[17] it operates as ideology that is (already) mobilized by political power. Treated instead as a type of contextualized language with a motivated form, it effectively reveals the workings of ideology. For Barthes, myth is an ideological representation in language, "speech defined by its intention": "Motivation," he writes, "is necessary to the very duplicity of myth: myth plays on the analogy between meaning and form, for there is no myth without motivated form."[18] Bakhtin as well stresses the "absolute bonding of ideological meaning to language, which is *the* defining factor of mythical and magical thought." The absolute fusion of word with concrete ideological meaning is one of the constitutive features of myth.[19] By focusing on the specific relation between mythical language and ideological meaning, these accounts reveal myth as a means of appropriating language for ideological ends. Mythic language is language whose ideological drive to bond word and meaning blocks dialogism, interpretation, and narrativity.

Some of these issues persist in literary criticism when myth, posed as the origin of literature or its archetypal narrative, functions as a universal symbolic system.[20] Whereas myth is proposed as the historical antecedent of literature, however, its universal and archetypal definition typically places it beyond the scope of history.[21] That is, myth is treated as if it were removed from the ideological representations that characterize the constitution of concrete historical situations in literature. In myth criticism, attributing a universal symbolic function to myth in literature privileges its structuring principle. To paraphrase Lévi-Strauss, the function of repetition (of myth) is to make the structure of the literary text apparent.[22] Myths have retained an essential epistemological function by virtue of their structuring power in characters, prefiguration, parody, and irony.[23] Some critics have sought to ground the contemporary significance of myth in interpretation as such.[24] Despite the changing fortunes of myth, myth and narrative are always contemporary with each other. A means of referring a literary work to both past and present, outside and inside, margin and center, myth appears to defy closure as well as to provide interpretation with a powerful model of narrative order that it can no longer claim for narrative representation as such. Myth, at once similar to and different from narrative representation, remains a problematic substitute for narrative coherence, thereby raising questions concerning its conditions and limits in postmodern writing.

Understandings of myth are based on the largely unexamined assumption that in telling myth no one speaks. In this sense, myth is like *histoire,* history/story as defined by Emile Benveniste, from which is absent the formal apparatus of discourse, that is, the relation of I and you, here and now. In *histoire,* and in the way in which myth is predominantly interpreted, "no one speaks here; the events seem to narrate themselves."[25] *Discours,* or discourse, is a type of language that always includes reference, whether explicit or not, to the discursive situation in which it is uttered or written. Myth, like *histoire,* is considered neither to provide nor to require such a reference. The absence of enunciative marks may be attributed to the fact that myth is communal, pervasive, and anonymous. However, this explanation ignores the discursive character of myth as well as the discursive dimension of community. By examining the narrative and discursive determinations of myth, a better sense can be gained of the cultural dimensions of Simon's rewritings of myth.

14 *Like a Narrative*

Le Vent is not one story but many. In the narrator's and characters' reflections on how a story can be told, the difficulty of assigning meaning to events is foregrounded as a problem of narrative. Simon's writing abuts simultaneously onto myth and narrative through the question of multiple, fragmentary versions. Because the novel always ties "what happened" to how it is retold, linking an occurrence to the genres it might belong to, readers progressively unlearn their fascination with plot and character. They begin to see that the fragmentary perceptions referred to are themselves fragments of a multiplicity of genres only dimly recognized as such, that individuals and events are informed by loose bundles of myths and genres. The logic of character, plot, space, and temporal development, the mainstays of conventional narrative, are displayed as mediated by their genres. Simon's writing shows characters' involvement in a hermeneutic project, which is a process of "trying out" different genres. Similarly, *Le Vent* is not about restoring a unified (mythical) subtext; rather, it is about tracing the mythical in the text's gaps and discontinuities. In its foregrounding of the conditions and forms of story telling, we recognize a postmodernist aesthetics that relativizes any unitary narrative order by fragmentation, discontinuity, multiple intertexts, and self-reflexivity.

Recasting Oedipus

In the opening scene of *Le Vent* the lawyer and the narrator discuss Montès. By returning to the town where he was conceived, Montès injects the past into the present. The town collectively recalls his departure and considers his return as scandalous and against reason. He reactivates what had become "a sort of legend," his mere presence acting as a catalyst for revolt, desire, discord, and wrath. The semantic register or discourse is that of Greek tragedy, a register to which belongs also the "paroxysm of passions" followed by a peace akin to the cathartic resolution of tragedy. Parodic versions of tragedy's chorus appear in the anonymous voice (the "town chronicle"), the lawyer ("a sort of chorus of antiquity"), the group of old men and the women in the beauty parlor ("at the top of their voices under their mitre-shaped dryers"), and finally, the narrator. The town has voice and memory. As in Sophocles' *Oedipus*

Rex, where society is compared to a vessel, a "reeling wreck" whose "timbers are rotten,"[26] the collectivity in the novel fears that without ritualistic forms of order "our universe would collapse like an old house whose beams have rotten through, would crumble in a few seconds into the abyss, the void" (21–22).

Narrating in *Le Vent* involves a communal desire to insert a fragmentary occurrence into an order of representation such as Greek tragedy and myth. Metaphors of the theater, for instance, are invoked as a common site to ground the discontinuous elements of the story. Theatrical references underscore the figural shifts (from particular to general, from fragmentary to motivated form) whereby narrative coherence is traditionally achieved. These references are treated negatively, however; they are called on precisely because they no longer function as ideology, defined by Louis Marin as "a system of representations, beliefs, and ideas whose systematic and arrested [*bloquée*] form is unconscious" (my translation).[27] The narrativity of tragedy emerges precisely when it fails to function as a naturalized narrative order. Simon's writing at once reinscribes and questions certain orders of representation, pointing up the ways a community reactivates tragedy and myth by reassembling disparate cultural fragments. Using these discursive artifacts it attempts to find a common interpretive frame for the creation of cultural ties. Myth elements in *Le Vent,* therefore, are related to genre and may be read: (1) in figures of desire that are repeated and displaced, (2) in figures of enigma and blindness, and (3) in narrative fragments disseminated in words. The question is whether fragment and narrative are simply embedded one within the other (fragment in narrative, narrative in fragment) in a relation of synecdoche (part for whole) or whether the fragment in Simon persists as a nontotalizable detail whose relation to narrative remains problematic because it involves an essentially cultural narrativity.

In the "recasting" reading I propose, certain words and descriptions, overdetermined by their repetition, establish links between figures. Montès perceives the waitress, Rose, sensually, intensely aware of blood pulsating through her veins (76). He has the impression of being reduced to something described as infinitely small, without body, without bones—a "brindille," which may be read mythically as a fecundating

16 *Like a Narrative*

twig or sprout. By figural substitution this scene stages both metaphorically and metonymically the instance of Montès's conception. In Montès's phantasm Rose's desirability combines with her function as mother figure, while he appears to himself as her lover and his own progenitor. This "blood" relation involves him in a triangular situation with Rose and her husband, the gypsy boxer, to the point of becoming indirectly responsible for their deaths. The figures of blood and desire are brought together in the scene where Montès contemplates in despair the bloodstained sheet that shrouds their bodies. Montès's desire, previously displaced, is recognized and needs to be read together with the earlier scene of Montès's conception in Rose. The son is here metaphorically born of the union with the (his) mother:

> As if, sitting there in a timeless space next to Rose dead, shut away, buried in that flesh, that heavy perfume of slowly fading lilacs, he found himself returning to a state that was virtually foetal, coiled in the painful and (supposedly) straining quietude of an intra-uterine life from which he was to be, from the second time from between a woman's thighs, although this one was five years younger than he—expelled, projected, screaming and terrified, into the void. (196)
>
> . . . he distinctly felt something break inside him, or rather, he said later, something like a disconnection, a rupture (the cord, I thought). (199, modified)

To the contemporary reader, these sequences cannot fail to suggest an Oedipal scenario of incest, a *causa sui* project, and a fantasy of patricide. Yet these elements of Montès's rebirth fantasy are also part of a broader reconfiguration of myth played out on the level of the semantic and narrative properties of language. The mythical fragment here is of two kinds: (1) fragments related to different versions of the Oedipus legend, including Sophocles' *Oedipus Rex* and *Oedipus at Colonus,* and other related legends and (2) mythical fragments of the Oedipus legend's pretext, the vast body of Greek myths. In both cases myth is recapitulated from within the fragments of Montès's story, functioning not as an abstract idea but as a narrative practice.

In the stories that the townspeople tell, Montès, like the Greek hero

Oedipus, grows up far from the place where he was conceived. His mother, in a sense, steals him away from his father in retribution for the latter's infidelity. The collectivity sees the return of the hero as a threat, sensing "in all forms of the unfamiliar the enemy: evil, numerous, fertile, and black" (35). In other words, the community transforms Montès into a mythic figure who, like Oedipus, fulfills the scapegoat function of ancient ritual. The expulsion of the scapegoat and the exposure of the unwanted child both relate to the Oedipus legend; the two forms of exposure, at sea and on the mountain, are variants of the same theme.[28] *Oedipus* can be taken to mean "child of the swelling waves" as well as "swell-foot."[29] These metaphors are crossed in Montès, who is compared to a drowning man struggling against a "liquid mountain" threatening to engulf him.[30] Like Oedipus, Montès limps.

Montès unconsciously embodies an enigma, and the answer to the famous riddle of the Sphinx is contained in his own mythical ordering of the world: "the human race reduced (reduced by him, recast, classified, divided up) to a series of myths, masculine and feminine subdividing vertically, first all into childhood, maturity, and old age" (154). The narrativity of Montès's blind order of cultural classifications must also be read in relation to a more extensive figurality.

Expiation and blindness, mythemes of Oedipus, occur in the links between certain figures of the text. Features of the Erinnyes, or Furies, appear in descriptions of the "avenging trio" (the bailiff, his daughter, and the woman) and the police, who are described as flies. Expiation emerges in figural repetitions and displacements that occur between flies, bloodstains, and the stain of Montès's guilt: "something like a stain, something obscure, black, irremediable." Blindness is suggested in scenes where figures of blood and tears are substituted for each other in a metaphorical act of blinding. Finally, Montès's own narration is qualified as myopic, while the narrator tells his account in the face of his inability to see. The more fundamental and constitutive blindness is that of the narrative discourse itself, which proceeds step by step in nonlinear and nonteleological fashion. In Simon, writing as cecity finds its exemplary figure in blind Orion, in the "aventure singulière du narrateur qui ne cesse de chercher, découvrant à tâtons le monde dans et par l'écriture" ("singular adventure of the narrator who never ceases to search, discovering the world gropingly in and through writing").[31]

Any translation into a singular archetypal myth such as that of Oedipus is effectively subverted because character, like decor and plot, is an unstable composite of different versions of narrative fictions and mythical fragments. Characters' names, for instance, have mythical resonances. Montès may be read as "from the mountain," bringing together *ores* (Greek for "mountain"), Orestes, and Montès. Anagrams of Rose are *eros* and *ores*, and she is called "montagneuse mère." Cécile is derived from *caecus* (in Latin, "blind"). Rose's daughter, Thérèse, pronounces her name as "térésaaspinas," a possible homonym for Tiresias, the blind seer. A number of Olympian myths are alluded to—Prometheus's creation of humankind, Hephaistos's destruction of the city, Hades' underworld, and so on. The name of the mercurial traveling salesman, Maurice, is a near anagram of *Mercure*, while Jep refers to Jupiter. The Jupiter myth appears in Jep's "lightning run," which ends in the stroke with which he stabs Rose. His "lightning" movement and the "metallic gleam, thin, cold, prolonging the fist" (191), produce Jupiter's thunderbolt on a metaphorical level, while the knife itself remains unnamed. The gypsy camp where Jep-Laius strikes Montès-Oedipus is described as a "crossroads" and is also the site where myths intersect. The description of the camp may be read as a *mise en abîme*, a reflection on the narrative and mythic fragments of which the novel is composed. The mystified reader is, like Montès, dazzled by the "thousands of splinters of glass, as if someone, some mad or idiotic decorator, had patiently ground up a pile of bottles and carefully spread the splinters everywhere" (127). Yet by identifying textual fragments as mythical ones, the reader is not necessarily demystified. The type of mythical reinscription at work in Simon's text raises further questions that bear on our understanding of the place of narrativity in reading.

The reader who attempts to determine the meaning that the mythical provides discovers that its meaning is another fragment belonging to yet another ensemble. In semiotic terms the signifier, itself plural, gives not onto the signified as immediately accessible meaning but rather onto a plurality of other signifiers. Semiotic systems are, moreover, also systems of narrativity. In other words, the discourse that considers the systematic character of signs is never simply a neutral description of the semiotic system and the regulated relationships within it. In constituting its object as an object of knowledge, semiotics sets into play a variety of specifically narrative positions on its borders and in its every part: discursive subject (both the *sujet d'énonciation* and the *sujet d'énoncé*), object of narration, writer, and reader.

By reactivating myths as fragments Simon's writing engages the issue of their narrative construction because reading myth (re)narrativizes these textual fragments. Distributed at the outset in words and figures, sentences and sequences, the fragments are assigned in reading to a mythic narrative order. But Montès's story reactivates many different and divergent narrative series. The narrator's discontinuous surface narrative both fragments and unifies other narrative levels; these in turn fragment and unify the surface narrative (Montès's story) as well. In reconstructing further narratives, be they theatrical, mythical or fictional, my reading in effect performs a repetition (in difference) of the narrative project described in *Le Vent*, with reading becoming yet another instance of the novel's fiction-making process. Clearly, this doubling effect between text and interpretation raises questions concerning the explanatory power of models of narrative order produced by interpretation.

By defining different levels of narrative—the surface structure as opposed to the deep structure—interpreters propose an *Ur*-narrative where the text's meaning or the law of its structure may be read. Jameson, in his critique of interpretation's master narratives, writes that these systems of allegorical interpretation radically impoverish one narrative line in order to rewrite it "according to the paradigm of another narrative, which is taken as the former's master code or *Ur*-narrative and proposed as the ultimate hidden or unconscious meaning of the first." Interpretation in this sense is "the forcible or imperceptible transformation of a given text into an allegory of its particular master code or 'transcendental signified.'"[32] The problems Jameson raises have a particular relevance for criticism that treats latent mythical narrative as an allegory providing the text's original meaning. The reactivation of mythic fragments in Simon's writing cannot be assigned to an archetypal *Ur*-narrative. To grasp the specific historical undertow of these heterogeneous mythic fragments that his work diverts from the linear flow of the master narratives of both myth and history, I propose we reconsider the role of bricolage.

For Lévi-Strauss, mythical thought as a form of bricolage works on "an already constituted set," which the bricoleur works to reorganize.[33] Simon's comparison of writing to bricolage stresses that it too is exercised upon preexisting artifacts: linguistic, cultural, historical, artistic, and not least of all, literary.[34] Simon critics have emphasized writing as formal assemblage at the expense of Lévi-Strauss's more interesting discussion of the historicity of the materials and instruments at the disposal of mythical thought. "But the possibilities always remain limited by the particular history of each piece." For Lévi-Strauss the elements which the "bricoleur" collects and uses are "pre-constrained" because, "like the constitutive units of myth . . . they are drawn from the language where they already possess a meaning, which sets a limit on their freedom of manoeuver."[35] Words and language bear the traces of their previous consignments; they are marked, or "preconstrained," by a history of their previous occurrences. Simon himself insists on this history in language when he states that "the writer works on a material—language—laden with history." "Our vocabulary," he writes, "is not a set of inert signs—each word carries a weight that is at once historical, cultural, phonetic."[36]

In his early work Barthes wrote of this history of writing, arguing that when history proposes or imposes a new set of concerns in literary language, "writing remains still full of the recollection of previous usage, for language is never innocent: words have a second-order memory which mysteriously persists in the middle of new meanings."[37] He calls this memory in language a "rémanence obstinée," a persistent afterimage. Such semantic overabundance, ignored or pushed aside by writing seeking to represent its object transparently, proves instead for Simon (and writers such as Mallarmé, Proust, Joyce, and Beckett) to be one of the foundations of his art. If history takes refuge in the slightest fragment, narrativity in the smallest figure, these figures of narrativity can unfold in the process of reading, like the Japanese paper flowers in Proust's evocation of involuntary memory. Fragments are assembled to compose other narratives, but not like ideological, mythical speech, which empties signs of their history.[38] In Simon's writing the historical and cultural sedimentation of writing, which I refer to as its narrativities, can be neither erased nor reduced to a unitary master narrative.

The "memory traces" or historical density, of Simon's art of bricolage may be grasped through the mythical, which is frequently brought together with the problem of knowing, that is, remembering. In *L'Herbe* a museum visitor stares blankly at a coded representation of a mythological subject. His inability to identify title, character, or legend attests to the dislocation of myth in modern times, when it no longer provides viewer and artist, reader and writer, with a common ground of shared knowledge. The retreat of myth, however, is not a simple absence, and its reemergence is not a simple presence. In *La Bataille de Pharsale* (*The Battle of Pharsalus*), for example, the mythical imposes itself on a scene of catastrophe ("In the *Aeneid* or wherever?") or a statue of trapped lovers, possibly Mars and Venus ("what pair of lovers surprised"). The narrator is unable to name the forgotten memory, although he remembers it as being mythical. Simon's practice of narrativity emerges most intensely in *Histoire,* which shows how the narrator's memory of his forgetting can be retransformed into remembrance through association of sounds, words, and images. The opening line of the text, "l'une d'elles"—"one of them," referring at once to branches of the acacia tree, old dowagers, and feathers—and its homophone *ailes* (birds or wings), leads by association to the narrator's attempt to recall the mythical birds that the old ladies evoke:

> déchirant le tympan, cherchant le nom de ce lac repère d'oiseaux aux serres d'airain aux plumes d'airain mangeurs de chair humaine Tympanon instrument de musique Stymphale noirs sans doute de plumage ou couleur acier hérissés de pointes les yeux semblables aux cabochons des longues épingles fichées dans leurs toques. (38–39)
> [splitting the tympanum, looking for the name of that lake haunt of bronze-beaked, bronze-feathered birds that feed on human flesh Tympanum musical instrument Stymphalus their plumage black probably or steel color bristling with barbs the eyes like the cabochons of long hatpins thrust into their toques. (27)]

Whereas the desire to remember an elusive myth often brings forgetting (until recalled by lateral associations of words and images), the desire to forget brings painful, intrusive remembrance. Instead of allowing the narrator to return to a womblike origin, to forget traumatic memories, his very utterances enclose him ever more surely in another order of narrative memory, that of the mythical text: "je voudrais je voudrais je voudrais si je pouvais l'enlever l'arracher de moi retrouver la fraîcheur l'oubli Déjanire" (365; "I want I want I want if I could just take it off tear it off be cool again forgetting Dejaneira at last" [309]). The mythical proper name is precisely that which threatens the subject's mastery over narrative; it appears as a supplement articulating the tension between memory as gain and memory as loss of desired oblivion.

Thus, in addition to showing the individual's dispossession of or by myth, Simon's texts contain a variety of reappropriations of myth.[39] From *Le Vent* onward myth is linked inseparably to Simon's critique of narrative and his experimentation with discursive modes and frames. In *La Route des Flandres* (*The Flanders Road*) mythical fabulation is presented as a product of the dialogues between Georges and Blum about de Reixach, the family legend, and history. At war and as prisoners, they and other soldiers invent stories, conjuring up erotically charged mythic images designed to sustain them in their disintegrating world. In their fictions they recombine stories about their tradition-bound Colonel de Reixach, his young wife Corinne, and their jockey, Iglesia, with the myths of rivalries, infidelities, and murders of the house of Atreus. Their dialogued fantasy makes up hybrid myths—Leda and the "peacock," for example, because they glimpse a woman behind a curtain embroidered with a peacock, and bestial versions of the infidelity of Venus with Mars because they witness a confrontation between two peasants over the woman. These stories are situated in the debacle of a bankrupt tradition of narrative explanations of war, peace, death, sexuality, and symbolization in general.

The evocation of woman as mythic figure is especially problematic in *La Route des Flandres*. The reference to the myth of Venus-Aphrodite occurs in the description of Corinne, who symbolizes the object of male desire and fantasy. Wearing a dazzling red robe that the myth associates with Aphrodite, she is described as "la femme la plus femme" ("the most womanly woman"). Her body, "impolluée, impolluable" ("unpolluted, unpollutable"), recalls the sea goddess's renewal of her virginity in the sea. The female organs are linked by paranomasia and assonance to figures of marine life: "moule poulpe pulpe vulve" ("mussel sponge valve vulva" [35]), "au goût de coquillage" ("tasting of shellfish").[40] Here the narrators assemble references and allusions without revealing or seeming to know the mythical figure's proper name, Aphrodite. Corinne's name also suggests *Coré*, another name for Persephone, meaning "maiden" or "virgin" in Greek, which yields Coré-Corinne (*reine*), queen of the underworld. Like Coré, who in the myth was said to inhabit both earth and Hades, Corinne provides the narrators with an imaginary escape from the living death of the camp.[41] Descriptive figures such as these undoubtedly generate through wordplay what Ricardou calls pivotal metaphors,[42] but these cannot alone account for the cultural narrativity involved in unbound clusters of "archaeological" figures. Generative readings are precisely "mythical," in Barthes's ideological sense of the term. Having emptied writing of its cultural specificity and historical density, they substitute forms of textuality and erotic wordplay for what they have excluded. My reading differs from myth criticism that claims that Simon merges female characters into mythological and archetypal images. On the contrary, his writing accounts for the cultural fabrication of feminine myth images in war by contextualizing their discursive and narrative determinations.[43]

Simon's texts replicate myths, yet parodically, thereby subverting their status as master narratives. In *La Bataille de Pharsale*, for example, a replication of myth occurs in the scene of a naked, drunken soldier who is compared to "a ridiculous parody, a ridiculous replica of every Perseus, Leonidas, the cohort of warriors frozen in the smoky paintings of the museums" (94, modified). As a reproduction of endless stereotypes, the soldier's actions are nothing more than imitations of iconographical conventions. In Simon's *Histoire* the narrator's attentive descriptions of banknotes and postage stamps reveal how myth is appropriated by capital and ideology; functioning only as a symbol, myth is reduced to "that inexhaustible and serene family of figures symbolizing labors and virtues under the aspects of eternally Georgic figures, summarily dressed and optimistic" (173). What is being told through this description is the way myth itself is appropriated by imperial power. The French postage stamp's *Sower*, a seemingly innocuous Ceres, is illustrated "spreading her civilizing manna above the palm-groves the pyramids the caravans the native markets the ragged swarms of Negroes or fellahin pasted now (the Sower) on the verso of the black and white photograph of the miraculous grotto" (189). The presence of an identical French stamp on postcards from the far reaches of the colonized world reveals that instead of being neutral "windows onto reality," these postcards figure a geopolitical narrative of the history of nineteenth-century colonialism. The stamped postcards become documents of the function of mythical figures in nineteenth-century empire building. In Simon mythical figures are shown to be linked to the historical narratives that appropriate them. Nonetheless, his writing of the detail disrupts those narratives even as it displays them, doing so by restoring to the mythic fragment its narrativity (the colonization of the other) while at the same time suspending its signification (the civilizing of the uncivilized) on behalf of the master narrative of empire.

These readings lead me to conclude that the narrativity of myth lies in (1) its fragmentation, (2) its reinscription in numerous, interlaced narrative contexts that thereby become readable, and (3) its diversion from serving either as mythical language or master myth. In *Les Géorgiques* (*The Georgics*) readers may find an archetypal master myth, the ritual murder of the sun king, which is thought to symbolize the cyclical renewal of nature. A remarkable coherence indeed exists between the Oedipus myth and the undying wind in *Le Vent,* Marie's monumental dying and the vegetal profusion in *L'Herbe,* the ritualized death of de Reixach and the renewal of the earth in *La Route des Flandres,* and *Les Géorgiques*' themes of regicide (General L.S.M. voting the death of Louis XVI) and the cycle of "semailles, saillies, mises en bouteille" ("seeding, breeding, and bottling"). Yet ritual death and cyclical renewal are also articulated with the narratives of war, history, writing, and labor, preventing the reader from isolating the eternal return as the master myth. Furthermore, in a post-Nietzschean perspective, the myth of the death of the god-king has as its corollary the problematization of transcendental truth and meaning, for it recounts the periodic dismembering or dissemination of sovereignty. Subject to the paradoxes of negation, the myth of the dismembering of sovereignty can be represented only as an assertion of negative value, which is then always susceptible to being recuperated as a positive one. Narrative can perhaps go no further in problematizing its own master myths than to take the paradox of meaning in (post)modernity as a reflection on the narrative process.

The analogy between myth in literary texts and the self-reflexive modes of modern writing is striking and reveals that they have in some significant sense become interchangeable. Myth is treated as a *mise en abîme* of the literary text. Interpretation that privileges texts' self-reflexivity, although it may not explicitly consider myth, is a model of essentially mythical interpretation. Because reflexivity involves a self-presentation in which literature turns back on itself, critics find that it provides an original and final reading. Thus, the analogy between myth and reflexivity in literary criticism brings into sharper focus their common function, which is to serve as privileged master narratives of interpretation. But they both perpetuate forms of narrative order that postmodern texts seek to undo. Claude Simon's reactivation of myth as fragment, text, *and* narrative provides insights into conventions of reading and writing precisely by disrupting them. In postmodernity mythical narrative does not provide a privileged law of narrative order, nor can it be "disengaged" from the major narratives of our times, such as those of language, desire, history, ideology, and technology, in which it is inscribed. Neither the forms nor the effects of narrativity can be contained by any general narrative order that would determine them once and for all. This disruption of narrative order can be seen in the challenge Montès represents to the community, which itself stands for fiction making in a society that lacks homogeneity, hierarchy, and any transcendent order. This challenge, and society's response to it, is what we must now consider.

Montès returns as an outsider to the town where he was conceived, and that return is marked by a hiatus and discontinuity in generations, legacies, and shared narratives. The narrator's fascination with him stems in part from Montès's undecidable duplicity: both young and old, rich and poor, an insider and outsider, conscious and unconscious, agent and victim, actor and spectator. He subverts the rigid oppositions that in a conventional narrative would be resolved at some level, most likely in the unity of the individual subject or of narrative omniscience. The problem of reconstructing his story is not resolved in this novel, which sets into play the discourses, genres, codes, and forms on which the telling of stories depends. Montès's fragmentary perception of people and events brackets recent history, while his synchronous, photographic view of the world suggests a crisis of historical intelligibility. His mythic and ahistorical perception, his "savage mind," are revealed to be inadequate but inevitable in a world where patriarchal legacy and narrative order break down at the same time. The wind may be read as the generalized figure for such a discontinuity in narrative legacies, such as those of a rational temporality and a continuity based on the subject's self-identity. Thus, the novel contributes to a critique of traditional narrative order and, implicitly, of the narrativity of historical representation. On the thematic level history is rather sketchily presented as "ordure" (refuse) rather than as "ordre," yet in its many figurations of narrative the novel anticipates Simon's subsequent reinvention of the narrative legacies of history. Challenging the limits of a formal, genre-specific understanding of narrative, Simon explores the broader narrativities involved in the construction of being, knowing, seeing, and writing.

Each of the community's versions of Montès's story, including the narrator's and Montès's own, is an attempt to eliminate the violent deaths of Rose and Jep by instituting them as a cultural or collective fact by means of which to restore order.[44] A narrative with this purpose would ascribe a beginning, middle, and end to events to recuperate those deaths into a meaningful order. Skeptical as the narrator is of the reliability of the accounts he hears, he lacks the authority to reject any version told. He emphasizes not the content or meaning of Montès's story but rather the very multiplicity and heterogeneity of its fragments and versions. In the aftermath of the war, society's old hierarchies have broken down, resulting in the mixing of classes and the increase in displaced persons and marginals. Society's story-telling drive persists in various instances of collective mythmaking: the lawyer, the town chronicle, the beauty parlor, the law court, and so on. The very absence of homogeneity in postwar society seems to spur the community's drive to identify and exclude its others, situating them as "outsiders" to the community (Montès, the Gypsies, the women).

Commentators have not remarked much on the particular setting of the novel, a town in southern France after World War II, yet references to the recent war and to the Holocaust abound, with Maurice acting like a Nazi collaborator and Montès himself being described as resembling a "survivor from Buchenwald." It could be argued that the novel's insistence on problems of legitimacy and citationality, order and disorder, and construction and reconstruction take on meaning only when read in that cultural and historical context as posing questions of individual and collective agency and responsibility. Simon's text, however, does not so much mimetically represent that situation as set up its narrative conditions of possibility, the role performed by narrative agency, and the function of conflicting narrative genres. In the postwar fictional world of *Le Vent* the idea of a unified, consensual narrative hearkens back to ideological and physical repression performed in the name of a singular truth and order, the dangers of which recent Nazi history and war had made manifest. Simon's novel refuses to represent as homogeneous and unified the voices of the community or the narrativization of its opinions, myths, and fictions. Indeed, diversity, transition, and displacement characterize its fictional world, in which the new town is still divided from the old, the landed bourgeoisie from the working people, marginals, and Gypsies. The story of Montès is also that of his disinheritance, of how he loses his vineyards through the legal maneuverings of the old order. In a society where hierarchies persist but are destabilized, classes are mixed, and characters' identification with any privileged discourse is tenuous, narrative itself is plural. As Simon's novel suggests, however, the narrative of scapegoating and exclusion returns here with a vengeance. With the waning of unqualified assent to the authority of any dominant discourse, several micronarratives emerge whose versions neither simply corroborate nor cancel one another. Series of nonexclusive versions come to supplant a consensus of meaning. In this sense Simon's novel rejoins current discussions on postmodern writing and the issues of pluralism in relation to the narrative dimensions of knowledge and power. While postmodern writing is characterized as multiplying narrative frames and points of view, their plurality is one not of relativized subjective apprehensions but of distinct, yet floating subject positions. This plurality occurs in the context of collective (re)actualization of genres and codes that are more or less shared, that overlap and conflict with one another. Absent from Simon's writing is any notion of narrative unity functioning as a modernist aesthetic principle dependent on, as well as promoting, social homogeneity and the exclusion of its others. Marginal discursive spaces come to occupy the center of the novel, just as the margins, frames, and the ways and means of narrative come to occupy the story itself.

Simon's novel deals explicitly with the problem of narrative appropriation and the failure of normalizing, mythic story telling in the face of local and historical events. (This may explain Simon's claim that on the one hand there is a chaotic reality and on the other an arbitrary order imposed by language.) In *Le Vent* Simon opens up the question of the figures and functions of narrative legacies in art, community, violence, and exclusion, a reflection that will continue in his ongoing experimentation with a writing of detail and description. Narrative legacies such as those of family history, revolution, ideology, gender, and history will be taken up by other novels, and their ties to the narrativity of writing further explored. *Le Vent* marks an important moment in Simon's development as a creative writer, for it shows that history, writing, and representation cannot be questioned before narrative order as such is refigured and its mystifications displayed. This novel defers Simon's "autobiographical" experiences such as those of World War II, the Spanish Revolution, and the family narrative and its involvement with the forces of history. This deferral appears to clear the ground, making possible the novel's more general reflection on narrativity. Simon's distancing of autobiographical elements opens onto questions of a general narrative, but the understanding gained produces long-range effects in his subsequent novels.

An important aspect of postmodern writing is the question of heterogeneity, that is, the mixing of genres, discourses, semiotic codes, and languages. Simon's insight is to have treated such heterogeneity as a problem not of relativized forms but of contingent and incommensurable narratives that engage questions of identity, power, sexuality, and history. As Lyotard writes: "The social bond is linguistic, but it is not woven with a single thread. It is formed by the intersection of at least two (and in reality an indeterminate number of) language games, obeying different rules."[45] As we have seen, Lyotard proposes that an avant-garde aesthetics of inappropriate micronarratives is an effective political response to the totalitarian uses of narrative. Each theory of the postmodern, it seems, proposes its own remedy to the uses and abuses of discursive hegemony in general. The difficulty confronting general theory at the present time, however, is that it cannot question totalities only from within its own totalizing, narrative hegemony. Yet general critical theory has no specific object of reference except as it arises from the intersections of different discursive and institutional fields. As opposed to this "mythic" situation, reading texts at the level of the narrativities of their figures allows us to retrace the construction of social, cultural, and historical dimensions in the very detail of descriptions and their tangents. By refiguring texts in this way, we can tackle the broader issues of the status of cultural legacies in postmodernism that then become readable, "like a narrative."

2

Refiguring Narrative and Cultural Legacies

These fragments I have shored against my ruins.—T. S. ELIOT

Much of contemporary fiction and theory implies an altered relation to both the narratives of legacy and the legacies of narrative. As readers' attention is drawn to the margins, modes of presentation, and conditions of possibility for representation, the notions of narrative and legacy together undergo radical changes. Yet the relationships in contemporary writing between fiction and culture cannot be treated solely as aleatory and mimetic, as some have claimed.[1] Postmodern writing does not imitate culture or provide an unmediated reflection of the real. Rather, it rewrites culture in terms of situated narratives. Viewed in this way, postmodern writing gives readers a means of gauging the extent to which the real is informed by the legacies of narrative.

In a general sense the emergence of new epistemologies and histories has to do with reclaiming and questioning legacies. Such is the case, for instance, in the critical rereadings of philosophy, feminist theory, cultural history, and psychoanalysis. In performing them critics neither replicate nor reject altogether the dominant histories and ideologies that have excluded entire histories and cultures and denied subjectivity to women and non-Western peoples. Their rereadings alter our understanding of the making and effects of cultural formations. Moreover, the critique of the master narratives of the transcendental subject, history, and truth has made it possible to reclaim the legacies situated on the borders and at the limits of traditional knowledge and representation. From these critical perspectives, former divisions are undone between disciplines and modes of inquiry such as philosophy, literature, cultural history, psychoanalysis, history, narrative, politics, and aesthetics. The outcome is the invention of new objects of knowledge, new ways of seeing the present by recombining narratives of the past. Cultural objects, even and especially those based on new technologies of vision, do not arise without their legacies. In other words, new cultural objects are produced in the recombining of epistemologies, discourses, and techniques but not emptied of their historical and cultural specificity. They emerge with problematic legacies and not as simply present simulacra whose historicity has been amputated.

The legacies in postmodernity that appear to be the most difficult to grasp involve its relation to narrativity. For many the postmodern is thought to have put an end to interpretation and the hermeneutic project per se, yet such a belief fails to recognize the full reach of narrativity into such "postmodern" dimensions as the technological, image culture, and the media. Feminist critiques have shown that systematic gender exclusions and positionings can be resisted only once their discursive and narrative strategies are understood and dismantled. Among the legacies of the postmodern in general must be included critical discourses that seek to establish points of contact between separate realms in unauthorized yet essential ways, but if such discourses strip figures of their narrativities, that very exclusion returns and comes to define the critical project itself. This chapter elaborates the particular and general narratives at work in cultural, historical, and family legacies in order to bring out their problematic narrativity. It proposes to reevaluate in Simon the narratives of legacy as well as the legacies of narrative. Through this permutation of terms, Simon's reinvention of cultural legacies makes tangible the figures organizing their narrative determinations.

Narratives of Legacy

As *Le Vent*'s narrativized myths make apparent, not only do genres have a disciplinary, institutional force, but they also carry and constitute a cultural legacy. In other words, their disciplinary force derives from their actuality as legacies, which are at once cultural, historical, ideological, and internalized in the psyche. In Simon the legacies of history, sexuality, visibility, and mobilization are not held apart but shown instead in the tensions of their encounter. They come to bear on individual, family, institutional, and cultural histories, grasped in their particular figures, details, and traces. Simon's work brings together these problematic and incommensurable legacies in a writing that reinvents fiction as a different kind of cultural object. His inventions acknowledge not only that different histories may be discontinuous but also that they are linked through the detail and the trace, their tangents and their figural narrativities. He does not reduce these legacies either to the certitudes of a historical model of cause and effect or to a too general and hence homogeneous intertextuality. Instead, his writing works to recontextualize cultural formations and their texts symbolically, materially, and discursively.

The critique of narrative representation undertaken in *Le Vent* continues in Simon's subsequent fiction, which presents a thoroughgoing interrogation of the narrative legacies at work in descriptive and historical writing. When canonical histories are thematized, the narrative voice enunciating a critique of them is skeptical, outraged, and yet not invulnerable to their seductions. That is perhaps why Simon seeks so persistently to trace the figures by which these histories transform the "real" events of what happens into their own terms of order and disorder. Canonical narratives set elements either outside or inside their space of representation.[2] The resistance Simon offers to these narratives of (dis)order is to reinvent them from the ground up, from the detail and the trace, detecting in and inventing from their dispersed figures the intricate workings of a narrativity that is at once personal, familial, cultural, and historical. It is a narrativity of fragment, detail, and tangent.

Simon's work explores the relationship between history (as a narrative order of representation) and the legacies that inhabit history, but on its margins, in its modes of presentation, and in its conditions of narrativity. In other words, his writing with and on legacies cannot be reduced to the terms of historical representation, nor does it lie outside those terms. Legacies in Simon are at once cultural and linguistic, traditional and antitraditional, conscious and unconscious, historical and mythical. Rather than reject out of hand the challenge of representing culture, politics, and history in postmodernity, Simon refigures their narrative legacies in the very movement of his writing. His critique of narrative representation and its legacies is directed as much at internalized, subjective versions as at externalized, institutionalized ones. What is more, he explores the intersections between them. Therefore, his project cannot be equated with the avant-garde fiction that takes the simulacra of the world of images and permutes them as external stimuli, leaving the subject either wholly immune to their mobilizing effects or entirely determined by them. Certain questions arise from Simon's reinventions of narrative. Does he restore master narratives? Is his work driven by nostalgia for master narratives that can no longer be told? Does his writing aestheticize, and thus monumentalize, the vestiges of a world of sense no longer available and in this way attempt to recuperate that world? I claim that as it sifts through the material traces of language and memory, his writing does not so much recuperate or reproduce a lost past as it writes an archaeology of its fragments, that is, the cultural narrativity linking its traces.

Someone receives something and doesn't know what to make of it. Or rather, something is received, but the receiver doesn't know what it is, or what to do with it, or what it makes of her or him. A legacy is always fragmented, composed of partial objects themselves fragmented, deriving from many different sources, and having innumerable possible destinations. Because of the complex links that Simon establishes between the question of writing and the "matter" of the various legacies he receives, his readers have been challenged to find a way of dealing with both, that is, with his innovative writing and its status as representation and reference. They have often formalized his writing and reduced to themes what are possibly the very workings of legacy, legitimation, and narrativity. His writing of legacies involves readers in a double reading that brings together figures and their narratives in a movement of reading at once discontinuous and linking. In other words, narrativity provides the conditions of readability for writing and (its) legacies. In the novels of his de Reixach cycle (*L'Herbe, La Route des Flandres, Histoire, Les Géorgiques,* and *L'Acacia*), Simon elaborates a poetics of narrativity against the ideological power exercised by discredited orders of narrative representation. These novels take up the legacies of autobiography and family, sexuality and gender, violence and legitimation.

L'Herbe concerns the legacy that a dying old woman, Aunt Marie, passes on to Louise, who is her nephew's wife (the third-person narrator). Louise receives a box containing Marie's ledgers, photographs, shoe buckles, and cheap rings. She cannot communicate with the giver, who lies in a coma. For Louise the writing in Marie's ledgers may be identified with time itself, "the very weave of existence." Its endless rows of entries inscribe

> the trivial events (and not even events: facts, incidents—and not even incidents: the everyday, the commonplace—and not even the trivial: minuscule, insignificant) rising again to the surface of time, of the past, like pilings stuck here and there in the gray immensity that had no beginning or end, their insignificance, their very tininess, out of all proportion with the frame in which they were set, according them a kind of unexpected grandeur, a majesty. (102)

This "infrahistory" is reproduced in the novel as entire pages of credits and debits, receipts and expenditures. As Louise scans the columns that convert the material costs of life and death into an enumeration without narrative causes and effects, beginnings or ends, she reflects on the absolute incommensurability between what she reads and any conventional (narrative) quest for meaning: "Yes: like the idiot sons shovelling up the ground yard by yard looking for buried treasure. Except that I'm still more of an idiot than they are, since I know ahead of time that there's nothing" (177). On page after page she sees a terrifying repetition of interchangeable dates in which time's passing appears only in the seasonal recurrence of fruits, expenditures, and the inflation of currency.

The novel traces Louise's initial resistance to the narrative of legacy and her ultimate recognition that Marie's sheer endurance has a historical dimension from which a different historical understanding may be derived. In other words, Marie's legacy emerges from the margins of her history. If, as the epigraph taken from Boris Pasternak suggests, "no one makes history, no one sees it happen, no one sees the grass grow," *L'Herbe* is less a reconstruction of Marie's history or of Louise's identification with her than a refiguring of a problematic legacy. It is the first of Simon's works to foreground the productive function of writing, as Roubichou has argued, but it cannot be limited to a one-dimensional linguistic formalism. The thesis of productive writing defines itself only in relation to the present, formal context of language as process, whereas the novel's figurations of legacies work to link language to its referential contexts.

"Legacy" constitutes the narrative trope par excellence. Simon's work as a whole may be read as various rewritings of legacy in an ever-increasing discursive and narrative complexity. In *Le Vent* the legacy of the vineyard is one that cannot simply be "assumed," and the novel separates historical and family narratives from the narrator's commentaries on story telling. The novel recounts the impossibility of occupying either a "landed" legacy or the legacies of narrative order. It rewrites legacy in the form of the mythic subtext without allowing mythic repetition to become a means of denying the break in inheritance that has occurred. A convergence between historical, familial, and narrative legacies does not come about in Simon's novels until *L'Herbe,* where it takes the form of a divergence in the sense that its fiction bypasses the legitimated legacies of official history and family tradition. The displacement of the family legacy from the Oedipal triangle (Pierre, Sabine, Georges) to its woman-focused periphery, the aunt and the in-law (Marie, Louise), may be taken to symbolize Simon's resistance to the reproduction of tradition as a consecrated narrative order. The burden of tradition (literary, familial, cultural, historical) is here displaced by the legacy one woman gives to another. Marie's gift to Louise may of course not be a woman's legacy per se, just as women and women's desire may well be absent from the novel. Nevertheless, the transfer of the legacy onto "women" signifies a break with patriarchal narrative orders—those of generation, genealogy, and reproduction. In this sense the novel recounts Louise's resistance to and her rewriting of opposing, yet intersecting, legacies: writing and the land, Pierre's writing and Marie's ledgers, Marie's and Europe's history, Marie's death and Louise's sexuality. Situated by a tradition, a past both fragmented and powerful, and yet not occupying the position of legitimate heir, Louise bears analogies to Simon as writer. Her conflicts with legacy play out on a different level what the writer deals with on the level of writing, discourse, and narrativity. As it was in novels such as *La Route des Flandres, Le Palace, Histoire, Les Géorgiques,* and *L'Acacia,* the question is that of the protagonists' separation from, yet enclosure within, an archaeology of stories, values, and times—in short, the narrative legacies of the past and the present.

Simon's writing as a whole may be described as a poetics of the detail in which words reveal diverse "facets" that connect in myriads of ways with other times and places. Such a poetics cannot be restricted to the terms of self-generative writing dictated by criticism whose concerns do not address the temporal dimensions of narrativity. Descriptions of characters, places, and objects are subject to shifts and displacements in which the described is, as it were, always underwritten by a plurality of other references, other images, other times, other people, other deeds, other texts. This underwriting engages writing with the diverse legacies of narratives. (Some of the hallmarks of Simon's writing, for instance, such as his complex use of parentheses within parentheses and present participles, are temporal and narrative dimensions of his writing rather than a technique of writing in the present.) Such an underwriting by other narratives is figured when Louise compares Sabine's sense of time to a dial "apparently made up of several superimposed or even concentric clock faces like those of the astronomical clocks . . . the hand pointing at the same moment to several indications." She continues by describing the watch case "decorated with interlaced initials so complicated that they are indecipherable," whose detail is "like those heavy monograms embroidered on sheets . . . the machinery of time and that of reproduction both developing, then, under the symbolic vestiges of other times and other copulations" (168–69). The metaphor for Sabine's mind is relayed by an extended reflection on the untold narratives of time, reproduction, and the undecidable identities symbolized by monogrammed initials. Simon's writing, too, unfolds under the vestiges of other times and other linkings. Like the two faces of a watch whose back and face figure a writing linked to the movement of time, his writing presents a narrative that cannot be reduced to any single plane of reference. The narrative dimensions of the figural detail may be grasped in a reading of its phantomatic legacies.

38 *Refiguring Narrative and Cultural Legacies*

La Route des Flandres opens with these words: "He was holding a letter in his hand, he raised his eyes looked at me then the letter again then once more at me" (11). These phrases plunge the reader into a paradigmatic narrative situation from which fictions will be elaborated. "He" is Captain de Reixach, a distant relative of the narrator, who serves in de Reixach's squadron, and the recipient of a letter from the narrator's mother, Sabine. Her letter, invoking a private family tie, intrudes here on the all-male military world, an intrusion that breaks down partitions. This scene has analogies with that of *Les Géorgiques*'s prologue, which shows an older man reading a letter in the presence of a younger man, depicted in the style of David's drawings for his painting of Galton. These scenes of an older man reading a letter he receives from or gives to a younger man who looks on emblematize the narrative dimension of the scene of reading and legacy in Simon's work. It is a dimension that, from *L'Herbe* to *Histoire*, and from *Les Géorgiques* to *L'Acacia*, privileges figurations of the legacy as correspondence, destination, and reception in the form of stories, letters, postcards, photographs, paintings, histories, and family archives.

Thus, the opening of *La Route des Flandres* immediately situates the novel in terms of destination and reception. The narrator articulates these poles as a general narrative condition for him to be able (or unable) to narrate his experience of war and the POW camp. There appears to be no common measure, no common denominator, for naming his fragmentary perceptions, and he invokes various genres (novel, myth, history, lyric poetry, exposition) with which to compare what remains for him unpresentable in their terms. For instance, imagining shimmering scenes involving Iglésia, de Reixach, and Corinne at the Auteuil racetracks before the war, he suggests:

> probably that was the truth: in other words not an idyll, an intrigue, verbose, concerted, orderly, starting, developing according to a harmonious and reasonable crescendo interrupted by the indispensable halts and false moves, and a culminating point and after that the obligatory decrescendo again: no, nothing organized, nothing coherent, no words, no preparatory phrases, no declara-

tions or descriptions, only that: those few mute images hardly moving, seen from far away. (41)

The scenes that he describes as bearing no resemblance to any traditional romance-quest structure, one founded on a fully orchestrated narrative logos, nevertheless acquire their specific character in their distance from such a narrative rhetoric. In this sense, the narrator's reference to a general narrative order subtending an array of different genres and artistic media (visual, musical, and verbal) also raises questions about figures of narrative. *La Route des Flandres*'s refusal of conventional narrative codes has the paradoxical effect of multiplying references to narrative orders of different kinds. As in *Le Vent*, the narrators (Georges and Blum) proceed by matching a scene to codes and genres with which it is in fact incompatible. Their invention of incommensurate narratives is a strategy for surviving during the wartime cavalcade, the cattle-train transport, the field of prisoners, and the POW camp, a strategy that extends to the postwar encounters with Corinne.

The story-telling drive emerges from a situation of near annihilation in which the tellers (Georges, Blum, and the soldiers) are spiritually and physically destitute, radically severed from any link to their former identities and realities. In the camp they attempt to remember and to invent various pasts in the face of an absolute effacement of difference, that is, in the camp's institutionalization of pure repetition in the endless monotony of hunger, cold, inaction, and deprivation:

> while trying to transfer themselves by proxy (that is, by means of their imagination, that is, by assembling and combining all they could find in their memory by way of things seen, heard or read, so that—here, among the wet and gleaming rails, the black wagons, the black and soaking tree trunks in the cold pale daylight of a Saxon winter—summoning up the iridescent and luminous images by means of the ephemeral, incantatory magic of language, words invented in the hope of making palatable . . . the unmentionable reality [l'innommable réalité] in that futile, mysterious and violent universe in which, in the absence of their bodies, their minds moved . .). (137)

40 *Refiguring Narrative and Cultural Legacies*

Georges's and Blum's stories of Corinne, Iglésia, de Reixach, and Georges's distant ancestors are concocted from mixed sources. They bear an ironic resemblance to the heterogeneous genres of the Reixach family archives that comprise "a huge mass of poems, philosophic digressions, sketches for tragedies, travel narratives" (45). Lucien Dällenbach, discussing the reader's disorientation in the vast number of embedded, interdependent genres and narrative modes that overturn the formal distinctions of poetics, asks what the text narrates, which story it tells (Georges's or de Reixach's), and who the narrator is. "To which literary genre or super-genre does it belong? Novel of memory, initiation, epic, lyrical evocation?"[3] His questions show that the novel as both text and memory maintains its undecidable discursive and generic character. He goes on, however, to resolve the undecidable, heterogeneous text by arguing that its lesson or "teaching" is that a text must be credible on an aesthetic level. Aesthetic order, he claims, is guaranteed by the text's triptych structure, its specular composition, pivot words, the account of the night spent with Corinne, and recurrent episodes of the dead horse and de Reixach's death. These counter the dispersion from which the text would otherwise suffer. In terms of narrativity Dällenbach's opposition between the safeguards of formal order and the novel's undecidable heterogeneity is a problematic one. Are the narrative perspectives that are opened up by the narrators' grasping at materials of all kinds (and the many positions from which the text derives) finally to be read as a formal error that can successfully be overcome or resolved on the aesthetic level? Can narrative questions be separated from the so-called aesthetic questions of formal symmetry, specularity, and repetition?

A reading of the text's narrative dimensions suggests otherwise. Any such resolution, based on the centering power of form, is itself dismantled in Simon's writing. No fixed narrative center may be ascribed to the novel, for every narrative position is disrupted, rendered partial by the intrusion of other narrative situations. For instance, Georges's experiences and his recounting of the unnameable realities of war and incarceration evolve against the backdrop of many narratives: his father's academic writings and speeches ("as if his father had never stopped talking"), his mother's obsessive chatter about her aristocratic Reixach ancestry, his endless dialogues with the skeptical Blum, and not least, his

Refiguring Narrative and Cultural Legacies   41

attempt to resolve his crisis of legacies on Corinne's body. The last of these, in which Corinne rejects Georges's Oedipal narrative quest, shows that she is not the sole object of desire. He believes that her body will provide him access to de Reixach and the narrative legacy as such. Such narrative intrusions and their effects of disruption do not arise as inessential supplements to the aesthetic forms of the novel; instead, they are constitutive of those forms and testify to the broad reach of different narrativities.

General narrative orders are reinscribed with a view to revealing and dismantling the specific fabrication they involve. The narrative quest of romance is identified as being unusable and mystifying, as is the "shimmering, exalted vision" of history. In one of the POW camp exchanges, Blum says that the law of history is to leave behind it "a residue excessively confiscated, disinfected and finally edible, for the use of official school manuals and pedigreed families. . . . But actually what do you know?" (140). Postwar peace is described as a process of covering over events in a kind of simulated transcendence. By means of history's narrative order, the war's violent dissociation of subjects, matter, things, values, and their representation is dissimulated or repressed by being made the same:

> after it had all come to an end, that is, had closed over, formed a scar, or rather (not formed a scar, for already no trace of what had happened was visible any longer) readjusted, mended, and so perfectly that you could no longer detect the least crack, the way the surface of the water closes over a pebble, the landscape that had been reflected for a moment broken, fractured, splintered into an incoherent multitude of fragments, of pieces of sky and trees . . . recomposing, the blue, the green, the black regrouping, coagulating so to speak, organizing, still undulating a little like dangerous serpents, then motionless, and then nothing but the varnished perfidious surface serene and mysterious, in which was ordered the calm opulence of the branches, the sky, the calm slow clouds, nothing more now than that lacquered and impenetrable surface. (172)

That this landscape, in its fragmented and recomposed forms, also figures the narrative representation of war and peace is confirmed when

Georges pursues the oxymoron of this "writing" as a solid liquid. The vacuous phrases of his father's academic writing are "as smooth, as polished, as frozen and as insubstantial as the shiny surface of the water, discreetly hiding" (172). (Such writing recalls the act of the narrator's great-grandmother, who in *Les Géorgiques* adds layer upon layer of wallpaper to the hidden trapdoor behind which lie the explosive archives of her regicide ancestor and the death sentence of his royalist brother.) Narrative history is a process of layering designed to ensure forgetting by covering over the traces. *La Route des Flandres* challenges its dissimulation by including this historical-literary discourse and its shattering within its own text and by not exempting the narrative situation from that upheaval's effects.

The preceding analysis suggests that every narrative situation is one that the characters have to tease out of a tangled web of fragmented voices, images, odors, phantasms, feelings, and texts. In other words, narrative situation cannot be said to constitute a given, a still center in the midst of the fragmented reality of representations. When the prisoners lose their sense of time, space, and identity in the camp, narrative situations are just barely recovered by the soldiers in the process of "restoring" or "extracting" from Iglésia the details of his involvement with Corinne: "so that it wasn't day after day but somehow from place to place (like the surface of a painting darkened by varnish and filth and that a restorer might reveal in sections—testing, experimenting here and there on different areas with different cleaning solutions) that Georges and Blum gradually reconstituted, piece by piece or more accurately onomatopoeia by onomatopoeia wrung one by one by ruse and guile" (104). Although such reflexive commentary has been taken to refer to the spatial and formal character of Simon's writing, the figure of "restoration" cannot really be understood outside the legacies of narrativity, ushered in here by metaphors of discourse such as onomatopoeia, experimentation, and different formulas.

The characters in *La Route des Flandres* are situated by discourses and genres having a variety of possible narrative permutations. For them, narrative dislocation is not a formal matter alone; rather, it is also tied to cultural, social, and historical legacies that are themselves in permutation. The posts of the principal narrators, Georges and Blum, become interchange-

Refiguring Narrative and Cultural Legacies 43

able as senders and receivers, with each occupying both posts, at times simultaneously. Such permutation involves the voice of the Other, here the Jewish soldier, in a dialogical exchange of different legacies. Although the de Reixach family legacy, despite (or because of) its confusions and fictions, is certainly privileged over Blum's, the latter's is not absent, and it is precisely Blum's skepticism that intervenes to problematize Georges's tendency to reproduce uncritically the legacies of his origins. Georges internalizes their dialogue to such a degree that it continues long after his friend's death, even in the lovemaking scenes between him and Corinne after the war.

During the war Georges's and Blum's quest for sense produces Corinne as a fictional, phantasmatic reference, which Georges later pursues to her very body: "what had I looked for in her hoped for pursued upon her body in her body words sounds as crazy as he is with his illusory sheets of paper" (203). While he makes love to her he also pursues dialogues with Blum, recalling through linked images of water and earth his experience of being an animal in flight. For Georges, sexual experience is designed to recuperate the pure loss of war and dehumanization by transmuting death into an affirmation of life and sense.[4] Corinne is not only a sexualized body but also a fictional referent invented by the narrator's desire to achieve narrative closure in de Reixach's story. Simon's writing displays the particular process whereby she is permuted into an object of desire as the referent of the narrative quest. In addition his writing makes of that fantasy referent an individual who can and does refuse to occupy the position of "a soldiers' prostitute" assigned to her by Georges's repetition of the Oedipal narrative. (Note the reference as well to his father's writing.) Certainly, there is as much risk of overstatement as of understatement in characterizing Corinne's power to reject her transformation into Woman as the required lack constituting male subjectivity. Finally, however, "Corinne" is the result of a bricolage of cultural stereotypes who is not represented as a woman with her own desires to express and narratives to send. Her reality as a woman remains as unpresentable as the traumas of the war that produced her. She provides an anchoring for the soldiers' stories in the midst of the debacle and for the narrator's failed attempt to continue telling in a conventional form during and after it. In sum, the shifting positions of senders, receivers, and referents become extraordinarily refined in this novel, causing the legacies of sexual and cultural constructs to emerge with extraordinary force in the very permutations of their narrativities.

As I have defined it, the paradigmatic situation of legacy in Simon is an exchange or correspondence between two men, a symbolic Oedipal pair (father/son, brother/brother, uncle/nephew), suggesting that narrative relationships (involving narratees and readers as well) might also be between men. This paradigm is true for Montès and the narrator, Georges and Blum, Georges and the male de Reixach legacy, the narrator and uncle Charles, and the narrator and L.S.M. However, other narrative exchanges must be considered—the voices of the community, Marie's legacy and Louise's voice, Sabine's chatter and Corinne's interventions, and Batti's position as addressee. As we will see, the paradigm is internally differentiated by means of a permutation of narrative posts that rewrites the workings of culture and its descriptions, as well as the orders of language and history.

The focus on narrative legacies leads to the following question: what forms of understanding do they provide? Do these legacies help to answer the hermeneutic question asked by Georges and Blum, "Mais comment savoir? Que savoir?" ("But how to know? What to know?"), pertaining to the problem both of knowing and of representing. "Mais comment était-ce, comment était-ce?" ("But how was it, how was it?") is asked in *Le Palace* because a breech exists between the events of the Spanish Revolution and their telling fifteen years later. In *Histoire* the question "Mais exactement, exactement?" ("But exactly, exactly?") describes the narrator's desire to grasp his imaginary museum of memories, memorabilia, and the fragmented bodies and texts in which these are held. *L'Acacia*'s refrain, "but there was something he could not see," addresses itself to what escapes vision and representation. These questions go to the heart of the problem of knowing and of acceding to the real.

Simon has contrasted the "magma" of sensations to the problematic order imposed by language, and he has recalled Jean Dubuffet's view that our thinking receives only a coded translation of conventional forms unless we make an effort of attention and reflection.[5] In Simon's writing this effort is presented in the work of narrativity. Does the permutation of narrative po-

Refiguring Narrative and Cultural Legacies 45

sitions provide more truthful knowledge of the world, or does narrative rewriting of any kind endlessly represent nothing but its own limits as knowledge and representation? Simon's work on narrativity may be related to the Nietzschean legacy in contemporary thought according to which one can accede to knowledge not of the real but only of the conditions of interpretation.[6] In a less absolutist way, my analysis attempts to retrace and redefine the limits of narrative and the ways in which his writing engages them. Simon's displacement of legacies, permutation of posts, refiguring of detail and description—these are some of the ways of linking phenomenology and narrative, knowing and telling, understanding and representing, interpretation and reference. In the next section I read the narrativities of memory and history and their relation to the figures of women.

Legacies of Narratives

Les branches passent à travers moi, sortent de par les oreilles,
par ma bouche, par mes yeux, les dispensant de regarder.
[Branches pass through me, come out through my ears,
my mouth, my eyes, dispensing them from looking (my
translation).]—CLAUDE SIMON

At the beginning of *Histoire* mention is made of work done by the narrator that relates in some sense to the acacia branches:

> One of them was almost touching the house and in summer when I worked late into the night sitting in front of the open window I could see it or at least its farthest twigs in the lamplight with their feathery leaves trembling faintly against the darkness beyond, the oval folioles dyed a raw unreal green by the electric light stirring occasionally like plumes as though suddenly animated by a movement of their own. (1)

The dense branches ("intersecting superseding overlapping") evoke the work of memory and its relation to language and writing. Phantoms of the past, "feeble ghosts gagged by time death," inhabit the narrator's memory and perception, condemned to survive as long as they acquire a fragile reanimation through his thoughts and writing.

The fragments in *Histoire* are those of the past, a legacy of virtual narratives that inform its writing. Submerged by postcards, stamps, photographs, and inscriptions of all kinds, the narrator appears as a survivor of an endless process of dissolution and reorganization, death and desire. The text's epigraph reads: "It submerges us. We organize it. It falls to pieces. We reorganize it again and fall to pieces ourselves—Rilke." Writing cannot impose pastness on these *survivances*, however, this accumulation of family stories, memories, postcards, history books, and inscriptions. Instead of passing into a history of meaning, they persist as fragments and become intensified as texts, refusing to become historically past, that is, to become part of a narrative history. The narrative stakes of legacy are immediately put forward in the text's ambiguous title, *Histoire*, which refers to the historical and the fictional and links them. Ultimately, the novel's writing does not resolve whether *histoire* refers to truth or knowledge as meaningful process, as diachronic narrative of memorable events, an anecdote, untruth, affair, or, in familiar French, a rather ordinary object that one cannot or does not want to name.[7] *Histoire*'s insight is not that history is but a fiction or that fiction is a sort of history. Rather, the novel brings forth the narrativities of both, and in so doing it questions monological narratives.

The narrator's "reading" of postcards and old photographs, "fragments, flakes? (scales) torn from the surface of the enormous earth: rectangular windows in which were framed one after the other" (10), brings together their descriptive and narrative properties.[8] The sliding from description to narrative occurs because the narrative situation from which a description is elaborated is itself subject to a (narrative) sliding that decenters the subject. Contrary to a narrative poetics in which narrating and describing are separate and hierarchized terms, Simon's work reveals that the text of memory can never successfully hold at bay the intrusion of description in narration and narration in description. Narrative and description repeatedly cross each other in what Simon has called the "present of writing," a present that in fact opens onto innumerable series of other descriptions and other dimensions of narrativity. In *Histoire*, as in his other works, the density of figural associations, correspondences, and discontinuities can emerge only when read within the larger problematics of the legacies of narratives.

An important cluster of figures appears in the return of certain

Refiguring Narrative and Cultural Legacies 47

sounds, words, and images related to the narrator's mother, her illness, and her death. Overwhelmed by his memories, the narrator edges, word by word, sometimes phoneme by phoneme, to the absence that haunts the novel as a whole and the double impossibility of gaining access to or escaping (from or into) his mother's memory. Since the work of memory does not conform to any prescribed narrative order, however, its movement encounters a series of obstacles at once blocking his view of her emaciated face ("like a knifeblade") and opening the paths through which his evocation may pass. As the priest's back blocks his (memory of) seeing, the narrator recalls the symbolic embroidery on his vestments depicting a climbing rose and drops of blood, which evoke a fall he had as a child. (He later relates the drops of blood to a memory of sensual awakening associated with Corinne who, when they played together as children, grazed her leg while climbing the forbidden cherry tree.) For now, the narrator evokes the priest's chasuble with roses embroidered on its moiré fabric: "on the mauve background of the watered-silk chasuble eyes following the rows of delicate shifting reflections shade over shade zigzagging slender whiplashes tracing on the fabric a motionless series of flaunting waves" (7). As the priest shifts position, "behind the motionless tide of purple waves the drops of blood the leaves for a second I could also see or rather glimpse Maman's face on the pillows between the lace sleeve and the edge of the bed" (7).

In one of Simon's early attempts at a conventional novel, *Le Tricheur* (The cheat; 1945), scenes simply describe the narrator's dying mother's face as being "like a knifeblade." Louis affirms his own power to evoke her image: "Je savais ce que j'avais à faire pour me faire mal: épuisée dans son grand lit blanc, son nez si maigre et sa bouche de douleur comme une entaille" (31; "I knew what I had to do to hurt myself: exhausted in her large white bed, her nose so thin, and her mouth in pain like a slash"). Despite analogies between Louis and the narrator in *Histoire*, whose fathers are killed in World War I and whose mothers substitute religious adoration for them in their absence, the two texts deal entirely differently with similar fictional material. In *Le Tricheur*, for instance, Louis proposes to explain the process of substitution in the psychological terms of motivation: "Et voilà par quoi elle l'avait remplacé: on dressait l'autel au pied de son lit, nappe brodée blanche et les bougies allumées et le prêtre" (31; "And here's what she had replaced him with: the altar was raised at the foot of her bed, white embroidered tablecloth, and lighted candles and the priest"). *Histoire*, by contrast, evokes the myriad details of ritual substitution (body, blood, icon, and symbol) that provide the context for the figural displacements in which the mother substitutes INRI for Henri, her absent husband. Because Simon's writing of the detail situates these paternal symbolic substitutions in the psycho-cultural, aesthetic, and historical contexts of the years before and after World War I, these substitutions are shown to be meaningful both within and beyond the subject's desire. They are effects of *histoire* in the most general and particular senses of the word. An enormous photographic enlargement of the father's face looms above the mother's bed, seemingly suspended, "like one of those apparitions surrounded with a halo of light . . . like some divinity with curly silken hair" (8–9). The process whereby Henri gradually becomes confused with and displaced by the divinity is shown to be based on his continual absence—first in his peregrinations around the colonized world and then in his death at Verdun.[9] "She had doubtless never stopped seeing him ever-present the unforgettable image floating immaterial and aureoled with mist down through the years their interminable engagement had lasted and in which he had already existed for her only in this impalpable and aerial form" (9). A far cry from the early novel's simple assertion of male-divine interchangeability in the female imagination, the later work explores through visual and material detail the social and historical situation of the symbolic substitutions involved. It portrays the narrator's memory as an immersion in his parents' imaginary history through its cultural legacies, which are narrative ones as well.

Direct access to the past is illusory, yet the narrator traces innumerable figural paths that mediate his severed relation to women. (The text also shows the process whereby the father, who dies in the narrator's infancy, is recuperated as the Father in the symbolic order. The narrator cannot be said to be distanced from him in the same way as he is from women.) In the movement of reading, the repetitions of words such as *moiré, mer, mère, mur, murmure, mourante,* and *moi?* come to figure verbal *revenants* or phantoms of the loss of both his mother and his wife. A comparison of his mother as a young fiancée to a high wall, the woman enclosed by patriarchal culture and her capacity to wait (20), recurs later with reference to his wife, Hélène, whose despair walls her off from the narrator. The most developed chain of consonances among *mère/mur/marbrures/marée* comes together in the following passage:

ma maman est malade dis-je
il faisait presque noir dans la maison à présent l'ombre du toit était déjà à mi-hauteur du mur qu'éclairait le couchant la partie encore ensoleillée d'une couleur orange foncé sur quoi les ombres entremêlées des branches de l'acacia dessinaient des marbrures bleuâtres des triangles des trapèzes se défaisant et se reformant le ciel commençant à foncer entièrement vide sauf un petit nuage effiloché rebroussé qui filait à toute vitesse les ténèbres envahissaient la vieille maison commençant par le bas s'élevant comme une marée noire glaciale le vent hurlait par moments sous les portes il y avait toujours quelque part un volet mal fixé qui grinçait sur ses charnières cognait contre le mur et se rabattait grinçait de nouveau après un moment de silence le son était différent selon qu'il s'écartait du mur ou s'en rapprochait quelquefois les deux grincements semblaient lutter alternant parfois il se passait un moment pendant lequel on n'entendait rien puis il semblait pousser un gémissement aigu bref et frappait violemment contre le mur. (223)
[my mother's sick I said
It was almost dark in the house now the shadow of the roof was already halfway down the wall the part still in sunlight was dark orange on which the interlacing shadows of the acacia branches drew bluish lines triangles trapezoids dissolving and reforming the sky began to darken empty now except for one tiny fraying cloud rushing across it shadows were invading the old house beginning at the bottom rising like a black icy tide the wind howled under the doors there was always a loose shutter somewhere that creaked on its hinges bumped against the wall and swung back creaked again after a moment's silence the sound was different when it moved away from the wall and when it swung back sometimes the two creaks seemed to struggle alternating sometimes there came a moment during which you heard nothing then it seemed to heave a short sharp groan and struck the wall violently. (187)]

This densely woven passage of remembrance brings together the wall, the branches of the acacia, and images of a rising black tide, as well as the noise of loose shutters rattling in the wind. The phonic repetition of fricatives (*gr, tr, br, pr*), *m*'s, and *n*'s (together with the nasals *en, ent, ant, on, an, ment*) creates an intense register of grinding and moaning that doubles the words' semantic resonances. The sense of the passage's narrativity is thus created by discontinuous elements that at once conceal and reveal the mother's agony, as well as the narrator's anger and pain: *hurlait, grinçait, cognait, silence, pousser un gémissement aigu bref et frappait violemment le mur.*

In the novel's closing phrases, the narrator evokes an earlier image of his mother, whom he imagines to be already pregnant with him, writing postcards on her honeymoon in Félicité Island in the Seychelles: "the lady bending over, her mysterious bust of white flesh swathed in lace that bosom which already perhaps was bearing me in its shadowy tabernacle a kind of gelatinous tadpole coiled around itself with its two enormous eyes its silkworm head its toothless mouth its cartilaginous insect's forehead, me?" (341). The final graphic question mark simultaneously figures the outline of an embryonic form and puts that mark of origin into question. Thus, while the narrator's attempt to write his way into his mother's body cannot guarantee him knowledge of his biological or family history, it provides readers with a dense figure bringing together previously dispersed evocations of its components: the desire for and fear of envelopment, breast as lack of nourishment, the toothless, masticating mouth remembered from Barcelona, emergence from sleep as from a womb.

These *renvois*, or referrals, only appear to be generated by the text, for they engage reading in the novel's figurations of the body, desire, memory, history, religion, politics, gender, and culture. For instance, as the narrator contemplates a photograph of his mother as a young woman, her arched and corseted body evokes a memory of a woman's breasts imagined to be as translucent and veined as the marble of funerary monuments:

> like those breasts of statues scored with signatures of tourists
> graffiti clumsily inscribed with a sharp point (knife, nail) which
> slips and skids
> marble scratched, scored. (139)

Refiguring Narrative and Cultural Legacies 51

The inscriptions of the pointed instrument referred to here are taken up in descriptive details elsewhere: the hourglass shapes of women's corseted bodies, which are fashioned into what is a deformity, "a lump a preeminent gibbosity," making the narrator wonder why they are not pulled forward; these shapes evoke the lettering on advertisements for old-fashioned pep pills, its capital *B* recalling that of Barcelona, and these shapes in turn recall a drawing in a women's fashion magazine depicting a gigantic soup bowl filled with pabulum, being taken by assault by tiny figures of children, some of whom fall into the milky substance. As Simon's writing slips from one female image to another, its sense emerges from yet another passage in which the fear of falling, of being drawn down, is clearly motivated by the fear of being entrapped and suffocated by the mother's breast. These figures are associated with the notion of writing as violent fashioning (nail or knife), a notion itself linked to the social "corseting" of the female body. Since the narrator's actual memory of his mother's body is of her wracked by illness, in no way resembling a nourishing maternal body, the fear of being smothered by such a body must be generated as a fiction, fabricated from ready-made images of constricted women's bodies, that is, from prior forms of cultural suffocation and entrapment that are as grotesque as they are violent: "swept on by the weight would fall capsize collapse and bury me smother me under the shapeless and sexless mass of her soft maternal bosom" (140). Simon's writing, in its figures, actualizes the minimal elements composing the cultural narrativities that block and reveal the desire for the maternal.

Despite critics' claims that the dying mother's knife-edged face has a phallic signification, these figures resist being interpreted in a·conventional way so as to conform to the castrating, phallic mother in Freud. In Simon's fiction characters are never described without their *revenants,* phantoms, and the legacies of their other representations. If any one image or part of an image may be assigned a simple metaphorical or symbolic meaning, others—before, during, and after—emerge to recontextualize both the image and its meanings. In other words, a psychoanalytic reading cannot be limited to the Oedipal family romance but must be further integrated with the effects of slippage and recontextualization that together compose the cultural and historical meaningfulness of its narrativity.

Distributed throughout *Histoire*, figures of women nursing their infants recur to intimate the severance signified by the narrator's mother's death. On a postcard of Tonkin, for example, he notes especially the stagnant water on which appear to float the decapitated head of a young boy and the nude bust of a woman "cut off at the breasts the twin hemispheres completed by their reversed and paler reflections" (111). Later, his intense scrutiny of a banknote, revealing the double image of a watermark, recalls an image on banknotes now out of circulation: "allegorical figures a woman giving suck sitting like the ones" (170). The next chapter pursues the figure of the nursing mother, who is now no longer appropriated as symbolic value of maternal reproduction but described as a figure of poverty: "The ones (or the one, since you might have thought it was always the same one) always standing on the steps of churches of banks . . . pressing the baby to the heavy breast . . . the open mouth exposing toothless gums still smeared with milk" (171). (The detail in the Barcelona scenes describing the revolutionaries' mouths and chewing connects those political scenes to the maternal ones.) These figures reveal obscurely the narrativity of their own "watermark," so to speak, in that they become readable in the movement of reading between discontinuous evocations. The narrator's loss of his mother's nurturing presence, like the repressed scene of her intolerable agony, scripted in palimpsest as a watermark of memory, cannot be represented as such. Its narrative is unpresentable in any conventional narrative order and can be only phantomatically marked in the process of writing and reading that traces out these figures of narrativity.

The difference must be emphasized between a reading of textual generators in Simon and one in which figures are always (re)contextualized as a social and political narrativity. For instance, when Ralph Sarkonak traces with remarkable precision the textual generators in *Histoire*, he claims that the notion needs to be "expanded" so as to account for "(infra-)linguistic criteria."[10] By *expansion* he means the valorization of the phonic and graphic levels. The links that his reading generates between "mother-breasts-knifeblade-tears" identify the dying mother ("knifeblade face") as the phallic mother who cuts, kills, and dispenses death. For Sarkonak, it is she who "kills" the narrator's wife and carries with her the family tradition of widowhood. In this reading, the narrative line has not been dispensed with but has been shifted onto a formal plane sustained by the Oedipal family romance. In Britton's Lacanian reading of *Histoire* in terms of the narrator's repressed desire for the mother, she speaks of the fetishization of the mother's body, noting repetitions of words occurring in scenes describing both the mother and the artist's model.[11] If Sarkonak and Britton are right, however, then Simon only repeats the tradition that divides woman into available prostitutes and unavailable saints (mothers), into purveyors of life and death. Because their readings of *Histoire* tend to downplay the cultural and historical specificity of his writing, however, their focus is on women as objects of male desire figuring desire as lack. But these are perhaps secondary effects of what he shows to be the cultural reproduction of women and mothers. Simon's writing on women does not simply repeat ready-made, culturally reproduced representations, because it succeeds in rewriting the modes and figures of narrativity that reproduce them.

The evocative power of names and images that commentators take to exemplify linguistic play must be read together with their conditions of emergence and reinscription, which are narrative ones. The memory of a Spanish revolutionary poster representing freedom from oppression (hands raised, chains severed), for example, recalls another image reproduced on a stamp:

> the name (Memel) suggesting the French word mamelle and in its very aspect (the two e's perhaps) something icy a black city snow-crowned beside a frozen livid sea inhabited by Slavonic women with flaxen hair and heavy snowy breasts (the two l's in mamelle suggesting a vision of twin forms, jumeLLes, balancing) able to see the tombstones raised pushed back falling over in an explosion of crystals and the Sistine bodies male and female marvelously beautiful pale and naked leaping up springing forward arms outstretched toward that shadowy apocalyptic sun. (178, modified)

The political "message" of the poster (freedom from chains) at first appears pushed aside by the child's fascination with words for a woman's body (as well as his desire for a Cratylian mimetism), but that political sense returns reframed as a figure of redemption in an apocalyptic iconography. The wordplay (Memel-Mamelle-jumeLLes) is situated in terms of desire for the mother, for language, and for images. The narrator's memory of his desire when he was a child emerges here in contiguity with a political iconography and a Christian one, in the interplay between the master narratives of emancipation and redemption. He goes on to describe Lambert, the schoolboy with the "arsenal of puns" who criticizes the young narrator's bourgeois family, makes suggestive remarks about his cousin Corinne's sexual availability, and later derides what he calls the narrator's "romantic" involvement in the Spanish Revolution. The narrativity of writing thus maintains a political dimension without severing it from the legacies of the narrator's past, that is, the realm of memory, awakening sensuality, failed revolutionary engagement, and the experience of absence and lack.

In *Histoire* the narrator attempts to reconstitute the individual figures of his family, the past, and his experience of war and revolution without merely reinscribing their simulacra, ready-made images, and fictions. Simon's writing, as opposed to the narrator's desire, inevitably recounts its encounter with these images and explores the tenuous narrativity bordering the fragmented figures of the narrator's past. In so doing Simon traces the narrative legacies inherent in conventionalized signs and forms (money, the activity of writing, language, etc.), as well as those narrative figures in memory that resist being reduced to a system of (re)production, commodification, and waste. By resisting the conventional narrative forms that prescribe a reductive frame for past and present, Simon opens up the text to the potential narrativity, or *histoire,* of memory fragments through detail and description. The same old story proves to be inadequate for dealing with the polyphony of voices from the past or for the complex (dis)harmonies that link them to the present. Since narration is a work of (re)animation or exhumation, the narrator's task is to forestall the reduction of the past's difference and diversity (of which the acacia tree is one of the privileged figures) to the Same, to his memory of the formulas in old ladies' voices and faces:

> as if here too all the tumult of the world died away, faded, insignificant, all equally confounded in the same incoherent, monotonous complaint through which all events, happy, unhappy or neutral occasions . . . were indiscriminately reduced to those snatches of desolate sentences, those commentaries hanging in the motionless air

Refiguring Narrative and Cultural Legacies 55

like those vibrations which persist long after the bells have stopped ringing, circling back, repeating themselves, . . . the monotonous and eternal lamentations and the same images, the same maze of interlacing wrinkles. (15–16)

An irreducible tension arises in Simon between the reductiveness of consecrated narratives (of family, history, politics, and social rituals) and the possibility of finding another way of telling from within the ruins of traditional narrative order. *Histoire*, therefore, may be read as the narrator's resistance to the narrative legacy of the Same (economy, war, and death) and the paradoxical movement of writing toward the (m)other by means of a now ruined, fragmented sameness.

The novel describes a certain world coming to an end, destroyed as much by external events (war, dislocations, commodification, etc.) as by an internal, voracious monster (memory? time? death?) eating away at the contents of things to leave only their forms. The narrator's memory of chamber music evenings, held when he was a child and attended by his dying mother, evokes in him a composite of dazzling sights and sounds that become powerful figures for memory and writing. The memory of the scene simultaneously includes its destruction by what the narrator imagines as an invisible army of termites:

> attacking now the final remains, the carapaces, the fabrics, everything crumbling, peeling, dissolving until the whole salon, the guests, the musicians, the pictures, the lights blur, disappear
> Thinking: not dissolve, fall to pieces
> Where, how? Recapitulation: chairs chromium-plated tubes, imitation leather, marble partition behind me. (71)

The disintegration of the world of childhood memories is superseded or relayed by the bank's hard, new technological order, whose commodification transforms material and symbolic legacies into immaterial shifts of capital. The narrator here calls for a narrative "recapitulation" of details to counter the danger of total dissolution of legacy as difference into the commodification (or capitalization) of the Same.

When the intensity of memory threatens to overwhelm the narrator, he asks: "But exactly, exactly?" Such attempts to restore order characterize his uncle Charles, who represents the belief that exact description is the only hope for narratively controlling memory. For the narrator, on the contrary, the problem of memory, "everything returning at the same time," cannot be resolved by relying on a purely phenomenal description or epochē. When Charles insists that his nephew tell him about his experience in revolutionary Spain, he demands a particular kind of story, an eyewitness description: "But tell me again. If you still haven't managed to decide what you were going to do there at least try to remember not how it happened (that you'll never know—at least tell me what you saw") (143). Narrativity arises from within the request to be told how it was; description contains a narrativity irreducible to conventional narrative chronology or sequencing: "tout en même temps recommençons premièrement deuxièmement troisièmement impossible" (175; "everything happened at the same time let's start over first second third impossible" [145]). Thus, memory in Simon occurs as phantomatic *"revenants"* whose own legacies of narrativity elude simultaneously the demands for either a narrative or descriptive order in which each could remain separate from or opposed to the other. From the narrator's "account" of his myopic perceptions during a shoot-out in a Barcelona square, his uncle concludes ironically: "the only indications of action—of History in the making—being reduced to those few ephemeral mushrooms of yellow dust that from time to time exploded in clusters on the façade behind the banner" (150). The narrator's inability to relate his experience to the prescribed order of narrative history reveals not simply the demise of an obsolete form but also his active resistance to the lures of its explanatory order. Nevertheless, his recollection of a brief, violent episode of the revolution in its stark details cannot be dismissed as being nonnarrative. The play of light and shade, silence and noise, and movement and immobility combine to create a complex scene endowed with a different type of narrativity, one whose links to the narrator's past and present are forged through the recurrence of their figures. The question of description and memory brings reading to the heart of a dispersed narrativity.

The novel's narrativity concerns, therefore, not its formal composition but rather the conditions of possibility for a writing that links the figures of a fragmented cultural narrativity. Scenes of bodies exhumed and marble figures being defaced contribute to our understanding of that narrativity. These episodes, situated during the Spanish Revolution, are thoroughly linked by the reference to the slipping of a writing instrument, which we earlier read as figuring a writing (constricting) of women and their bodies. Anamnesis in the novel is figured as a double activity of exhumation and reinscription, for the narrator's work of memory is a process of unearthing, breaking, and tracing. Although the narrator does not yet acknowledge in these scenes that his activity of remembering is involved, his descriptions suggest the narrative movement of his exhumation of the cadavers of his family's past and those of history. He is at once the sender, receiver, and referent of legacies of narrativity that situate him and that he does not control.

As receiver of the collection of postcards, his situation has analogies with that of his mother, whom he imagines on her deathbed: "it was all over now present immobilized everything here in the same moment forever the images the moments the voices the fragments of time of the multiple sumptuous inexhaustible world scattered on a dying woman's bed" (326). The similarities between their positions imply that narrative legacies also involve a process of mourning, an identification with absence. He symbolically attempts to occupy her position but is unable to grasp the "destination" of her legacies. Desiring to hold everything together in the present, a present imaginable only at the very threshold of his mother's absence, he attempts momentarily to arrest the past, to prevent it from escaping him. Since particular memories such as those of the revolution do not lie outside time, they are threatened with a double disappearance ("escaping me") due as much to the narrator's own desire to escape them as to their escape from him.

In the final evocations of the voices of the past in the acacia tree's rustling, the novel's figure of a narrative memory par excellence, which is related to the gesticulating Spanish activists, it becomes clear that the narrator's "reliquary" of phantoms is also threatened with disappearing:

> able to perceive behind them something like a murmur spreading running through the inextricable tangle of branches as if the whole tree were shaking itself shivering then everything quieting down the murmurs of their desolate arrogant voices around Grand-mère ... (334–35)

then they'll collapse again sink down continuing to gesticulate another moment like the passengers of a ship slowly submerged vanishing little by little into the depths of time and me impotent watching them slowly engulfed effaced. (335)[12]

The narrator's final re-vision or reanimation of a phantomatic past situates him as a guilty survivor, powerless to arrest the submerging and final effacement of his individual, collective, and historical past. The novel closes, as we have seen, on his attempt to encrypt his embryonic origin ("me?") in his mother's body.

In the work of narrativity remembrance does not simply restore the past to the present. The writing that exhumes memory also buries it anew, immersing it in (a new) language whose narrativity emerges in the figurations of details and their tangents. The narrator no longer repeats the same formulaic stories, whose nightmare of rememoration opens and blocks the narrator's memories at the beginning of the novel.[13] His memories become inseparable from the narrativities linking them, which cannot be discarded, for they are themselves both a condition and an effect of memories. In sum, Simon's *Histoire* is a remarkably dense and illuminating reinvention of the workings of memory in its narrative conditions of possibility. Its writing tells much about the narrativities of cultural legacies and memory, which cannot be made to conform to a universal, homogeneous narrative text.

Simon's *Les Géorgiques* recapitulates the major themes of his previous novels such as war, the land, labor, the family, and desire. Along with *L'Acacia*, which I will treat in the final chapter, *Les Géorgiques* must also be read as the most thoroughly elaborated version in his work to date of the narrative conditions of legacy. Three men and a woman are brought together in this text; each is involved in a decisive historical moment: the history of Europe from the French Revolution to the Restoration (the General L.S.M. and Batti his overseer), the Spanish Revolution (O.), and the debacle of the French army in World War II (the cavalryman). From the very opening of the novel Simon's writing explores the conditions of legacies and the narrativities that subtend them.

The prologue describes two male figures in the style of David's drawings for the *Oath of the Jeu de Paume*, with the older one holding a letter. From the prologue two dimensions of reading unfold. (1) Contrasting with the uncertainties of time and sequence in the prologue, the first chapter opens with laconic sentences cataloguing the ancestor's historical exploits. Different dates, places, and events in L.S.M.'s career appear jumbled together, epitomizing the fragments of a minimal and discontinuous narrative history from which description has been eliminated, except for the fact that the fragments are in the present tense associated with description. (2) Description returns when a second narrative, in italics, intrudes on the minimal archives of the first and begins to tell the cavalryman's story of the debacle in Flanders. While at first appearing to mimic the historical rhetoric of L.S.M.'s titanesque exploits, the second narrative in fact constitutes a particular "reading" of the General's archives and hence provides an opening for the return of description and detail. Despite the historical gap separating them, the recounting of one soldier's experience "reads" another's archival legacy. As the text moves on, the first *he*'s history alternates with the recent war-related "historical" experiences of the second *he*. The novel introduces a third *he*, later identified as O., the Orwellian volunteer in the Spanish Revolution. But it would be a mistake to limit the situations of destination and reception to only the male protagonists. Present throughout as the first addressee of the General's letters, Batti is the one whose situation most closely resembles that of the narrator who inherits the archives. Moreover, the reader is given to understand that many other situations and effects of destination in turn frame these *histoires*.[14]

The activities of reading and writing open up and are opened up by the narrative dimensions of legacies, dimensions that the novel figures first as the hand, whose skin is "furrowed [*sillonnée*] with hundreds of wrinkles, like crepe georgette" (17), of someone reading or writing archival registers. The hands and eyes may belong either to the aged General or to his now aged descendant, the cavalryman as reader and writer: "He is tired. He closes his eyes. The luminous imprint of the register, its pages brightened by sunlight, lingers on his retina" (17). The word *sillon* ("furrow") configures different narrativities of the novel: the wrinkled hand poised over the written page, the furrows of cultivated land, trenches in warfare, and the wake left in the General's path (and that of his marble bust) as he streaks across Europe like a meteorite. In other words, the details of the hand's texture or an afterimage imprinted on the retina partake also of narrativity, coming to emblematize the narrative paths or *sillons* of events as well.

Typographically, there occurs a break in the continuity of the printed page. In a quotation of the General's lament at the death of his beloved first wife, the archival fragment is seemingly torn or shattered along a jagged line that divides the memorial in two parts, with half on one page of Simon's text and half on the next:

>   night heard my complaints
>   on a coffin when
>   changed the face of Europe
>   movement of the revolution
>   run every kind of risk
>   the greatest dangers I succeeded.
>   (23)

He screws up his eyes to read the words:
> a tomb; the
> dawn found me
> the event which
> the great
> led me to
> in the midst of.
>   (24)

The line that shatters the incomplete epitaph is in fact cast by a hand whose shadow creates yet another *sillon* in a novel that is, like the Europe that the General crosses with his armies, "sillonnée . . . en tous sens" ("furrowed . . . in all directions/senses"). The integral text of legacy cannot be recomposed or unified without passing over the writing and reading that divide it, thereby creating its very narrativity. The narrator observes:

> When the registers are held up at an angle and the pages turned, fine rust-coloured particles, with glinting, golden facets like mica, fall from the letters and slide down the leaves. It is as if the assembled words, sentences and very marks left on the paper by the troop movements, battles, intrigues and speeches flake, crumble and fall

Refiguring Narrative and Cultural Legacies 61

into dust, leaving on one's hands nothing but an impalpable powder, the colour of dried blood. (51)

The timeworn materiality of the writing, whose ink traces are reduced to dust, appears to contrast with the apparently timeless dimensions of the narrative legacies opened up by the writing.

Nevertheless, the narrativity elaborated in *Les Géorgiques* does not remain untouched by time, history, and context. The scene of writing and reading becomes the site of convergences and divergences that alter the shapes of time and experience. Whereas these scenes remain for the most part unassignable to any one source or origin, belonging with equal probability to the General (referred to as "il") or to the cavalryman who inherits his archives also referred to as ("il"), they provide a common ground for a bare minimum of shared elements such as a wrinkled hand, the play of optical effects of light and color, the spectacle of Glück's *Orpheus*, cavalry warfare, and flight from the enemy. Related metaphorically, these scenes provide a figure of passage for one character to link up with another, for one epoch to connect with another, without closing the historical gap separating them or erasing their differences. In contrast, O. is a mystifying narrator who casts his experiences of the revolution in a pregiven narrative, chronological, and causal order. There is no common measure between the events and the conventional narrative structure he ascribes to them later in London as he pores over conflicting newspaper articles on the revolution. Reading Simon's novel together with George Orwell's "eyewitness" account, *Homage to Catalonia*, which it recapitulates intertextually, we note that the scene of writing in the novel presents O. voicing his story hoarsely because a neck injury during the revolution damaged his vocal chords. By staging in this way the event's mark on the narrative "voice," Simon subverts the type of conventional narrative such as O.(rwell)'s that works to silence it. In so doing, he welds the narrative situation inseparably to the revolution O. describes, whereas that scene is absent from Orwell's text.

Les Géorgiques is not only a story of men. Batti, whose "milk brothers" are the two L.S.M. brothers, is very much involved in the problematics of legacy. The narrator first suggests that she herself is part of the inheritance L.S.M. leaves to his son, Eugène, that is, an object to be handed down in the family (459). But he corrects himself: "Or rather no. The opposite. That is to say it was she who had inherited him" (311). Like the narrator, then, she is the receiver and agent of a family and revolutionary legacy. Besides being an addressee of the General's personal correspondence, she is also the one who, in managing the land, converts his words into actions. Significantly, the novel's final scenes focus on the narrator imagining her standing, reading L.S.M.'s tyrannical letters (the standing position being that of destination and reception, described in detail in the prologue, rather than that of writing or reading seated at a table). After his death, the General's monologue to her turns into a dialogue with her when Batti, rebelling, is said to treat him as an equal. The revolution's legacies are intimated in the shift in Batti's position from that of obedient receiver and executor of the General's instructions to that of interlocutor and sender in her own right. As an essential part of the structure of destination, she breaks the seals placed by law on the General's possessions after his death. Transcripts of legal proceedings reproduced in the novel ascribe various classist motives to her, yet her action may simply signify her postrevolutionary equality. Through Batti and the narrator (as child, cavalryman, and aged reader/writer), Simon refigures the narrative of legacy. The legacy of the archives is not a privileged theory of the past to be handed down intact but rather the signs of divisions, dissimulations, and diversions (*détournements*) from mainstream history. The reception of such legacies, then, is a critical rewriting, a reevaluation of legacy through a refiguring of its narrativity. In retrospect, the prologue's scene of destination signals something essential—that we cannot tell whether the letter is being sent or received. The questions raised by such a focus on destination, reception, and referent involve the effects of the General's legacy. Is the narrator, like Batti, being *ordered* to conserve some legacy; is he, like her, supposed to preserve and "secure [his] hedges"? And what about the text's readers: how are they situated with respect to the legacies of narratives? In other words, what legacies are being narrated (transmitted and altered in the transmission) through the process of destination?

With its emphasis on destination and reception, my reading diverges from two readings of the relation between history and writing in Simon: that of the invisibility of history (Britton) and history as cyclical repetition (Dällenbach).[15] I shall discuss Britton first, in whose reading "fiction, mirage, image, representation, the visible... refer to different but interchangeable versions of the imaginary" (168). For Britton, Simon's writing oscillates between a visual and a generative discourse, the former constructing fantasy in the imaginary order and the latter constructing the subject in the symbolic order. The difference between the two discourses "is immediately evident in reading the novels, in the sense that the presence or absence of a fictional referent is always observable" (168). This claim can be made only because her valorization of the visible applies to the imaginary order alone, the consequences of which become clear once she engages the problem of history. Arguing that for Simon there are no structures that underpin or go beyond individual consciousness (whose awareness is either perceptual or formal), Britton seems to have no recourse but to treat history itself as invisible, as an empty space that corresponds to the real in Lacan (the "missed encounter"). She finds that the invisibility of history is confirmed by what she calls the nonhistory of space and the modes of exchange. History, culture, and change, I submit, must be located within the problematics opened up by the writing of the detail and the destinations of narrative legacies, all of which must be ignored if history is the "figure of the unpresentable," "an empty space in the text" (164), or "an area of shadow lying on the text: only as things emerge from it do they become visible" (157). But this is to take narrative legacy to be a scene of pure textuality, without any posts of destination, reception, or reference. There is, in my sense, no nonhistory in Simon, because everything is historical, especially the question of land and the modalities of exchange that underlie war, legacies, and revolution. What his texts describe as millennial or prehistorical, such as violence and exchange (and exchange as violence), is designated as such from within war and the crisis of history, not from an empty, neutral space lying outside it.

The privileging of history as cyclical repetition is attributed to the narrator's uncle Charles, but can his interpretation be taken as the privileged model of history? Simon's writing puts Charles's discourse and the narrator's commentary into italics, upsetting once again the code assigned to italics as, first, the mark of description (as opposed to the archives' minimal narrative history) and then the mark of citation (of the authenticity of legal documents). For Dällenbach the passage confirms his belief that Simon privileges history and writing as repetition and analogy. Interestingly, it is this passage that appears to found an analogy between the cyclicality of nature and that of war, but it is a dangerous analogy that, in attributing to nature a warlike character, ushers in the notion that war is part of the natural order as well. A closer examination of the passage suggests a different understanding of its narrative dimension.

Set in context, the passage refers to a legal document, the judgment against the General's brother Jean-Marie L.S.M. for desertion and emigration, the text of which is one of many legal documents reproduced in the novel. The irony of the judgment is that it involves verifying his identity in order to condemn him to death. Charles situates the judgment with respect to L.S.M.'s having voted the death of the king, "the first vote entailing the second" (301). He goes on to suggest that maybe the narrator is still too young, that as he gets older he will feel rather than understand certain things for having himself experienced them. He then says:

> *As if History were above all an accountant's affair with long additions of figures where the balance sheet is summed up in a few moments of commotion and murder [. . .] All those letters during all those years . . . A real handbook of agriculture. It was just as cyclic, just as regular as the hands of a watch returning to pass over the same figures on its face, month after month, season after season, while he hurried in all directions from one end of Europe to the other.* (302–3; italics in the original)

Charles adds ironically that the *personal* qualities required for war and agriculture are perhaps not that different.

> What I am getting at is this eternal renewal, this tireless patience or, no doubt, passion, which makes it possible to return every so often to the same places in order to carry out the same tasks: the same meadows, the same fields, the same vines, the same hedges needing replanting, the same fences to check, the same towns to besiege, the same rivers to cross or defend, the same trenches periodically opened up under the same ramparts: Koblenz, Pavia, Namur, the

Meuse, Mantua, the Ijsel, Antwerp, the Adige, Verona, Peschiera, Mainz. (303)

The return of the Same as an abstract model of repetitive history is concatenated with the repetitious tasks performed both by agricultural projects and by those of war. Simon's writing, by naming these tasks, constructions, and historical places one by one, displays their appalling monotony and thereby suspends their immediate inclusion in the totalizing master narrative of eternal return.

Thus, cyclical repetition is not *the* privileged narrative model of nature, revolution, and history in Simon, because that model is itself situated within and bordered by other narratives of legacy: that of divisions within the law (opposing brother and brother, the general and the particular, the public and the private); of history as the family's repression of an intimate yet historical truth (regicide generating fratricide); and of the problematic status of the legacy for the men and women who receive it. The novel's figurations of the narrative relation as an operator of differences (youth and old age, historical agents and victims, male and female, sender and receiver) need to be elaborated as the critical point of an encounter between Same and Other.

The novel stages, once again but differently, the scene represented in the prologue of an older and a younger man exchanging correspondence. As in the prologue, the question as to which of the two is the sender or the receiver remains undecidable, and the novel explores the movement of destination itself. Uncle Charles may believe that it is he who passes the General's archives to his nephew, framing them with his own interpretation in terms of individual acts and history as pure repetition and continuity. His belief entails a cycle of male-centered identifications from generation to generation within the family, with the grandmother reenacting the repression of the family's divisions. In the narrator's *dis-position* of and by the archives, what he makes of them and they of him, the significance of different narrative legacies emerges. He includes, for instance, Batti's importance not only as a receiver but as a historical agent (transforming signs into labor and change), the divisive effects of repression, and his own dispositions with respect to these legacies. So, beside the "imaginary order" of identifications (history as pure repetition) between the General and his distant descendant, the cavalryman, lies another order into which the individual subject is plunged, a (postrevolutionary) history governed by the law as division. History exists in a tension between repetition and imaginary doublings on one hand and difference, division, and dissimulation on the other.

Times of Narrative Legacies

The excavalryman's attempt to recount the debacle in which he was involved in World War II leads him directly to an impasse. In retracing the events that may have caused the total disintegration of his division, he finds himself compelled to fall back on a conventional narrative form: "the affair then (or the phenomenon) divisible into three phases, namely: the early hints of disaggregation, the threat of disaggregation (the first instance of break-up), and finally the disaggregation itself, consummated as it were, confirmed as an accomplished, irreversible fact, the ending of all cohesion, of all discipline" (65–66). Supported by a skeletal temporal framework, his description of the three phases proceeds in an orderly enough fashion until he reaches the final phase, which he claims "can only be described in a fragmentary manner mirroring the phenomenon of fragmentation itself" (67). Having made this rather radical statement on a catastrophic writing that would mime disaster itself, however, the excavalryman pursues in sequence: "To start with . . . there is a halt. . . . From that point onwards . . . it is necessary (since there is no organized unit any more) to pass from the plural to the particular" (67, modified). Able neither to apply nor to discard the conventional narrative framework whose credibility the catastrophic undermines, he shifts from a notion of general order to that of particular states, from plural to singular. As he tries to understand his total solitude and disorientation, he moves back to the written orders, the particular instrument that must have caused the catastrophe. The orders, he suggests, were designed to teach the soldiers "the names of history": "the same roadsigns the grayish ferruginous names which recur at every page in French history books: Bazeilles, Sedan, Mézières, Rocroy, Givet, Wattignies, Meuse, Moselle, Ardennes, Longwy" (74).

The glacial cold and unbearable conditions are likewise described as prerequisites having their assigned place in ritualized forms of historical narrative and memoirs: "no doubt so that everything could be put in order, so that the phrases in the textbooks or the memoirs of the victors could be there too, in their appointed place, like a ritual . . . as if it were necessary for the brief mention of winter quarters . . . to be made within the regular sequence of chapters between the proud accounts of campaigns and the lists of casualties" (74). The sparest details of disaster are already generated and contained by the formulas of the historical narrative that situates these details outside narrative, as the realist details guaranteeing its representation of "real war." Ritualized and replicated, the very elements of the experience of war (death, filth, unbearable cold, excrement, rust, exploding sulfur and carbon) become an instrument appropriated by the ideological ends of history as (re)production. Nonetheless, despite his feeling that the soldiers are present simply to enact some useless and deadly ceremony, the narrator persists in describing "how it was," from examining in detail the myriad colors of snow crystal formations to imagining what laws could govern such unthinkable events:

> Perhaps laws (an order or rather an ordinance which it was impossible to detect but which was just as imprescriptible, as mathematical in nature as those that govern the spirals of shells, that shape snow crystals into stars, or that structure the most minute living particles) laid it down that the different phases, the different stages of the process (or of the ritual) which had been set in train should be observed. Or perhaps, having struck a first blow, and appalled herself, History had given herself a respite, had put off . . . the moment after which the din of thousands of houses crashing down, the deaths of children by the thousand (and by the thousand thousands) the screaming of thousands upon thousands of men and women under torture, would count for no more than the daily ration of news items killings. (90)

The laws pertaining to war are first attributed an order, which is then qualified as being instead an *ordonnance* (ordinance), a word whose resonances are at issue in the novel as a whole: a *placing* into order, a *disposition* according to an order; in painting, the overall *composition* considered as a grouping and balance of masses; a *prescription* ordered by legislative or medical authority; and, suggestively in this context, the older sense of a cavalryman serving as *messenger* to a superior officer or general. The narrator presents war's ritualized slaughter in the modes of a variety of discourses and genres: the morphology, or *ordonnance*, of nature, the discourse of narrative form, allegory, and the reduction of genocide to a newpaper byline. These describe "orderings" for which no general or absolute law or order may be designated, not even the narrativities with respect to which they are nevertheless situated as an untranscendable limit.

The temporal dimensions of narrativity are pursued when the narrator permutes the biblical phrasing of the General's correspondence, which is also a poetic, Baudelairean one—"voici venir les temps."[16] The phrase illustrates the narrator's attempt to locate finality in the narrative order of antecedent models, laws, and texts. "Mais le temps n'était pas encore venu" ("But the time had not yet come") he states: "Those times, then, had not yet arrived, things (that is to say what was decided—or not decided—in their overheated offices by the school headmasters raised to the rank of masonic dignitaries, the worthy clergymen, the crafty millionaires, the former seminarist, the old American actor and the butchers strapped in leather) were probably not ripe" (90). The teleological narrative time of prophecy, here in a negative and plural form, provides a further model. Indeed, its force here derives from irony, since one narrativity (the time of biblical prophecy and redemption) is superimposed on another (the time of revolution, according to L.S.M.'s phrasing) and in turn on another (the time of arbitrary yet catastrophic [non]decisions by the war's perpetrators).

Les Géorgiques as a whole attempts to answer the enigma of the significant historical moment. The event always arrives too soon or too late, either "mais ce n'était pas encore le moment" ("but it was not yet time") or "il n'est plus temps" (meaning either "this is no time" or "there is no longer time"). Yet the words of the General's address to the National Convention on the judgment of Louis XVI are unequivocal: "the path you have trodden has sunk under your feet as you have walked: this is no time to retrace your steps" (158). The narrative structure of the General's idea of revolution is that of an irreversible history, a master narrative combining emancipation and teleological progress. His judgment on Louis XVI may therefore itself be read as figuring history as irreversible narrative time. The testy letters he writes to Batti, instructing her in the proper management of his land, signify that the revolution has not changed the narrative of property and confirm his belief in the power of performative language. The imperatives of this language determine time, situation, and act as unquestionably convergent: "Voici venir le printemps, ma chère Batti" (216; "Spring is coming, my dear Batti" [147]), and "Ma chère Batti, voilà le moment de garantir mes haies" (217; "My dear Batti, now is the time to secure my hedges" [147]). In L.S.M.'s old age the powerful words about the timeliness of time that emblematize the master narratives of redemption, emancipation, and property are echoed in a minor key by the narrator in the context of L.S.M.'s economy of time: "as if he knew that his days were numbered" (255; "Comme s'il savait que le temps lui était compté" [375]). In the final words of the novel, the narrator reads, after Batti, the General's regret for wines not made and fruits not preserved ("although my father was a very good fruit-preserver"), in which he asks her a question that ties these ways of preserving nature to the economy of preserving life in the face of death: "do you think I have so many years to throw out of the window?" (322).

The narrator's reading and writing of legacies, his different dis-position of them, seriously questions the general's faith in the conjuncture of time, place, and the determinism of history. He reworks the figures of convergence and divergence that are constitutive of the revolution, history, and the law. The law emerges as an instrument of division instead of the guarantor of the unity of truth and rights: the law that proclaims regicide legitimate also encrypts the law on emigrants that, in sentencing L.S.M.'s brother to be executed, brings fratricide along with regicide into the family's divided history. The law becomes the instrument creating the history of innumerable divisions, partitions, and conflictual tensions that affect the General's descendants and his legacy. Despite L.S.M.'s testament to his son, Eugène, as his sole inheritor and his resistance to the dividing and fragmenting of the legacy, "there had been apportionments, lots drawn, then sharing of apportionments, removals, displacements" (158). The act (over time) of the General's great-grand-daughter to suppress his archives, which confirm his part in writing an opinion on Louis Hugues's judgment and the law on emigrants, replicates the General's own attempt to erase his brother's name from his archives. In its virtual, divisive power, one law inevitably creates another law in which the effects of this power are enacted. The law itself divides, because one law legitimating regicide contains the division that generates the other law making the General a fratricide—that is, legitimation creates history as divergence and difference.

Simon's writing has never before gone so far in probing the diachronic dimensions and effects over time of narrative legacies. In *Les Géorgiques* the performative force of the revolutionary law is that of division, a decapitation that divides any unitary narrative. As it judges wrongs and competing rights and metes out punishment and compensation, the law designates the difference between the private and public realm, the personal and the historical, property and disappropriation, what is on the inside and on the outside of narrative legacies. Significantly, these legacies in Simon's writing take on a movement similar to the figure of the chiasmus as elaborated by Derrida. Applying the outside to the inside, the figure of the chiasmus is "a structure of referral (*renvoi*) that always divides a totality by what it believes to leave at its borders."[17]

In Simon the structure of referral is neither universalized nor ahistorical. It is situated in the novel's figures as the violent collision between the generality of the law and its particular effects on the general's brother, his succession, and his legacy. The suppression of the documentary evidence by the old lady and her family is programmed by the logic of referral that subtends the oppositions themselves (public/private, legality/death, general/particular, part/whole). The General's descendants repeat the gesture of effacement (of the truth of the brother's death) and in so doing reintroduce what was excluded from their history into the very core of their family's obsessions. The narrativity of the General's legacy implies that there is internal differentiation within, but not separation or opposition between, public and private realms, form and content, body and spirit, and sign and meaning. The archives, part of which are classified as the "Correspondance particulière du Général," therefore do not merely reconstitute the ideals and exploits of the revolutionary General and his descendants' decadence. Rather, in the narrativity that they ac-

Refiguring Narrative and Cultural Legacies 71

quire in the novel, the archives are shown to participate in and possess both a particular and a historical logic of referral that frames all correspondences.

The novel's scenes of exhumation figure the materiality of the body of the past. They create a variety of correspondences among the "exhumation" of the General's body, of the family's past, and of the narrator's reading/writing of the archives. (The narrator re-creates the scene of the General's body being brutally ejected from its tomb, the heart crudely sawed out of his body and placed in a jar of alcohol, and the cadaver sewn back up, "the gaping chest sewn up again with big cross-stitching like a laced shoe" [305, modified]). The "lacing" up of the General's body bears a remarkable resemblance to the old lady's lifelong destiny of repression, figured by her constant wallpapering of the door behind which lie the general's archives: "like a corpse buried behind the tangles of red leaves," "the evidence of something inexpiable (something monstrous?)" (32, modified). As the ultimate heir of the General's archives, the narrator reads and writes them in a process of exhumation that carries with it repression, effacement, and forgetting. Indeed, he reflects with irony on the process of reanimation whereby a marble bust or the papers of the General come to be substituted for his dead person. The legacies of narrative, in this sense, cannot be limited to formal analogies and imaginary identifications between characters (the narrator, the General, his brother, Batti, and O.). Reading and writing engage here with a radical division, or *partage*, that is the legacy of decrypting signs of the past, a narrative legacy casting its shadow onto the private and public realms of war, revolution, and time.

Is it possible, however, that Simon's work nevertheless ends up by producing a nostalgic vision of the monumentality represented by the ancestor's historical exploits? Does Simon perpetuate a monumental history in which readers are situated as unquestioning heirs to its narrative tradition? I think not, for the narrativity at work in the interstices and the fissures of that monumentality cannot be reconciled with such a nostalgic history. For a reading attentive to *revenance*, to the spectral figures of narrative legacies haunting the text with their remanence, the splits and divisions in legacies are at once the inescapable and enabling conditions of these figures' meaningfulness. A quotation from *La Corde raide* reflexively taking up a well-known phrase from Rimbaud, "Je est un autre," recalls this fissuring: "It's like trying to hold water in your hands. Try. to find yourself. 'I is another.' Not true: 'I am others. Other things, other smells, other sounds, other people, other places, other times.'"[18] The next chapter pursues the question of legacies through the parodic modes of Simon's writing, situating them in relation to the dialogic, the simulacrum, and cultural legacies.

3

*Parody in Postmodernity: Replication
and Cultural Critique*

*What could a parody be that did not advertise itself as such?
This is the problem facing modern writing: how to breach the wall
of utterance, the wall of origin, the wall of ownership?*
—ROLAND BARTHES

Discussions of postmodernism reveal considerable ambivalence with regard to parody, which nevertheless persists as one of its defining terms. There is a pervasive sense of "if only" where parody is concerned: if only it were not quite so masterful, so ironic, so authorized, and so distance creating, it would then be better able to account for postmodern practices and their articulation with critical theory. In a general sense, parody is always involved to some degree in postmodernism's tendency to reproduce systems of representation and to stress their replication. For some, however, it remains too closely bound to the certitudes of the modernist paradigms of ironic and aesthetic distance, subjectivity (Barthes), and style (Jameson). Nevertheless, a wholesale rejection of parody carries with it a loss of critical focus on questions of narrativity and the historical dimensions of discourses. In other words, if criticism dispenses with parody, it may well be led to treat the conditions of writing "from within" by defining them as a synchronic space of images and simulacra. Unless theory accepts being lost in the funhouse of what Guy Debord has called the "society of the spectacle," and in so doing losing its own purpose, it cannot abandon parody entirely. Parody thus comes into play in two spheres: (1) in the broad sweep of discussions concerning the Enlightenment,[1] romanticism, and modernism, whose controlled ironies and critical distance imply knowledge of the norm or law and its transgression, and (2) in debates on postmodernism where those certitudes are in question. But valorizing parody's critical effectiveness is not tantamount to occupying an exterior position of distance and mastery, a position systematically undone in contemporary art. To grasp postmodern writing we need to invent readings that neither ignore the real pervasiveness of simulacra in contemporary culture nor simply assent to their unbounded proliferation. Such readings would not replicate mimetically the workings of the various apparatuses that (re)produce simulacra. Parody works to provoke questions concerning replication, the crossing of cultural spaces, and the possibility of oppositional practices of writing; it needs to be recognized as a necessary participant in a critical practice of humor (Lyotard, Barthes) and pastiche (Jameson).

In 1966 Marcelin Pleynet, a member of *Tel Quel,* made what Susan Suleiman characterizes as a pessimistic prognosis for the avant-gardes of the 1960s: "In our time, no more transgression, no more subversion, no more rupture . . . or rather, in my opinion, a parody of transgression, a parody of subversion, a simulacrum, repetition of rupture."[2] Ihab Hassan remarks on the parodic and self-reflexiveness of the postmodern novel with its multiple, fractured, and ambiguous perspectives.[3] For most theorists, however, parody is deemed to be too "masterfully" transgressive for the postmodernist paradigm. Barthes, for one, argues against parody because of its association with classical irony, the trope that enacts the discrepancy between language and meaning but always presumes the institutionalization of the law.[4] He finds in Flaubert's novels the workings of a different irony marked by an uncertainty that discomforts classical irony's reliance on subjectivity.[5] Hence parody, for Barthes, is "irony at work," employed "in behalf of a subject who puts its own imaginary into the distance it pretends to take with regard to the language of others."[6] As a result, parody merely confirms the power of the subject of discourse. Nevertheless, as Barthes's question in the epigraph suggests, he seems unwilling to abandon it entirely.

Ambivalence toward parody emerges as well in Jameson's work on postmodernism,[7] in which Jameson seeks to trace the developments whereby modernist styles become postmodernist codes in the context of advanced capitalism where, as he writes quoting Debord, "the image has become the final form of commodity reification" (18). In postmodernism, Jameson argues, an autonomous culture is dissolved in "a prodigious expansion of culture throughout the social realm, to the point at which everything in our social life—from economic value and state power to practices and to the very structure of the psyche itself—can be said to have become "cultural" in some original and yet untheorized sense" (87).[8] The "micropolitics" of proliferating social codes have heterogeneous styles and discourses without a norm, which are "antithetical to parody which gives way to pastiche and humor." Although Jameson says that "pastiche is, like parody, the imitation of a peculiar or unique, idiosyncratic style, the wearing of a linguistic mask" (17), he claims that it is a neutral practice of "blank parody, a statue with blind eye-balls," without "any of parody's ulterior motives." My use of parody resembles what Jameson calls pastiche's heterogeneity.[9] I will retain the concept of parody, however, for the critical dimension he believes to be characterized by modernist distance and now unavailable in late capitalism. His understanding of the postmodern asserts the presence or immediacy of simulacra without the mediations of history, subjectivity, and memory. The narrativity of these mediations, I propose, requires that even a postmodern pastiche of forms still needs to be considered in terms of parody. Otherwise, the critical dimension of the postmodern itself is likely to dissipate.

Interestingly, parody makes a comeback as "parodic force" when Jameson discusses postmodern "fantastic historiography" (in Gabriel García Márquez and Thomas Pynchon) as free play with the past. Through the "inventiveness of fabulation" narratives gain an active relationship to praxis, despite their lack of control over events: "agency here steps out of the historical record itself into the process of devising it; and new multiple or alternate strings of events rattle the bars of the national tradition and the history manuals whose very constraints and necessities their parodic force indicts" (369). Thus, despite Jameson's conviction that the generalizing tendency of late capitalism erases depth, the subject, memory, and history, some indications of incompleteness appear in his totalizing view of image commodification in late capitalism. If the generalizing tendency of postmodernism were in fact accomplished absolutely, then there would probably be neither a need nor a means to critique it historically or culturally. Since this is not the case, parodic interventions continue to provide a necessary counterbalance to the totalizing aims of general theory. Postmodern parody would be a way of addressing the discursive underpinnings of identity and difference, same and other, model and copy.

For Lyotard the question of parody arises in the context of a call to elaborate theory-fictions.[10] It is not the derision of terroristic theory he is after but its parody, which undermines its model by becoming indistinguishable from it. Unlike Jameson, he argues against a *general* intelligibility, reality, concept, or definition: "because for a judgment to be true, a metalanguage must authorize it; and there is no master to pronounce this metadiscourse" (54, my translation). "Modernity is judgment without criteria," he writes later, "judgments are not regulated by categories."[11] The claim is a radical one and has fueled much debate concerning the dangers of abandoning general principles of judgment and value and the possibility of an aesthetics of the particular. The idea of judging without criteria still occupies the same field of concepts as the law and its transgression, critical distance and knowledge. Rather than parody, which is thoroughly mediated by the criteria of a universal genre, humor is modernity's essential tone for Lyotard (and his interlocutor, Jean-Loup Thébaud) (12). Humor is opposed to romantic irony, which for Lyotard "consists in going beyond the law of classicism in the matter of the reader, that is, the law of taste, by discovering a new reader above this law"; and Thébaud concludes that this reader "knows the law and parodies it. Whereas humor would be one of the characteristics of modernity" (12). Significantly, this discussion of humor versus parody follows on Lyotard's idea of the "evanescence of the addressee" in Diderot and modernity, which he reads in terms of substitutions in the pragmatic system of narration: "permutations of the author with the narrator, of the narratee with the speaker and with the one who is spoken of in the narrative, and so on" (12). Parody, humor, and narrative permutations are necessarily linked and need to be related to the broader epistemological and historical context of what Lyotard has called the waning of master narratives in postmodernity. Although Jameson now

Parody in Postmodernity 77

finds that eschatological schemata and not narratives are the real issue, he nevertheless detects a continued narrative understanding of the retreat of narrative epistemologies. To grasp this contradictory and paradoxical situation, the field of replication and repetition that parody opens up needs to be explored further.

Derrida's practice of deconstruction engages that field as difference in (re)iteration, supplementarity, translation, and original and copy, all of which are involved in parody. He distinguishes his project from a certain postmodern one when he claims that *écriture* is the "restance manquante du simulacre" ("lacking remainder of the simulacrum"). This absent remainder of the simulacrum is for Derrida a structural limit that does not close off a field of knowledge or define its exteriority because the remainder is at once the condition of and the opening of and onto any field. Parody is one of the means, he states, whereby writing and supplementarity always preclude any total control of sense and code. Heterogeneity and the parodic are not to be accepted passively as a way of affirming that the "maître sens, le sens unique et hors greffe est introuvable" ("the master sense, the singular and graftless sense, is irretrievable").[12] By doing so one would make of parody or the simulacrum an instrument at the service of truth or castration. Instead, Derrida links the workings of parody and the simulacrum, suggesting that both undo the subject of consciousness and knowledge, an undoing performed also by deconstruction: "la parodie suppose toujours quelque part une naïveté, adossée à un inconscient, et le vertige d'une non-maîtrise, une perte de connaissance. La parodie absolument calculée serait une confession ou une table de la loi" (100; "parody always supposes a naivety withdrawing into an unconscious, a vertiginous nonmastery, a loss of consciousness. Absolutely calculated parody would be a confession or a tablet of the law" [translation modified]. Derrida's deconstruction involves a form of parody that would be not be transgressive with respect to the law but rather translational. In this form of parody originals become such through their very translation. To the extent that the original may be said to parody its translation, copies without originals proliferate in this form of parodic writing.

Claude Simon's writing redirects these questions concerning postmodernity toward their narrative conditions. It recapitulates and reinvents the way in which the symbolic exchanges of discourse, history, and culture come into representation. And it is through parody that Simon's rewriting and critique of narrative representation may be read. Contemporary and postmodern novels do not simply recycle histories, myths, and the image-objects of mass culture in a passive, unmotivated, or neutral way. They reinvent the narrativity of these discourses in every dimension and on every level, production, destination, reception, and reference. I propose to extend the notion of parody beyond its formal definition so as to explore more fully its critical effects.

For the Russian formalists, parody's literary function is constantly at issue in their theories of *l'écart*, defamiliarization, and the "baring" of artifice and conventions. In fact, these theories of parody privilege what Iouri Tynianov calls its "quality of divergence" (*Differenzqualität*), a quality that accounts for the dynamism of literary change.[13] In his view such development proceeds not in a linear fashion but by means of a specific work of mechanization-destruction, divergence, and struggle through which the new material is organized.[14] Tynianov's model of parody is not only formally defined, however; his writing also narrates a dialectical struggle between destruction and construction bearing the marks of a social struggle. This conflict is itself modeled on the Oedipal narrative of the male writer locked in a struggle to supplant his "paternal" antecedents. Clearly, parody cannot be limited to serving an autonomous aesthetic function, since it relates instead to the cultural and social dimensions of literary and other signifying systems. Parody creates connections and *passages* between the aesthetic and the cultural, fiction and nonfiction, serious and nonserious, in short, between the discourses of fiction and the contexts in which they have their effects. In this perspective, parody works to undermine attempts to sever language from social discourse or formal experimentation from cultural and historical issues.

But why is it now a question of parody? Claude Abastado defines parody as dependent on a triangular situation of decoding (between parodist, parodied text, and reader) involving a communicative situation or "cultural community" that is subject to historical change.[15] The target of parody is a word, a set of words, a genre, or a style; parody turns, Abastado claims, on signifying systems, thus producing a language to the second degree. Parody organizes the fragmented discourses and topoi of modern writing as a space of tension and refraction, opening it onto the cultural totality that it shatters.[16] Whether what shatters or explodes under the pressure of parodic tensions is the cultural totality or only the work is left ambiguous in Abastado's formulation. I let this indeterminacy stand so that the effects of parody can extend well beyond the text to the multiple social texts whose discontinuities parody then replicates, refigures, and distorts.

Recent theory of metafiction that stresses only parody's link to self-representation loses this sense of the broader cultural contexts of parody. For instance, parody is defined by Linda Hutcheon as "an integrated structural modelling process of revising, replaying, inverting, and 'transcontextualizing' previous works of art."[17] Even though she claims not to deny to parody all social and ideological implications, this restriction of parody is in fact accomplished by the aesthetic limits assigned to its pragmatics of "formal difference." She dismisses wholesale, in a brief sentence, the relevance of poststructuralism for parody: "Nor, however, is parody simply a post-structural differential or relational kind of repetition that stresses only difference" (101). This reduction of difference and repetition in poststructuralism misses, of course, the fundamental relation of parody to writing and difference, to reiteration and supplementarity. (In her poetics of postmodernism, "ironic parody" is still defined as a formal self-reflexivity, in which the turning of art to its aesthetic past is the basis for a textual poetics of the historical and the social.[18] The terms of formal metafiction called on to textualize history and ideology, however, again end up by collapsing "aesthetic introversion" and "historical memory" into a single term.)

In Hutcheon's notion of "formal difference," irony maintains a critical distance between the parodied text and the parodying text, between stated and intended meaning. Irony is the means whereby parody is refocused on the "semiotic competence and intentionality of an inferred encoder."[19] In other words, ironic distance comes to supplement parody as a way of reaffirming the intentionality of the subject and its authorized transgressions. The paradoxical essence of parody lies for Hutcheon in the ambivalence it sets up between conservative repetition and revolutionary difference. Nonetheless, even as she limits the social and cultural significance of parody by closing it off as an "interarts" or "intramural" discourse, a controlled social view is brought back through the notion of the didacticism or the "teachings" of metafiction. These teachings instruct and manipulate readers while at the same time blocking their access to effective social critique.

The parodic might be rethought instead as the means by which postmodern art questions the validity of didacticism not only in art but in institutions in general. The parodic would then undo the simple opposition between an aesthetic understanding of culture and a social one, between form and its occasions. Claude Simon rejects the "fable" of conventional narrative precisely because of its didactic modes and aims. His parody of totalized systems of meaning such as the didactic proceeds by an attention to details, tangents, margins, remainders, and excesses. A way of reading the relation of narrative to the parodic needs to be found in order to grasp the cultural and social effects this relation creates in his novels.

For the critical model most apt to explain the place of parody in relation to the social as well as the aesthetic languages of the novel, I turn to Bakhtin, where we find not a rejection of modern parody but rather a lucid presentation of its dialogic conditions of *énonciation,* or utterance.[20] In his writing Bakhtin shows little of the ambivalence toward parody's modes of transgression that appears in Julia Kristeva's account of dialogue's role. In the distinction she draws between dialogue's "transgression giving itself a law" and parody's "law anticipating its transgression," she overlooks the necessary link in Bakhtin between the dialogic and the parodic.[21] Bakhtin's work on parody has considerable relevance for my interest in formulating the conditions of narrativity where such narrativity is grasped both as an image of language and an image of the Other's discourse. For Bakhtin stylization, parody, and "direct narration" are bivocal and bilingual phenomena. He states that to introduce a "parodic or polemical element into the narration is to make it more multi-voiced, more interruption prone, no longer gravitating towards itself or its literary object."[22] He does not limit the parodic to a purely narcissistic or reflexive narrative ("narration gravitating towards itself"). The parodic is more complex in that it is both the simplest example of "bivocal" language and the gauge of a general dialogics between genres (17). It is found in the "representation of the direct discourse of the other."[23] Parody is not itself a genre but rather the object of representation (not a sonnet, for instance, but the image of a sonnet); it is a *"travestissement"* in which the disguises of all genres come into play. Bakhtin's insight into the dialogism inherent in the represented image of a certain language or discourse is of particular interest to any discussion of parody in relation to social languages and their narrativities.

Rather than to define novelistic discourse in an essentializing way, his concern is to account for the "transmission of the discourse of the other." The privilege he gives to the transmission and reception of genres and discourses explains the pertinence that his theory of dialogism and the "cultural domain" continues to have. "The problem of a particular cultural domain in its entirety—knowledge, ethics, art—may be understood as that of the frontiers of that domain." For Bakhtin, "the cultural domain has no territory, it is entirely situated at the frontiers that pass everywhere, traversing each of its aspects" (40, my translation). He concludes that all cultural acts exist "on the borders." Returning repeatedly to the figures of border and frontier without territory, Bakhtin proposes that "discourse lives, one would say, at the limits of its context and that of another" (103). One of the constitutive traits of the style of humor is "the multiform play of *frontiers of discourses, languages, and perspectives*" (129).

Bakhtin points out that parodization exists in different degrees and that the degree of dialogical resistance on the part of the parodied discourse can vary from a literary parody having its end in itself to a quasi solidarity with the parodied discourse, as in the case of romantic irony (225). Parodied discourse, then, opposes an internal dialogical resistance to parodic intentions or intentionality because "the word is not inert, objectified material in the hands of the artist manipulating it."[24] Significantly, Bakhtin refers to parody not in the singular but in the plural, speaking of "parodic genres." These parodic genres do not belong to the genres they parody; instead, they are "modèles multiformes, 'horsgenres,' ou 'inter-genres'" (417; "multiform models, 'outside-genres,' or 'inter-genres'"). He describes "an immense multilingual, multistyled novel, pitilessly critical, lucidly ironic, reflecting the plenitude and diversity of languages, voices, of a culture, a people, and a given period"

(417). The notion of intergenre hearkens back to Bakhtin's important notion of cultural domains defined by their borders or frontiers, and it takes up again in a different way the modes of relaying at work in the "transmission" of the Other's discourse.

The novel of modern times, Bakhtin writes, conscious of its status as language and literature, is felt to be at the border of divergences between the literary and extraliterary and also at the edge of time (423–24). He insists on the internal divergences of language, divergences that are social and ideological struggles. The novel is never a finished, teleological genre for him, since it possesses no canon of its own that would ensure for it a finality of any kind. Thus, Bakhtin's dialogics of parody and its multilingual polyphony as an intergenre provide a more comprehensive way of understanding discourse as both internally and externally differentiated rather than as a simple critical distance from and a positive affirmation of the law of genre. Indeed, his theory of the novel is the only recent theory of narrative that successfully maintains the difference of dialogism paradigmatically, from the smallest units of signification to the largest cultural domains, without sacrificing either one.

By reading the workings of parody in Claude Simon's novels, narrative modes and genres of discourse can be understood in an open and nonautonomous manner.[25] Of course, parody is not the only mode in his work, and distinctions must be made between parody and satire, caricature, humor, and pastiche, which are all present to a significant degree. Parody becomes the exemplary mode for Simon's narrative critique of the society of the simulacrum and of the imaginary and phantasmatic relations (narratives) that it reproduces. As we shall see, parody reveals the pervasiveness of the work of simulacra in systems of representation, as well as in the discourses and figures that carry them, such as commodity, sexuality, war, and history. More precisely, it is Simon's art of the detail in description that initiates and carries the parodic registers of his writing. From the detail emerges a figure, a parodic counterfigure, or both. Details' extreme mobility and their tendency to divide and splinter are essential for elaborating a narrativity founded on what Naomi Schor has well named the "diegetic detail."[26]

Entre l'effroi et la dérision—CLAUDE SIMON

Parody of Narrative

Parody haunts all reproduction and formal replication. The analysis I develop considers the replica and modes of replication as fundamental conditions of parodic and readerly intelligibility. The Latin verbal form *replicare* means "to fold again or fold back" and has as well the figurative meaning of "to send back to, to refer to." The noun *replication* has two divergent meanings in French that enter into play in a parodic reading: the discursive and the nominative. According to Larousse, *réplique* refers to the action of responding (see *riposte*), to the protesting of an order (see *discussion*), and to the dialogued element in theater. In this way, replication as a property of the discursive opens it to the nominative "simulacrum," which then signifies a copy or reproduction similar to an original. Replication enters, therefore, into the general field of dialogism and double-voiced discourse, referring these specifically to the conditions of enunciation, to reiteration as an "answering back" rather than the pure replication of repetition, and to the problem of the simulacrum, connoting difference.

Rather limited in scope in the novels of Simon's first experimental period, which goes from *Le Vent* to *Histoire*, the work of replication becomes more generalized in the later novels (*La Bataille de Pharsale, Les Corps conducteurs* [*Conducting Bodies*], *Triptyque, Leçon de choses* [*The World about Us*]), which, as we shall see, have erroneously been called formalist. Through replication we can trace developments in Simon's parodic writing in such a way as to elaborate its extraordinary powers of transformation. The more formal replication, or what Bakhtin calls the image of representation, becomes generalized the more it engages reading in questions bearing on its social, economic, sexual, and historical implications. Formal replication and parody inhabit the very web of sociality, its productions as well as its gestures and actions. In this sense the cross-referencing of systems of signification, genres, and discourses cannot be reduced to a question of formal structuring alone. Parodic effects channel Simon's writing into areas of signification excluded from Ricardou's autonomous generators and from the signifier's formal play. Jameson's discussion of Simon's trilogy as being exemplary of postmodern pastiche and simulacrum is instructive, but it rests on the arbitrary opposition he sets up between the modernism of Simon's personal, Faulknerian novels and the postmodernism of his impersonal *nouveau roman* ones, an opposition moreover that parody undoes.[27]

In *Le Vent* the parody of narrative conventions appears in the narrator's explicit critiques of narrative's feigned solutions: unity, continuity, causality, resolution of conflict, and the recuperation of the tragic. In addition, Montès fulfills an important function of dialogical discourse, that of the idiot, who for Bakhtin represents an important parodic principle of the novel.[28] In describing the dialogism of stupidity he stresses the polemical nature of misunderstanding the Other's discourse, which founds its power to "singularize" the world of social conventions, that is, its languages. The agency of the idiot has its roots "in the heart of the internal dialogization of language itself," "in the mutual incomprehension of those who speak different languages" (217). Such incomprehension teaches both writer and reader, Bakhtin claims, to discover and construct representations of social languages (217). After *Le Vent*, *L'Herbe*'s meditations on writing, history, and narrative go even further to figure a general pervasiveness of the parodic, without this time relying on the character of the "idiot" or on narrative commentary.

Pierre and Sabine, Georges's parents, are pathetic and derisory characters who, it is said, unconsciously materialize parodic versions of the myth of Hercules and Dejaneira and the legend of Tristan and Isolde. As they struggle to grab hold of a bottle, their postures are shown in a perspectival space of representation already figured in innumerable paintings and fables. Similarly, the novel's story of Louise's love affair is intertextually described in a reference to Flaubert: "the rooms inhabited by the invisible, innumerable, and unappeasable cohort of pale Bovaryesque ghosts" (16). In fact, serial repetition, characterized by formal replication and mass production, provokes in the narrative a kind of anxiety, a sensation of vertigo: serial identities are identities performed, but in a form that negates, abolishes, and parodies them. The biscuit tin, which refers both to Louise's experience of sensuality and her dying aunt Marie's legacy, presents a series of images of young women and little dogs ad infinitum:

> the present from the dying woman, the old can on whose lid the picture of the young woman lying on the grass and the same curly

little dog with the blue ribbon repeated themselves, reproduced a size smaller on the lid of the same box the young woman was holding in her hand (actually, that is, visibly, only twice, the third cookie tin being already so small that the young woman was nothing more than a mere spot on the green of the grass, and the little dog a mere speck, but the idea of this endless repetition which escaped the senses, the sight, precipitating the mind into a kind of dizzying anguish.... (153)

The scene of Louise lying in the grass after making love is possibly allegorized as well as parodied in this *mise en abîme*, but the box, which is a legacy of the dying woman, also raises the question of the meaning effects of serial reproduction in general. What is striking is the absolute incommensurability between the rigorous, laborious life of Marie (who resembles in this respect Batti in *Les Géorgiques*) and the constraining, stereotyped images of young women. *In regression* both in a graphic and metaphorical sense, these images in series drive a wedge between the actual historical agency of women and the representation that "domesticates" them as much as it does the little frizzy-haired dog. The commodified image of the woman reflected on the lid as being "reduced to scale" remains as alien to Louise as it is to Aunt Marie. A parody of a parody, the multiplication of the reduced image signals the abyss that social replication creates between derisory imagery and history, between the seductions exercised by the ideological image and the real efficacy of the one who survives and helps her family survive history itself. One ought to say that Marie (and Louise as well) survives the history of representations of woman as much as she does the overwhelming events of history.

When Pierre the philologist takes up the narrative, his version of the events makes history itself an arena for the repetition of programmed destruction and war from which a "lesson" may be learned:

To remind us of what we should never have forgotten: that History is not, as the school books would like to make us think, a discontinuous series of dates, treaties, spectacular and clanking battles (something that would be, ultimately, assimilable to the diseases, epidemics, floods, and other kinds of scourges whose sporadic manifestations occur at well-defined hours, places, and dates, like bullfights, for instance, or the sempiternal death of Oedipus), but on the contrary limitless, not only in time (not stopping, not slowing down, never interrupting, permanent, like film showings—including the repetition of the same stupid plot), but also in its effects, without distinctions between the participants, war itself being no longer merely waged—that is, endured, that is, suffered. (30–31)

The parodic replication of the image and its relation to history may be seen as profoundly linked. Historical events themselves cannot be preserved from the work of reproduction and replication. They are, instead, constitutive of and determined by repetition, reproduction, and replication. In other words, Marie's experience of history, which she endures, cannot be maintained as purely exterior to the parodic conflicts of replication. There is no small measure of ambiguity involved here in Simon's relation to the narratives of history and revolution, a relation I will continue to develop.

La Route des Flandres elaborates a number of different narrative modalities, including the parody of narrative and narrative itself as a parodic modality. In the context of the debacle that sets the anachronistic de Reixach and French army against the technological superiority of German air power, all forms of military organization are revealed to be derisory, parodies of the very notion of "military order." Both derisory and tragic in its consequences, the shocking incommensurability between eras, systems, and orders provokes an effect of generalized parody in the novel.

The narrator and his fellow soldiers witness a violent confrontation between villagers that constitutes an unleashing of violence in the midst of the war's violence. This conflict serves as a powerful figure of the war itself; more specifically, it is a narrative model functioning as a derisory replica of the larger conflict. Georges and Blum's dialogues, full of inventions, suppositions, and arguments, take place against a backdrop of war, against the other disputing voices that figure the generalization of conflict between individuals and between armies:

> while we listened to the discordant echoes, the incoherent outbursts, fragments of rage of passion detached from that permanent

and inexhaustible stockpile or rather reservoir or rather principle of all violence and all passion that seems to wander imbecile and idle and objectless on the surface of the earth like those winds those gales without any other purpose than a blind and negative fury. (212)

Blum reconstructs the story of Georges's ancestors, including the Conventionnel Reixach, in a variety of literary and philosophical genres and pictorial art forms, such as the sentimental novel and the libertine engraving. That very diversity transforms the family history into its many parodic versions. Blum accuses Georges of inflating the fragments of family gossip to tragic and epic proportions: "Melodrama tragedy fiction, he said, you enjoy all that you add to it, and I No, and he And if need be you invent it, and I No it happens every day" (212). Blum serves as a dialogical foil to Georges's naive realism. Never simply representational or mimetic, narrative inventions resonate with the genres and systems to which they belong. Blum, a context- and class-conscious interlocutor, always makes his discourse double voiced, in Bakhtin's sense of the term, and satirical, the term Lyotard uses to define this mixing of genres.[29]

Parody in Simon is wedged between a laugh and a reaction of outrage,[30] between humor and critique; it is frequently represented as an effect provoked by replication, both comic and terrifying, derisory and sublime. The indignant, scandalized voice is also part of a general lack of identification with representations, a *mise hors soi* of which the parodic is the model. The expansion of parody to entire episodes is often set in motion by a permutation of narrative positions, namely, that of the sender, receiver, and referent. History is parodied in this way by its victims, just as the soldiers in *La Route des Flandres* are no longer the passive, unquestioning recipients of orders and representations addressed to them. At the level of narrativity, the situation of discourse at times remains suspended between different referents (war, captivity, flight, coitus). As I noted in chapter 2 these referents are even permuted into senders or vice versa. In the cases of Corinne and Blum referents and receivers are permuted into senders, and the space-times of reference (Flanders, Germany, France) are rendered mobile, becoming substituted both for one another and for the posts or positions of sender and receiver.

Parody is closely allied with these permutations because it involves the possibility of repeating, situating, and redistributing discourses (of history, for instance), codes, systems, and narratives. Once it is figured as citation, all narrative may be parodied. Since Simon's work never recounts an autonomous story, closed in on itself, but figures instead the multiple permutations of its versions and narrative modes, parody arises from within such a plurality. Resisting the military orders that dictate that they must be sacrificed, the soldiers use parody as a means of defense against that mortal representation. Similarly, when Corinne rejects her pornographic representation in the soldiers' stories, what she rejects is her own parodic reduction, her (re)production as a serialized object of fantasy. Defeat and the outrage at the loss of agency it entails generate reinscriptions of incommensurable narratives, systems, and organizations in ruins, from which arise untold inventions of writing. Humor is not absent from this parody, but it is a black humor whose parodic force is created in and by the debacle itself. Parody, therefore, cannot be interpreted in a limited formal context, even though it frequently relies on formal effects. In sum, rather than implying authority and critical distance, parody issues from the minute conditions of history, war, and sexuality figured in relation to their narrative conditions of possibility. From *La Route des Flandres* onward parody becomes inseparable from a repeated catastrophe and from catastrophic repetition, which are both figured as a generalized narrativity.

Je suis revenu pour la première fois en 1953, presque vingt ans après, évoquer des fantômes et des cadavres, et mon fantôme et mon cadavre.
[*I came back for the first time in 1953 after almost twenty years, to evoke phantoms and corpses, both my phantom and my corpse.*]
—CLAUDE SIMON[31]

Parody in Revolution

The parodic turn of serial reproductions raises questions concerning the historical and political dimension of (serial) writing and (serial) narrative. Indeed, the phenomenon of the same and the series that opens *Le*

Palace sets up one of the fundamental paradoxes of events. The grand hotel, its furnishings, its engravings, and the narrator himself all participate in a revolution in the mechanical sense of the novel's epigraph: "Revolution: The locus of a moving body which, describing a closed curve, successively passes through the same points. Dictionnaire Larousse." Periodically requisitioned, objects are subject to periodic migrations in much the same way that the text's writing turns to a rhetoric of inventory, litany, and series.

The gaze the narrator casts on himself fifteen years after the Spanish Revolution is in this sense a "revolutionary" gaze that materializes a derisory character, his parodic double: "he (the student, the homunculus, the fledgling, the distant and microscopic double)" (236), "that is, that part of himself that diminished, shrank, reduced itself as fast as it could until it had the size and absurd voice of a tiny doll dressed like a monkey, a Lilliputian and malevolent, fortune-telling mandrake" (241). Deprived in the present of any development and meaningfulness, whether historical or individual, the past is reduced to simulacra or phantoms that exist deformed yet intact in "the immobile and gray matter that is time past." A secondary or parasitic definition of revolution enters into conflict with the official versions of the events of the revolution, their authorized histories. This secondary definition, however minimal and technical it may appear, in fact opens the text onto the parodic and critical dimension that accompanies events. The "revolutionary" episodes evoked in the novel are accompanied by their reiterative versions, which are invariably parodic and theatrical: church/opera, funeral procession/operetta, revolutionaries/actors. A parody of political *engagement* and its prescribed solutions is offered, for instance, when the narrator represents materialist and dialectical history figuratively as a train that we are invited to board "dans le sens de la marche," that is, in the direction determined by the idea of progress.[32]

In Simon's writing all repetition produces the perception of an automatism that always risks turning into parody. Serial repetition, which I analyzed previously in *L'Herbe*, is also linked to death, to mortal repetition. The failure of the Spanish Revolution figured in *Le Palace*, however, is not recounted in terms of historical causes and political consequences. Rather, Simon's writing figures that failure (1) in scenes of anarchical clashes between its participants who are supposed to be allies in the revolutionary cause, (2) in the abortion of a macrocephalic "revolution" wrapped in the reams of newsprint of the liberal press, and (3) in the revolution as a woman's body hemorrhaging in childbirth, a devastating figure that pervades the last pages. The political statement contained in these figurations—as well as in the recursive movement of the "revolution" itself—is undeniably that of a disillusioned partisan, whose radical skepticism refuses *engagement*. Simon's refusal is directed against the type of political commitment that is actualized in a master narrative whose dogmatic narrative pragmatics belies its rhetoric of emancipation.

The opening of *Histoire* may be read as the narrator's awakening to citation, his recognition of his own nightmarish replication of myths, writings, and texts. The invisible palpitation of leaves, birds' wings, and cries evoke the powerfully haunting presence of his grandmother and her friends. Their stories, expressions, gazes, and dress all return to him in force, phantoms of a lost era reduced in his memory to a parodic sameness. Ready-made parodic and satirical representations succeed in rescuing the narrator for a brief moment, only to dissolve and fragment into further linguistic and mythical associations: "imagining them, dim and lugubrious, perched in the network of branches, as on that Orleanist caricature reproduced in the History textbook and which represented the genealogical tree of the royal family whose members hopped among the branches in the form of birds with human heads" (2).

Ritualized repetition frequently becomes the object of parody in Simon's novels. The character Lambert himself represents a specific type of parody in which is enacted the complicity between constraint and iconoclasm, the law and its transgression. For instance, his parody of the mass is highly scatological and pornographic but nevertheless recalls ancient forms of the parodied mass. The effect of Lambert's "arsenal of puns and spoonerisms," however, needs to be seen in relation not only to the mass it parodies but also to his own political conformism. Parodic distortion is limited because Lambert's transgressive "arsenal" confirms the relation between language and paternal authority. This analysis recalls Hutcheon's notion of the paradox of parody, according to which parody is transgressive precisely to the extent that it affirms the law, the tradition, that it opposes. Lambert's verbal aggression figures only one form of parody, however, a specific Oedipal regression to infantile language in order to gain power over the discourses of ritual. The novel as a whole actualizes a much broader play of parody as difference, satire (in Lyotard's sense), and humor. That parody remains conservative when its effects are limited to repetition and distortion is shown by Lambert's doctrinaire politics, which in adult life confirm his affirmation of the law. Through him the text marks out the limits of a certain form of parodic replication that remains subject to the original that it vehemently mocks.

Still, Lambert's transgressive play with language and his strategies of exchange (which always leave the young narrator feeling cheated) have analogies with the narrator's own replications. He exclaims a "ouais" ("Oh, yeah") of recognition when quotations begin to accumulate and proliferate in series. By reinventing citations he attempts to accomplish nothing less than an exorcism of the past (a new ritualized form?).[33] Yet neither quotation nor pastiche alone is guaranteed to exorcize the past and the narrative models through which it is represented. A particularly revealing scene in this regard shows the narrator seeking a loan at a bank. It unpacks the processes whereby matter is converted into exchange value, making possible the buying of money with money. The reduction of the multiple and diverse to the same takes place in terms of their sign function and exchangeability. Taking place at the bank's "LOAN SERVICE LONG & SHORT TERM," the scene requires a double narrative reading at least. On the one hand, the scene is clearly about the narrator's frustration at his powerlessness in a system of exchange where things are dematerialized and monetary signs are simply exchanged for other monetary signs. (When he fails to get a loan, he must sell off his family's material legacy, including the antique chest of drawers in which he finds his mother's postcard collection.) On the other hand, the bank is also the place providing money to conduct war, to "make history," the place from which money once again is rematerialized, converted into mud, conflict, and death. During this scene a conversation about illness takes place between two peasants who, like the narrator, have come to ask the "Sphinx in anthracite grey" for a bank loan. One of the men laments: "Sales histoires faut pas s'amuser à traîner ça, ça finit par" (90; "can be nasty you shouldn't fool around with it, it ends by" [72]). The bank scene is briefly eclipsed as the narrator evokes the chamber music concert of his childhood, a scene that recalls another illness and another ending, those of his dying mother, which are precisely the "histoires" haunting him and which he cannot get over. When the text returns to the bank scene, the snatches of conversation between the two men take on a very different range of meanings involving memory, family narratives, their endings, and the dubious remedies of attempted exorcisms of the past: ". . . pas traîner ça Ca finit par Devriez voir un médecin" (90; ". . . don't fool around It ends by You should see a doctor" [73]).

Histoire is not parodic in the limited sense of being merely formal or derisory parody.[34] Rather, parodic repetition is brought out as a general condition of possibility for memory and telling. The replication of narrative, understood as the necessity to reiterate its forms and genres, creates a proliferating parodic effect that touches all the text's idioms, discourses, genres, and models.

La Bataille de Pharsale has been considered to be a text in transition between the historical and personal narratives of the preceding novels and the so-called impersonal writing of the trilogy that follows it. The style of the last section of the novel, especially, is likened to the so-called neutrality of the trilogy. This view of Simon's style as impassive or neutral, however, is challenged by the writing of the detail, the motifs of translation, and the relation of both to replication and narrativity. His writing enacts the differences of genres in increasingly parodic modes, remapping the opposition between genres that are thought to be either exclusively narrative or nonnarrative.

Each of the novel's three sections bears a heading: "ACHILLE IMMOBILE A GRANDS PAS,"[35] "LEXIQUE," and "CHRONOLOGIE DES EVENEMENTS" ("ACHILLES RUNNING MOTIONLESS," "LEXICON," and "CHRONOLOGY OF EVENTS"). In part I a first-person narrator at a sidewalk café looks up at a building where, behind one of its windows, a red-haired painter makes love or is imagined to make love with the narrator's lover. The narrator's narrative position is increasingly taken over by a plurality

Parody in Postmodernity 93

of other spaces, times, paintings, and texts, yet despite these shifts, this part closes with the narrator at the café once more. It breaks off when the description of the passing show simply runs out of steam, out of associative details of particular traits, the particular being a condition of narrativity: "There is nothing particular about the couple" (65, modified). Both the first and second parts end, therefore, in different forms of a narrative impasse.

Part II, LEXICON, with its epigraph from Proust on the hieroglyph,[36] relates a lexical convention to a novelistic practice. Subdivided into seven shorter sections of discontinuous "entries" ("BATTLE," "CAESAR," "CONVERSATION," "GLADIATOR," "MACHINE," "TRAVEL," "O."), the alphabetical arrangement of the lexicon follows on from the *A* of Achilles, the *B* of Battle, and so on, to O. as the omega or end.[37] Besides this, the three major divisions of part II are arranged in alphabetical order as well ("Achilles," "Battle," and "Chronology of Events"). By grafting an arbitrary lexical ordering onto its narrative fragments, and vice versa, Simon's writing involves these different genres, ways of reading, and writing in a reciprocity they do not usually have. In this fashion literary narration is played off against a logic of lexical cross-referencing that undermines conventional narrative order and highlights figural links and their narrativities. The lexicon's lack of enunciative focus disturbs the reader's sense of the stability of represented time, space, and event, and performs as a narrative lack.[38]

Part II ends on a note of extreme precision, flatness, and control that implies a "view" of narrative composition in terms of a model of geometrical relationships: "we must represent the totality of the system as a moving body ceaselessly altering around a few fixed points, for example the intersection of the line OO' with the trajectory of the pigeon in flight, or again that of the itineraries of two journeys, or again the name of PHARSALUS figuring in a Latin textbook and disfigured on a signpost beside a road in Thessaly" (127). To interpret this passage as a reflexive statement concerning Simon's generative writing would be to accept that the "system" is based only on simple textual mirroring and repetitions. Yet when the same geometric description also crops up in the context of lovers' bodies, referred to as O–OO', it is certainly a parody of such "measured" language where

94 Parody in Postmodernity

bodies and passions are concerned. It might be possible to explain the reduction of living bodies to plane geometry ("Begin again, start over from zero" [123]) by calling on the narrator's psychological need to still his jealousy of the couple by gaining "distance" from them, but the collision between the two orders—bodies in coitus and geometry—itself shows the violence of incommensurability and is a powerful parody of "translation" into another system of representation in general. The gap between discourse and its referent is enacted here as a problem of narrativity. As far as narrative order is concerned, the geometrical ordering of space leads to an impasse in the face of which the narrator still charges himself to "start over, organize. First, second, third" (125). In no sense does he get outside narrative ordering, because even its parody in the stark geometry of coupling bodies is grasped as repetition, seriality, and sequentiality.

Part III, "CHRONOLOGY OF EVENTS," opens with what is a minimal travel narrative and closes with O. (re)writing the first lines of the first part of *La Bataille de Pharsale*. Once more, a play of genres exists in the disparity between chronological order and another narrative mode, which one would be hasty to label simply achronological. In the terms of the epigraph from Heidegger,[39] what is in question is a certain "uncovering" of the conventional chronological system rather than its absence in an idealistic, atemporal form.

From the outset the novel's turbulence displaces it from a singular narrative position in a particular space and time to other occasions (texts, paintings, graffiti, a comic strip, journeys, etc.). The issues raised by such displacement from one cultural language to another are well summed up as a problem of translation: Greek and Latin into French, images into texts, past into present, events into history, texts into writing, one genre or code into another. In *La Bataille de Pharsale* the narrator emerges as "I" in the novel's scene of translation and dictation. He replays a childhood scene in which he was required to translate classical Latin texts on the Battle of Pharsalus (Caesar, Lucan, Plutarch, Livy, etc.), all of which are treated as intertextual fragments. His tutor is an older man who resembles Uncle Charles of *Histoire* and *Les Géorgiques*. Attempting to convince the child to apply himself, the uncle first defends linguistic necessity and semantic stability ("Work or Duty"), but he finally recognizes the open-ended drift and absence of finality in language, saying: "but perhaps you're right after all knowing everything never leads to anything but learning something more and words lead to other words" (9). Such an endless internal replication of knowledge and discourse threatens the myth of semantic stability he attempts to transmit to the child. To arrest the absolute discontinuity of the word-for-word transposition that the boy produces, the tutor dictates translation to him: "Latin assignments I droned through word by word like some disgusting pap until for the sake of peace and quiet he ended by taking the book out of my hands and translating himself" (9). The work of translation produces texts without originals, as Walter Benjamin would argue,[40] and Simon's writing traces the process whereby a text is metaphorized or "carried over" from one site to another. It does so, however, without erasing the difference between the translating and the translated text, and the parodic emerges precisely in the transfer or passage from one site or cultural context to another.

Elsewhere in the novel, repetition and writing are related to fields of dispersed and shifting figures, which are constantly related to a cry that is suppressed. Thus, a warrior is described with "one of them piercing his open mouth just as he rushed forward sword raised leading his men transfixing him stabbing the shout in his throat" (3). Figures of open mouths, wounds, vagina, and so on, are combined with the vectorial trait of the bird's wing, arrows, phalli, and a pointing hand (reproduced as an ideogram in the text). These figures of designation-piercing are related to a cry-wound they penetrate and suppress. Another link brings together spear-phallus-arrow with the death or suppression of a "tongue" or a language itself. "Caesar the Gallic War the Civil War➳ thrusting into the open mouth nailing the tongue of that. Latin dead language. Dead secret. Living death" (9). These sexual symbols may, of course, be referred back to the narrator's psychology and to the threat of castration that since Freud (in the essay "The Medusa's Head," for instance) is signified by the multiplication of phallic and vaginal symbols. But the context of translation in which they arise situates them as a problem of translation without unified terms. Translation is thus opposed to the dictatorship of mortal repetition and castration rather than being its confirmation.

Repetition of an anterior text always creates a space of translation and a potential opening for parody. The novel's work on Proust's *A la recherche du temps perdu* shows a number of sizable fragments appearing both as direct quotation (sometimes italicized) and in the process of being translated into the figures of Simon's novel.[41] The meaning of Proust's phrases and words, diffused throughout, is not given; rather, their semantic potential (in the main, erotic) is brought out in their reworking and transformation. Since the motifs of both Simon's and Proust's novels concern the pain of jealousy, infidelity, memory, and writing, Simon might have sought an approximate repetition of his themes. Instead, in another act of writing, the parodied signifier "jealousy" is resituated within a volume, a signifying textual space: "jealousy where was it right-hand page near the top" (60). To avoid repetition of an anterior text, the narrator paradoxically performs an act of rereading that at once replicates and displaces the other's text. In the process, Simon's writing brings out an affective dimension linking language, parody, and desire.

The affective dimension emerges especially in a passage evoking an Italian translation of Graham Greene's *Force of Destiny*, whose "naturalness" is actually a convention-bound fiction. It is described as "something British and Christian and moist and . . . profound" (121). Then, in a veritable paroxysm of parody, the novel's title is linked to a scatological wordplay ("forza del destino le tragicaca de consciença"), a fragment of Faure's *Histoire de l'art*, and a quasi-phonetic transcription of a passage of *La Recherche:* "Sodome et Gonhorrée page combien *tous laids souvenir voluptueu kil emporté de chézelle lui permetté de sefer unidé dé zatitudezardante zoupâmé kel pouvé tavoir avek d'otre*" (177–78; "Sodom and Gonorrhea what page *all ugly voluptuous memories he brought away from her allowdhim tomagine the ardent or faintpose she might assume with others*" [121–22]). The humor of this parodic reinscription stages both the dictation effect of other texts and their ludic distortion. The language of allegorical painting is linked to the clichés of romance and the aesthetics of socialist realism: hope and faith (Faure), the force of destiny (romance), and art symbolizing courage, hope, the people or glory (Belgrade). Simon's parody takes the allegorized abstract noun and renarrativizes its work of replication and redundancy.

A quotation in *La Bataille* from Faure on Caravaggio has been taken to reflect Simon's own "glorification of form" and his writing's calm indifference in the face of massacre and passion: "Painter of bacchanals too *slaughter as well as love is a pretext to glorify the body whose calm splendor appears only to those who have penetrated nature's indifference to slaughter and love*" (81). No such neutrality is ever established as a given in Simon's writing. Instead, parody is a mode of critique that accounts precisely for the intergenre mobility of the detail and the powerful effects of trying it out in different genres and narrative frames. Therefore, parody is neither a mode of critical distance nor an instrument of arbitrary and violent displacements. It is the exemplary means for a critical replication of their narrative conditions of possibility.

After the attempted exorcism of a personal past in *Histoire*, *La Bataille de Pharsale* appears to orient itself more decisively toward the resolute *mise à nu* of narrative processes that comes to dominate the thematics and writing of the later novels. Before engaging more fully with the serial figures that pervade postmodern and contemporary space, Simon seems to turn back in *La Bataille* toward the paintings, texts, and scenes of the past—"that painting (where was it?)"—by marking out the replications involved. The tension between formal repetition and parodic replication cannot be resolved within the text alone. Readings of the formal repetition of figures in Simon cannot account for the general issues of replication involved in history, in the commodification of people and ideas, and in aesthetic representation. Ultimately, neither the minimal elements nor the larger structures of Simon's novel remain impervious to the play of parodic replication. Rather than take *La Bataille* to be the beginning of a "formalist period" or impersonal mode in Simon's writing, I find its joining of parodic replication to translation to take a decisive step toward a critique of the society of reproduction, a critique taken up in the trilogy (*Les Corps conducteurs*, *Triptyque*, and *Leçon de choses*) and in the novels about history. Historical events are not immune to the work of reproduction, and parody, as writing's defense against mortal replication, inhabits the material representations of revolution, war, and technology.

a sensation of vacuity, anonymity, and desolation, as if the protagonists were there only in transit, in a temporary and artificial setting of which they had no part—CLAUDE SIMON

Les Corps conducteurs formulates in exemplary fashion the broader cultural dimensions of the proliferation of simulacra, pursuing the critical function of their parody. It opens on a Warhollike description of a series of identical women's legs, typical of mass-media advertising, serial (re)production, and commodification. The writing then describes what turns out to be a painting in which doctors are grouped around the body of a smiling female figure in plastic. The novel's opening onto replicas contrasts with the nearly indeterminate presence of a sick man who supposedly perceives them. It has been debated whether the man's presence constitutes a minimal narrative focus, thus making the novel subject centered, that is, the antithesis of Ricardou's generative text. But what of the man's pain and fear? By way of a response, the text proposes a replica of an anatomical plate representing a man's torso: from the outside as well as the inside, simultaneously. We are told that the organic body of the man suffers extremely painful attacks, but his suffering remains absolutely without continuity in the world surrounding him. Isolated from the outside world by his extreme pain, the man comes to figure a more pervasive alienation from objects and individuals, all of which are reduced to closed circuits of reproduced simulacra.

In its descriptions of external details Simon's novel clearly privileges exteriority in general. Not surprisingly, this emphasis has encouraged critics to pursue a uniquely formal coherence based on isomorphic repetition and prescribed by the text's apparently formal detours and links. It may be argued, however, that bodies, the city, communications, political discourses, and finally the text as a whole are turned toward an exteriority that is not simply formal, impersonal, and impassive but instead forcefully parodic, at once derisory and terrifying.

On the journey the sick man makes to get back to his hotel, a short distance that is expanded inordinately by his painful progress, his eyes encounter gazes that automatically turn away from his. Masks void of expression, these gazes project an unreality about them just as much as they themselves seem to be the products of a hyperreal environment. Alone in the city, the man experiences a phantasm of catastrophe, which appears as an immaterial but heavy, gray mass advancing like an avalanche. The man is surprised that others (the doctors, for instance) do not seem to be able to see it. His hallucination is generated as much by his terror of cancer as by the anonymous, stereotyped space that surrounds him. The city here is not really inhabited; instead, it is an uninhabitable, vacant space entirely given over to passage, transitions, waiting, and commerce. It is an urban landscape that is as unlivable as the jungle the novel refers to, a jungle in a film or story traversed by explorers who suffer, like the sick man, from solitude, dereliction, nightmares, and delirium. Lost in the Amazon, "man in his fundamental state of solitude" exists both in the jungle and the modern city. The cultural catastrophe occurring in an urban landscape as well as in a jungle consists of the loss of the Other. The loss is a radical one signifying nothing less than the lack of community whose mediations sustain the subject.

Clearly then, Simon's writing does more than consecrate pure description as such. Instead, the descriptive-compositional mode of his writing invents passages from one space-time to another, shifts from one discourse to another, and the virtual interference of one cultural domain in another. His entire text is constituted by resonances and echoes that create delays, redundancies, and iterations. This process cannot be understood in terms of a simple notion of imitation ("pure description"), despite the fact that, as Benjamin has argued, the process of commodification relies on such a notion. In his essay on art in the age of technological reproduction, Benjamin claims that industry and commerce reinforce "the older epistemological concept of imitation," where "the identity of the imitation with its model is also a criterion for its success."[42] This return of mimesis occurs despite what he calls the anti-imitative movements of antiart and antiliterature in the modernist period.[43] Jean Baudrillard's definition of the term *simulacrum* is relevant here in defining the status of imitation in the era developing from Benjamin's age of reproduction, which one might call postmodernism.[44] For Baudrillard simulation involves "the liquidation of all referentials—worse: by their artificial resurrection in systems of signs. . . . It is no longer a question of imitation, nor of reduplication, nor even of parody. It is rather a question of substituting signs of the real for the real itself; that is, an operation to deter every real process. . . . Never again will the real

100 *Parody in Postmodernity*

have to be produced." He calls this substitution the simulacrum, a "hyperreal henceforth sheltered from the imaginary, and from any distinction between the real and the imaginary, leaving room only for the orbital recurrence of models and the simulated generation of differences" (167).[45] His notion of simulation excludes parody, at least of the kind implying the possibility of a critical distancing, yet parody reappears in Baudrillard's discussion of the disappearance of what Antonin Artaud termed the theater of cruelty: "All dramaturgy, and even all real writing of cruelty has disappeared. Simulation is in charge [*maîtresse*], and we have right only to what is retro, to the phantomatic and parodic rehabilitation of all the lost referentials."[46] For Baudrillard another kind of parody does exist, then, in the gap or void left by the disappearance of the referent, as a reminder of its loss.

My analysis of parody differs from Baudrillard's in a number of respects. First of all, it is not possible to isolate the simulacrum from parody because each is the effect of the other, operating in the same cultural space. In other words, both the simulacrum and parody are produced by iterative processes that are the basis of signifying systems. When Baudrillard speaks of the absolute precedence of simulacra over representation (166), he falls back on an aesthetic and cultural model of productivity that is essentially homogeneous and totalitarian in that it radically excludes differences, tensions, refractions, and dissonances of all kinds. In other words, his monological model, affirming what he calls the implosion of antagonistic poles, banishes in a conservative fashion all differences from a social dimension that, despite such attempts to reduce its differences, remains complex, diverse, and dynamic in its resistances to pure reproduction.

The heterogeneity that Baudrillard's theory would restrict is one of the hallmarks of Simon's writing. Descriptions of scenes that are apparently simply present are regularly referred to as being repeated elsewhere, in the form of their replicas and other frames of representation. This is the case, for instance, when embracing bodies are at first described in realistic enough fashion and then shown to have a windowlike opening, that reveals assemblages of plastic organs. *Les Corps conducteurs* illustrates how in this space of sectioned bodies and texts any gaze onto the outside world encounters only empty gazes and an absence of reciprocity. The narrative itself becomes caught up in a febrile movement that passes from object to object without finality, without a subject to carry the narrative, and without other subjects to reflect it back. The gaze proceeds from simulacrum to simulacrum, driven by a mechanical and self-generating movement that seems to enact the conditions of reproduction itself. Such encounters, in which there is a lack of reciprocity between individuals, are wholly phantasmatic and prone to being particularly violent. These relations are no longer to be understood within the limits of a metaphysical opposition between subject and object. Instead, a physics of bodies (or conducting bodies) and seemingly autonomous mechanisms of replication have so exteriorized the subject that it can no longer be divided into a conscious and unconscious subject. The space in which such a deindividualized subject is located is a catastrophic city, reduced to being unreal and jerky in its discontinuous reflexes, closed in on its own representation. Anything or nothing can happen in such a space, a space where everything has potential links with everything else and yet nothing at all has a necessary link with anything. In *Triptyque,* for instance, an irredeemable and tragic event is actually secreted or generated by the isolation of different spheres, by both space and writing developing out of a series of simulacra embedded one within the other.

This space of extreme discontinuity and extreme connectedness becomes the privileged site of Simon's critique of the economy of reproduction, a critique that is thoroughly parodic in its conditions and effects. Take, for instance, the description of an electric billboard: "Framed in rectangles, in sunbursts dripping with gold, in red moons or ephemeral cascades of diamonds, [emblems] are endlessly repeated like admonitions or lessons being drummed into the heads of idiots or retarded children" (68). The description addresses itself not to what the advertisements mean but to the massive material and discursive apparatuses that produce them, the public networks of communication and the electronic conditions of transmission and passage. His novel does not describe the arbitrary content of the message, which merely restates the prescriptive "consume!" The power of injunction and interpellation deployed by advertising signs (reproduced in English in the text) frequently exists in an ironic relationship with the sick man himself: "IT'S

NEVER TOO LATE" (78) or "SOMEBODY IS ALWAYS WINNING. IT MIGHT AS WELL BE YOU" (80). If Simon's *Les Corps conducteurs* can be said to have a subject, it may be the disquieting pervasiveness of simulacra in the technological age. At the same time, however, the book struggles to avoid falling into the traps of simulacra, one of the most powerful being their repetition. In this sense, Simon's writing is far less formalist than is supposed by readings that trace linguistic generators and thereby simply reproduce the intrinsic logic of simulacra. Is there an alternative to such entrapment? Jameson's reading of pastiche in *Les Corps conducteurs* suggests that there is none. This question may be reconsidered, however, from the perspectives of parody that I am developing here, taking the example of the Latin-American writers' congress.

In the absence of a community in the modern city, the congress of writers becomes the community's parodic substitute. It is there that definitions of different political positions are debated in discourses that are massively predetermined and thus subject to repetition, to becoming mired in their own terms. A radical critique of modern alienation emerges in Simon's writing, one that resists literary prescriptions such as those proposed in the delegates' speeches. By forging links in his writing between the illness of the body, the absence of community, the politico-literary discourses at the congress, and the conventional representations of exotic adventures (the story of the jungle explorers), Simon succeeds in breaking down the arbitrary and artificial separations between these domains. Links articulated in this way create what I call narrativities without narrative, which cannot be accounted for according to a conventional understanding of either image or narrative.

A number of examples of such a narrativity without narrative appear in the text. Women are absent from the delegation of writers, and when a woman from the audience intervenes, she is ruled out of order. Their absence from the official "platform" has different meanings and effects. The delegates make proto-Marxist speeches on the question of representation, calling for a literature that will bear witness to the oppressed in general, "by giving voice to their legitimate aspirations." In their political discourse they argue for abolishing political censure, which would then make possible "free speech," the telling of other stories. Yet Simon's writing demonstrates the continuing effects of other forms of censure working in political institutions and through political discourse. These forms of censure are reproduced in the commodifications of images and the manipulation of simulacra. In a humorous yet critical way, Simon places under the very eyes of the delegates a newspaper advertising a film. A link is intimated, therefore, between the two cultural domains as spaces of reproduction: the advertisement of a busty, sensual woman with closed eyes—LA VENUS MALIDA (the damned Venus)—and the discourse on the oppressed claiming to speak in their stead. Further descriptions of women in pornographic magazines take up similar images of naked women, highlighting the details of their frozen smiles and uncomfortable, contorted positions. These descriptions' focus on the conditions of image making subverts the illusion of female availability that the images seek to produce in their male readers. The image in Simon replicates the stereotyped, ideological image of "woman" but subverts it by calling attention to it as a contrived image. It is presented as an object not of desire but of manipulation and commodification.[47] The site and description of the image subvert the way in which political discourse ignores the culture of images and yet claims to speak in the name of the oppressed. The text makes it possible for the manipulation and commodification of women's bodies to break into and interrupt the closed, stereotyped discourses of political rhetoric. Readers cannot ignore the irruption of one genre or medium into another, an irruption that exercises a powerful and parodic critical effect.

We should note the links between the commercial exploitation of women's bodies, the representation of the open medicalized body, and the lovers' bodies opened up by means of a window to expose their plastic internal organs. The idealism of political discourses, founded on the conscious intentionality of the engaged and committed writer, is shown to be overtaken on all sides by image culture and technology. The proliferation of phantasmatic simulacra of the body shows how they elude the subjectivist and predicative categories of the uttered political discourse. By means of its figures the novel reveals that although this discourse seeks to be impermeable to the age of simulacra, it is nevertheless thoroughly traversed by its political problematics.

Simon's writing thus parodies the pervasive generalization of formalism in its most immediate and least avoidable consequences—the culture of simulacra. It does so without simply reproducing their formal systems. It is therefore misleading to speak of the autonomy of language or writing in Simon's texts. What is involved, rather, is a writing that at once situates and questions all automatisms in mechanically reproduced discourses and representations. The real issue is not the autonomy of writing but the automatisms involved in codes of replication, automatisms against which the writing struggles step by step, word by word, figure by figure. The critical dimensions of this struggle appear especially in the parodic narrativity that accompanies and doubles all replication. This parodic mode is played out in a particularly suggestive figure: that of a solitary man in the city speaking to a mirror that he lifts to his lips with mechanical gestures. On the back of the mirror is the image of a woman, and it is not clear whether this urban Narcissus kisses his own image or that of the woman. Like other images of reproduced simulacra that proliferate in the text, this solitary figure raises the question of whether internal duplications in the text (and its reading) are bound to be continuous with the modes of replication in culture.

In the absence of a dominant narrative of legitimation (of the subject, representation, being, or history), which would establish authorized relations and hierarchies, the most immediate linkages seem to pass through language and the figures of writing. Passages between different images, spaces, and times thus result from punctual, unauthorized connections. These connections may well be symptoms of what Jameson has called a more general "waning of affect" in the postmodern, where "human subjects are commodified and transformed into their own images."[48] One way to gauge these simulacra effects is in relation to the question of violence and its narrativity.

The kinds of narrative linkages I have been analyzing produce at times scenes of considerable violence. Semantic recurrences in *Triptyque* establish virtual connections on the level of writing between a skinned rabbit, Corinne stretched out, and a drowned little girl. Although performed on the level of word and image, these linkages involve a relation of violence that can be limited neither to the fiction's content nor to its formal structure. Whence then does the violence derive? Is it possible that as the text's writing turns replicated form into meaning, there occurs at once a production and a sublimation of violence? Two critics

(Mark Andrews and Aline Baehler) react with some consternation to formalist and "indifferent" readings of *Triptyque*.[49] It is clearly necessary to avoid returning the text's sublimated violence to a formal analysis. As I have proposed, the task of relating that violence to the narrativity of its figures can be achieved by recognizing that the violence in the text may be located in its iterative and parodic structures. A fictional world in which characters, things, images, spaces, views, and so on, are indefinitely replicated leaves no interpretive ground on which to situate a reading, except perhaps a reading that retraces this very process of replication. Nevertheless, we cannot separate the text's sublimated violence from the fact that its three stories ("a wedding celebration that ends badly, the accidental drowning of a child, a by-line in a seaside resort") are repeated and specularized one within the other. Any reading that does not explicitly establish the complicity between the formal construction and the violence repeatedly veiled and unveiled remains trapped by the web of the text's formal structure.

Parody provides a way of establishing such a link. If we consider the structuring of *Triptyque* as three series where each is represented in the two others, the resemblance between this mode of composition and the very functioning of the parodic mode is striking: in both cases, we find a model according to which one frame of reference is embedded in another, shown, that is, to belong to another that permits the "reading" of the first. Borrowing a term from Andrews, one could call this a distributed reading. For Andrews, a distributed reading of nontotalizable figural and intertextual repetition would not remain enclosed within the three major narrative series. He argues that a distributed reading is required precisely because it allows affect to be reintroduced into the "micro ephemera of love and death." "Allegory at the micronarrative level," he argues, "dramatizes the reintrojection of affect into the neutralized textual fabric of *Triptyque*." In his formulation, the affect revealed in micronarrative activity "takes indifferentism to be an evasion, and exposes pure form graphically as counterfeit death."[50] Baehler, in her analysis of Corinne and the flaying of the rabbit, links affect and form, stressing the extraordinary violence of the indiscretions committed at the narrative level.[51]

What precisely is the impact of these discontinuous but apparently closed series of frames of reference (or macronarratives) that allow neither a principal narrative nor an ultimate frame of reference to emerge? The text shows that the danger is that anything can happen; someone might even die. In fiction, this violence seems to be without consequences, yet one must ask what kinds of readings are complicit with it. When codes are linked in apparently unmediated fashion to other codes, images to other images, fragments to other fragments, phonemes to other phonemes, we need to consider what mediates these passages and how they are made. In *Triptyque*, for example, there exists considerable tension between the excessive stress laid on links at the formal level and the understated, minute gestures of progressive abandonment leading to the child's death. Indeed, the novel describes a death that cannot be recuperated by a narrative order that would attempt to transcend it dialectically. Such a recuperation proves to be impossible, since the violence is not so much sublimated in this text as it is staged in the very links that join one story to another by means of parodic simulation. Any transition from the scene of the couple on the outskirts of the city to that of the ravaged actress, the couple in the barn, and the drowning of the child interrupts the development of one scene to the benefit of another. But discontinuity does not prevent the occurrence of events. The type of parodic reading I have proposed is a way of not sublimating violence in the name of affectless form, even a postmodern multiplicity of forms.

In Simon's writing a change of medium or a reframing of a scene in a different genre—written text, photograph, sculpture, painting, comic strip, stamp, advertisement, opera—is always potentially parodic. In *Triptyque* the descriptions in each of the three episodes are also part of another series, be it a painting, postcard, film, novel, or puzzle. This fashion of knotting one medium into another in an impermeable formal closure has something decidedly excessive, fantastic, and phantasmatic about it. It is a writing that designates in this way not only the pervasiveness of simulacra in modern culture but also the parodic replications that accompany and effectively question simulacra at the level of their narrative figures of representation. At the core of these questions is that of the relationships between simulacra, replication, and the possibility of a parodic rewriting. From *Histoire* and *La Bataille de Pharsale* to *Leçon de choses* and *Les Géorgiques*, Simon's work has accounted increasingly for the proliferation of replication.

Parody in Postmodernity 107

It has developed and staged parodic narrativities as a defense against loss, alienation, betrayal, and death.[52] Therefore, the celebrated return to history and the archives in *Les Géorgiques* may be read not only as a continuation of the historical novels (*L'Herbe*, *La Route des Flandres*, *Le Palace*, and *Histoire*) but also as part of Simon's ongoing elaboration of the connections between violence, parody, and history in the contexts of revolution and war.

le monde à présent pour ainsi dire retourné à la façon d'un gant
[*the world at present so to speak turned inside out like a glove*]
—CLAUDE SIMON

Following an epigraph drawn from Rousseau's *Confessions*, the prologue of *Les Géorgiques* describes a painting/drawing in the style of David's sketches for *The Oath of the Jeu de Paume*. The drawing in neoclassical style portrays an older man holding a sheet of paper while a younger man looks on, a scene of destination and reception that I have read as the scene of legacy in Simon's work. As if to parody a familiar topos of a modernist aesthetic of self-reference,[53] the description of the sketch suggests that the figures and decor have a deliberate coldness, a dryness resembling that of architectural drawings,

> which similarly offer the spectator not existing monuments but combinations and collections of forms that are purely imaginary, referring only to themselves, and the grey lines, incredibly fine, straight as a bowstring or rounded in perfect curves, mark the division not between solids (flesh, wood or marble) and the air around them, but between white surfaces that interlock as their inflexions or their angles dictate. It is obvious that the interpretation of such a drawing is possible only through the use of a representational code which is accepted in advance by each of the two parties, the draughtsman and the observer. (8)

Rather than being a confirmation of Simon's formalist aesthetics, this passage describing a drawing/painting based on pregiven codes refers to a type of academic study that is antithetical to Simon's writing.

In rereading the epigraph from Rousseau's *Confessions*, I again find something quite different from the formal purity of autonomous, interlocking aesthetic codes: "Climates, seasons, sounds, colors, darkness, light, elements, aliments, sound, silence, motion, rest, everything acts upon our machine and consequently upon our soul" (translation modified). The neoclassical aesthetics detailed in the prologue resonates in a critical and parodic fashion with Rousseau's sensationalist description of the effects of a multiplicity of phenomena on the human body and on the soul. The ending "consequently" (*par conséquent*) suggests a narrative temporality where first the body (machine) and then the spirit are affected by phenomena. In fact, it is precisely the sequence of actions in the drawing, the destination or reception involved, that creates uncertainties concerning its meaning:

> Indeed, although it has been carefully rubbed out and now shows up only as a very pale, almost shadowy grey, the right hand of the seated figure was visibly drawn in a different position originally. . . . The question still remains as to whether this gesture (this dismissal) occurs before the addressee has taken cognisance of the terms of the letter . . . or during his reading, or after it. (10–11)

After the prologue, the novel comes back repeatedly to the scene of reading, not to determine which actions came first in L.S.M.'s archives, O.'s account or the cavalryman's unpresentable experience of war, but rather to emphasize that scenes of reading and writing signify through their narrativity and figures.

To trace the figures of parodic replication, I return to the figures of divergence, *partage,* and division, which provide an understanding of postrevolutionary historical and family legacies. Legal texts concerning a dispute of L.S.M.'s inheritance, reproduced in the novel, claim to distinguish by typeface between facts or the text of the law (roman) and suppositions (italics), creating what Britton has called a parody of legal documents. Since the novel also alternates between typefaces, without assigning either truth or the lack of it to that difference, parody comes about as "knowledge-versus-imagination inscribed in the materiality of writing."[54] However, the legal text that disputes L.S.M.'s material legacy itself replicates parodically the law condemning the king:

> The pompous language of the speech for the defence printed by courtesy of the barrister which seemed (with the same letters carved

and cast by hand, the same typography) to be a ludicrous riposte to the Declaration of Opinion which twenty years earlier he . . . had drafted and presented to an assembly so that his memory would remain indissolubly linked to what in his eyes was not simply a speech for the prosecution of a man but the proclamation of the end of one world and the advent of another. (260)

In terms of a master narrative L.S.M.'s belief in emancipation rests on the possibility that a performative death sentence would actualize the end of one world and inaugurate a new order. The narrativity of the document disputing inheritance is the parodic inversion of the performative power of revolutionary discourse. Instead of accomplishing a complete break and the advent of an origin, the legal text is a repetition in difference (in derision) of the Revolution itself as a performative writing. Ten years after the Revolution, the General returns periodically from the front to find that the conspiracies and betrayals of the Terror have turned the architects of the Revolution into parodies of themselves. He sees the idea of a unified Revolution diverging into two distinct histories, those of military action and political parody:

as if during his absence History had diverged, had, unseen, split, continuing on the one hand in broad daylight, openly, with cannon fire, on the other hand forced to make itself up, disregarding all known rules, groping along, faltering, slipping, suddenly losing its head, hurrying, spinning free, out of control, veering towards parody, towards the farcical. (262, modified)

History already moving away, abandoning their truncated corpses, the headless monster in a never-finished death . . . time both static and runaway, History beginning to spin on one spot, without moving forward, with sudden flashbacks, unforeseeable detours, wandering aimlessly, sweeping away everything within reach of this kind of whirlpool, snatching him on the way, by surprise, casting him (or hurling him) into the very centre of the maelstrom. (262–63)

In these extraordinary pages, the excavalryman or narrator rewrites the general's archives in such a way as to explore its figures of an historical dynamic as parody and difference. He echoes Marx's dictum in *The Eighteenth Brumaire of Louis Bonaparte*: "Hegel says somewhere that all great historic facts and personages recur twice. He forgot to add: 'Once as tragedy, and again as farce.'"[55] It is interesting that Marx goes on to write that "man makes his own history, but he does not make it out of whole cloth . . . [but] out of [conditions] such as he finds close at hand. The tradition of all past generations weighs like an alp upon the brain of the living." Marx finds in the Revolution's reliance on the ghosts of past epochs the signs of a recurrence of the same: "a whole people, which imagines it has imparted to itself accelerated powers of motion through revolution, suddenly finds itself transferred back to a dead epoch . . . the old dates turn up again, the old calendars, the old names" (12). In Simon's writing the parodic doubling of the Revolution at its very inception makes it at once a form of stasis and accelerated movement. The meanings of the word *tourbillon* (tornado, maelstrom, or vortex) include the sense it has in the history of science: a material system animated by a movement of rotation. The novel remetaphorizes Marx's dialectical definition of revolution as both "accelerated powers of motion through revolution" and a return to past forms. The Larousse definition in *Le Palace*'s epigraph—"Revolution: The locus of a moving body which, describing a closed curve, successively passes through the same points"—takes on added meaning in the later novel's replication. In *Les Géorgiques* the distance separating one "revolution" from another is not a simple recurrence of the same within a closed system but rather a parodic replication (repetition in difference) measured in the split between stasis and acceleration, immobilization and mobilization.

In re-creating the Revolution as war, terror, and parody, the narrator speaks of Jean-Marie L.S.M.'s experience of exclusion from history as one in which everything is turned inside out. The general's brother is doubly erased from history, by the revolutionary laws on exiles as well as by Jean-Pierre L.S.M. and succeeding generations of his descendants: "*the world at present so to speak turned inside out like a glove, a garment shown the wrong side up, or rather perverted in the sense that nothing in it had the same meaning any more, if any meaning at all*" (298, modified). Interestingly, this image of history as radical inversion, where what was inside is applied to the outside and what was exterior is applied

Parody in Postmodernity 111

to the interior, recalls invagination, one of the terms for the logic and movement of Derrida's deconstruction.[56] In Simon this inversion accounts for the effects of revolutionary history grasped in its very narrativity. It is a narrativity in which the former signifieds become signifiers, past becomes present, content becomes form, the former public domain invades the private one, and vice versa. In its radical perversion this revolutionary history recalls very nearly Bakhtin's definition of parody: "parody is the creation of a *decrowning double*; it is that same 'world turned inside out.'"[57]

Simon's writing is not dictated by a didactic urge to impose on the reader a moral position, a predication, or a teaching, whether of the formalist or *engagé* variety. Rather, its critical dimension results from the modes of parodic narrativity set into play in his work on replication. Without ever claiming the high ground of an aesthetic-formalist "position," parody is that which works at the limits of cultural narratives and creates new passages or narrative links between them in unexpected ways.

4

General and Particular Mobilizations:
Gender, War, and Narrative

Simon's radical skepticism with respect to traditional narrative orders, their ideological motivations, and powers of mobilization has gained in range and focus throughout his writing. In his most recent work he has continued to dismantle the explicit and implicit master narratives of militarization, dogmatism, and technology. An important aspect of his understanding of prewar, wartime, and postwar situations is their particular technological mobilizations, which turn out to be narrative ones as well. Of all his works of fiction, *L'Acacia* is the first to elaborate the rise of fascism and totalitarianism and the conditions before the two world wars that led up to mobilization.

Simon is exemplary of the European male writer who, instead of becoming an unquestioned heir of the Western tradition, was cut off from its full privileges and sacrificed to a dying world as it transformed itself into the modern technological world order. Certain of the promises of empowerment made by traditional master narratives of male subjectivity and heroism were not kept. Simon's biography shows that, like the narrator's father in *L'Acacia*, his own father was killed in World War I. Like the narrator, Simon was trapped on a horse in an anachronistic cavalry under aerial attack, a sacrificial victim to the mobilization of the war machine.[1] The collapse of military order he describes in his novels is inextricably bound up with the collapse of the ideological narratives of heroism and power. For his part, Simon the writer never "gets beyond" these experiences, which are some of the most formative for a European man whose lifetime spans much of the twentieth century. The connection between an experience of war and the narrative tradition of which that war is an integral part is made most tellingly in *L'Acacia*. The narrator, a brigadier in World War II, recognizes with horror that the death drive in his colonel's madness is actually an internalized "heroic" narrative that the colonel enacts by leading his soldiers into a technological death trap in search of a hieratic and anachronistic death or telos. From the experience of being first a body mobilized, incarcerated, and then a body in flight, a human being hunted like an animal, Simon the writer derives an aesthetics of detail through which people, situations, and events become linked to one another. Certain of these links in his writing are based on a shared privation in which human beings are denied their humanity: the specific segregation of the ghetto as a prelude to general mobilization, the enclosure of women by a reproduction-oriented tradition, and the amputation of soldiers from the community. Simon's art of the detail engages his readers in the minute examination of the violent effects of the *mise à l'écart* in general: that of soldiers, Jews, blacks, mulattos, women (the mother), peasants, and the poor. He explores the points of contact between different, segregated worlds despite their distance in time, space, culture, and discourse.

L'Acacia is not the first of Simon's novels to treat the question of the individual who, entangled in cataclysmic events, becomes dispossessed of the old certitudes of his subject position in narrative. This loss does not mean, however, that legacies of family, land, and history are simply rejected or denied. On the contrary, Simon reinvents these legacies with extraordinary patience and pleasure by questioning the false innocuousness of their most insignificant artifacts and remainders, through which narratives are subsequently linked to one another. As this study has shown, the narrativities of legacy are central to his work as a whole. As far back as *Le Sacre du printemps* [The rite of spring] and *Le Vent*, but especially since *La Route des Flandres*, Simon's novels of history and the family return to a crucial question: how is it that a man who was supposed to be heir to the Western tradition of knowledge and power, who was designated to be the measure of identity and selfhood, cannot simply lay claim to that legacy? The reason rests in part on the fact that the "one" becomes the "Other" and "Others." Simon's narrators, many of whom are young soldiers, are segregated from the community, cut off from the privileged identity that comes from the convergence of subject, space, time, and language proposed by the narratives of the Western tradition. Their mobilization is presented as a useless sacrifice to a dying world order attempting to preserve itself by means of a radical mutation so as to enter the technological age. Simon's writing shows, in its intense detail, how people's bodies, as well as their art, instruments, beliefs, thoughts, stories, and language, "become mobilized" into the general war machine.

In *L'Acacia* Simon reinvents the novel of the family, voyage, and war through the details linking it with vast narrative ensembles and traditions. This time the novel traces the story of the improbable encounter between the narrator's parents. At the turn of the century two individuals separated by everything—geography, milieu, class, and religion—are finally united after a long engagement and leave for the colonies where they conceive a child, the future narrator. The voyage that brings them back from the colonies on the eve of World War I becomes a gauge of the time separating them from the father's death. Simon takes up again certain stories told elsewhere, elaborating in valuable ways—providing what he calls complementary information—the two critical prewar and wartime periods of this century. (A possible title and subtitle he considered for the novel were "sentimental education," a "novel of apprenticeship").[2]

The first part of the novel opens in 1919, and the first page presents women in movement. "They went from village to village" ("Elles allaient d'un village à l'autre"). Their progress is hampered by the yellow mud in which they twist their ankles. Whereas the presence of the acacia tree in the title and "elles" recalls the opening of *Histoire* (the branches, the old ladies), the evocation of the muddy roads echoes the beginning of *La Route des Flandres,* where the soldiers twist their ankles in the mud. The descent into the inferno is here the search for the lost body of the soldier by his widow, sisters, and child. The group of four women replicates and displaces the four surviving horsemen of *La Route des Flandres*, with the difference that here the soldier is dead, survived by the family that attempts to find traces of the dead person, to accomplish a ritual of mourning at the possible sites of his disappearance. The voyage constitutes for the future narrator-writer a formative experience of having been "dragged through an apocalyptic landscape in search of an elusive skeleton" (122). This movement toward an absent end irremediably modifies his belief in teleological quests in general.

Whereas in *La Route des Flandres* the narrator attempts to draw to himself the captain, the paternal figure, to make him a part of his own family's narrative legacy, in *L'Acacia* there occurs a distancing and rapprochement of this problematic figure through its doubling.[3] In the earlier novel the "suicides" of the captain and the de Reixach ancestor are themselves the object of the narrative quest. Read as an Oedipal family narrative, *La Route des Flandres* suggests that by making love with Corinne (the "father's" wife), the "son" in fact sleeps with a mother figure. The telling of much of the war story from within the scene of lovemaking, with the language hovering between an escape into woman and an absorption into the earth, signifies that the Oedipal narrative is figured as the dominant narrative strategy of the text. Significantly, Corinne walks out of the narrative quest, whose real object is in fact the "father" and the patriarchal narrative order.[4] In *L'Acacia* Simon retells the story of the colonel's "suicide," but he severs the family tie to the captain as a symbolic father. The rejection of the fiction of the family narrative (the paternal de Reixach and Corinne) can possibly be accomplished only once the story of the "real" father's disappearance is allowed to emerge. The intensity with which the ancestor's and de Reixach's deaths are treated in *La Route des Flandres* may now be understood as a screen for the father's death recounted in *L'Acacia*. In other words, the quest for the father's body (by his widow, sisters, and son) comes to replace the substitute (symbolic) quest for the mad, paternal, death-dealing captain so obsessively pursued in *La Route des Flandres*. The colonel is not named here, no family tie is claimed, and the unnamed woman sought after the narrator's escape is a prostitute. The narrative itself does not have a woman as its principal addressee, which suggests that the consequences of Corinne's refusal to be used as a "soldiers' girl" in a tradi-

General and Particular Mobilizations 117

tional narrative quest have been carried over to *L'Acacia*'s narrative structure itself. An important difference between the two novels is that the encounter with Corinne is situated in a time supposedly beyond the war, whereas the encounter with the prostitute occurs in a France still occupied and in Perpignan, which is only apparently outside of the conflict. In a more general way the structure of address and destination in the two novels differs widely. In *L'Acacia* the widow and her husband's family go in search of the man's body. Thus, the woman's own symbolic quest for the man (husband, father, and brother) obviates the need for the son to repeat the quest in which dead authority figures are made into ambivalent fathers. Unlike in the earlier novel, the "good" father and the "bad" father can here be distinguished. The good, privatized father, though a military man, becomes a victim of the war machine, whereas the bad, mobilizing father is the mad murderer who sacrifices his sons, leading them to their deaths in his hieratic suicide quest. The bad father's infanticide and genocide is symbolized through the colonel's enactment of the narrative of sacrifice, an immolation to a moribund world.

The 1919 voyage as quest involves the search for the body of the father who is unpresentable; it is an attempt to constitute through displacement a sepulcher or monument to the disappeared. However, the symbolic quest for the man's body, which may be termed the absent paternal signifier, is never completed. All witnessing is already secondary, at a remove from the original event and already generated according to the model of received images fabricated by the heroic war propaganda of the period. The failure of that quest, then, is due as much to the absence of material traces as to the ideological narratives that frame the search itself. But it is precisely by means of the voyage of mourning of the three women and child, whose movements retrace the steps of their husband-brother-father, that the text replicates the classical symbolic quest. By reinscribing that quest, the novel questions its monumentalizing narratives. In other words, from these initial images of women in movement there emerge the many dimensions of different spaces and times from which are elaborated the general and particular figures of "mobilization" in history and personal story.

The difficulty of presenting the unpresentable father lies in the problem of contact. The woman, her husband's sisters, and the child have no access to the reality of the man's death. Their quest for his body is a voyage of mourning whose sustaining images are based on iconographical fragments from traditional narrative representations of the dead hero:

> the account given to the widow and the sisters (or the account which they made of the episode subsequently), though doubtless in good faith, perhaps somewhat embellishing the matter or rather theatricalizing it according to the stereotype impressed on their imagination by the illustrations in history books or the paintings representing the death of more or less legendary warriors, almost always dying in a semi-recumbent position on the grass, head and torso more or less leaning against a tree trunk, surrounded by knights. . . . Nothing else, then, but these vague accounts (perhaps at second hand, perhaps poeticizing the facts, either out of pity or kindness in order to flatter . . . or again because the witnesses—those who had been there or those who had repeated their accounts—were themselves deceived, glorifying the episode, obeying that need to transcend the events . . . : hence we have seen the performers of brilliant actions distort the facts, though these were to their advantage, with the sole unconscious goal of making them agree with pre-established models). (248)

More likely than this, the narrator adds, the body was

> in the imprecise form these shapeless heaps offer to the eye, more or less soiled with mud and blood, and where the first thing that strikes the eye is most often the excessive size of the shoes, forming a V when the body is lying on its back, or else parallel, showing their hobnailed soles to which still adhere clots of earth and grass if the dead man is lying face down, or stuck together, drawn up toward the buttocks by the bent legs, the body itself in a fetal position, distractedly turned over with one foot by the man arriving on the scene. (248)

Narrative models and stereotypes block the possibility of contact with the reality of the father's death, but Simon's writing insistently details the real they exclude. The woman who drags her child and husband's sisters across the muddy war-torn fields of Verdun performs the part assigned to her in the narrative quest structure; she is the spouse who immolates herself in the symbolic narrative of mourning. Her voyage, in other words, is an effect and reproduction of the narrative quest structure. Simon shows that the quest for the absent father's body itself belongs to a narrative mobilizing war images and stories that is designed to dissimulate real events and death. Indeed, in the narrator's inability and refusal to narrate his own wartime experience according to the dictates of the quest model, we also see the end of the narrative of symbolic mourning for a disappeared world order.

Women and the War Machine

Whereas Simon would be the last writer to claim any knowledge of his characters, male or female, in terms of their psychology or motivations, his work nevertheless contains significant figurations of the material and symbolic condition of women and men. One could say that in Simon's novels women remain other, beyond reach, and inaccessible to the narrators' scrutiny of women's legacy. The significance of Simon's work as a writing of the cultural figuration of women, however, the details and social narratives by which they are constituted, has been sorely underestimated. His novels in fact account for some fundamental yet discrete elements of the constitution and situatedness of woman: as mother, beloved, wife, model, teacher, prostitute, farmer, intendant of estates, questor. The understanding of women that readers derive comes from the aesthetic detail, which is never isolated from its context(s) and is reconfigured as women's condition in relation to the forces of war, sexuality, power, authority, economy, and history. Sometimes, as in *Histoire* and *L'Acacia*, the position of the male narrator resembles, up to a point, that of the mother in certain situations, yet their two narratives diverge in important respects. Simon's tendency to represent strong, male-identified, hardworking women in certain novels (Aunt Marie in *L'Herbe*, Gatti in *Les Géorgiques*, and the two sisters in *L'Acacia*) contrasts with the significant absence of such women in the so-called formalist novels. In the latter, women are presented as desubjectivized, and their presentation includes a critique of the commodification of and the violence against women at the level of cultural narrativity. In general, formalism generates conventional representations and simulacra whose effects are countered by the replications of parody.

Opposed to such formal writing, *L'Acacia*'s historical and cultural perspectives make the connection, more firmly than any of the previous novels except *Histoire*, between the enclosure of women at the turn of the century and the loss of agency experienced by soldiers and prisoners of war. Although the opening pages of the novel show us "women in movement," their progress through the war-torn landscape is, on closer reading, merely an illusion. In a passage that is vintage Simon, the double figure of the woman and the river seems to emerge from the historicized landscape itself, from its recent catastrophe:

> comme si depuis sa source, tout le long de son cours et de ses méandres, elle draînait les retombées de quelque pluie de cendres, de quelque cataclysme définitif, total, condamné à laver sans espoir de fin ces terres vouées à l'infertilité et ces gravats parmi lequels les deux femmes et l'enfant suivaient l'implacable errance de celle qui les traînait derrière elle. (14–15)
> [as if, from its very source, down its entire length and along all its meanders, it were draining the remains of some rain of ashes, some definitive, total cataclysm doomed to wash without hope of an end this earth consigned to sterility and these heaps of rubble among which the two women and the child followed the implacable odyssey of the woman who was dragging them behind her. (6)]

In this evocation of the river ferrying the debris of war, the river's meanders and the woman's implacable quest are linked through the words themselves (*draînait/traînait, méandres/errance, condamné/implacable*). Despite her movement, the widow is revealed to be fixed in a position of mourning and identification with the dead man she seeks. What Freud calls mourning is accomplished here not only through a mimetic identification with the dead body, blocked at the intimate mirror stage in the imaginary order. In a more ample sense, the woman's work of mourning is figured by a symbolic voyage that in its very movement goes beyond the private limits of an individual loss, ultimately involving the location of that loss in social history and ritual. Simon's writing describes the widow's immobility in the midst of her apparent movement from place to place. Enclosed by her crepe veil and withdrawn from others by her loss and her class, she never addresses directly those from whom the sisters request information and directions. She is placed outside the "destinations" of communication with others: "as if she herself had not spoken the same language or as if some ceremony forbade her to speak to strangers directly . . . only the eyes . . . gleaming in the shadow of the veil with a sort of wasted ardor, a charred luster, a fever" (7). While the widow enacts the dictates of the narrative of mourning, one of the sisters takes care of the child. The story that she tells him, contrary to (and yet ironically like) the teleological quest of the widow, seems not to have any ending, for "tirelessly, her exhausted face stamped with a passive desolation, she would add new episodes every day" (9).

Thus, in spite of her movement, the narrator's mother is identified with the dead, "mortally calm, monumental, black, mortally resolved, still filled with that unappeasable distress and that inflexible determination," forcing her "from one charnel house to the next" (14). When she finally stops her quest for the body, Simon's writing details the intricate narrativity, the impossible finality, involved: "And in the end she found it. Or rather she found an end—or at least something she could consider (or that her exhaustion, the degree of fatigue she had attained, obliged her to consider) as able to put an end to what was making her scour, these ten days, the ruined roads, the half-abandoned farms, and the canteens stinking of drunken men" (14). The cemetery scene, which portrays the widow and the child kneeling before the burial site of two unknown French soldiers, is one of a pervasive immobility. It shows the other two women "motionless, their lips motionless in their motionless wrinkled faces" (15). The telos of the narrative quest for the absent father is reached here in a ritualized scene of mourning that, in its absolute stillness and irrecuperable loss, ought to have put an end to a world governed by the sacrificial narrative. Chronologically, however, the sacrificial motif begins before this scene and continues after it. In retrospect, what is buried here is a traditional narrative of quest, and it is that "ending" that provides the thread joining the segregationist and sacrificial motifs of the novel.

As the following chapter shifts to May 17, 1940, the immobility of the 1919 tableau of mourning is linked to that of the soldiers on the eve of the debacle. Figures of "passivity" and "indolence" first appear, paradoxically, in reference not to the soldiers but to the bombers flying overhead: "(... nothing but the mixture of black and white: iron gray, funereal) lazy, indolent" (17). Exposed in the middle of the countryside, the soldiers mechanically take note of the planes' flight: "all they knew was that what was circling so lazily over their heads in the cloudless sky still vaguely tinged with the dawn's pink was the portent of their death . . . , their eyes following it without slackening their gait, without trying to escape or scatter, their torsos continuing docilely to sway back and forth in their saddles" (17, modified). The novel's extended figuration of immobility, passivity, and docility begins as a conflation of human and mechanical attributes, soldiers reduced to mechanical movements (referred to also as the movement of chess pieces) and technology seen anthropomorphically as lazy and deadly.[5] The attack occurs soon after. In a tableau of suddenly arrested movement, the narrator evokes the frozen immobility of the soldiers in the face of the aerial attack that sacrifices the whole army. Although they appear only in a later chapter, the "gardes mobiles," or MPs, might be mentioned here. Those who share the young reservists' compartment combine a machinelike efficiency and a tranquil violence. They act according to what seems to be a regulated series of gestures: "the whole episode (bursting in, taking off equipment, settling down, opening packages of cheese, chewing) concatenated with a sort of calm, innate, somehow mechanical violence, that is the violence natural to former farmhands, plowmen, or laborers . . . somehow domesticated, the way gunpowder packed into the cartridge casing is domesticated" (147). The details of Simon's description stress the guards' response to orders as being a "savage docility." These are the professionals, mobilized into the military in such a way that they seem to belong to "a world apart, marginal to the groaning and fearful human race" (148). They are hybridized, halfway between humans and "spiny shellfish," between men and machines.

The next chapter, "August 27, 1914," pursues the sacrificial motif in the story of the father's two sisters who, abandoning their youth and their ambitions to be teachers or mothers, toil the land to meet their brother's expenses at the military academy of Saint-Cyr. Devoid of self-pity, in old age they simply state the facts in the telling (to the narrator in

1982). Thus, while the apathy and immurement of the woman who is to become the narrator's mother is an important aspect of the representation of women in *L'Acacia*, it is not the only one. It is the sacrificial motif that brings together the laborious destiny of the sisters with the indolence and apathy of the young woman who is described as having done nothing in all her life: "It was as if she had no desires, no regrets, no thoughts, no plans. She was neither sad, nor melancholy, nor dreamy. Rather gay, according to those who knew her at the time, greedy (and therefore doubtless sensual)" (82). Yet we are also told by the narrator that "she was not chaste but somehow asexual" (84). He appears to accept the nineteenth-century narrative of woman that denies her all attributes defining identity and subjectivity. Nevertheless, he deftly avoids making of her a melancholic "Emma Bovary" heroine. From the material remainders and stories of his mother's life, therefore, the narrator invents a figure fraught with contradictions, the same contradictions that pervaded the lives of upper bourgeois women at the turn of the century.

The sacrificial motif emerges forcefully when the young woman's liking for bullfighting is evoked: "she described the blindfolded horses, their bellies ripped open by the bull's horns and their guts hurriedly stuffed back in with straw before being sewn up and offered to the bull all over again. Apparently she was utterly unconscious that she possessed a body and what such a thing might be used for, aside from being fed with delicacies or dressed in laces" (82). Simon's writing makes the transition elliptically between the horses' and the woman's "function," relating one sacrificial figure to the other. The word *blindfold* is echoed by *unconscious*, the horses' bellies being ripped open by horns are related to her body's use in a figure suggesting deflowering and perhaps childbirth, the horses' guts being stuffed back are linked with her appetite, and the sewing up of the horses is continued through the laces in which she is dressed. The writing suggests an analogy that the novel takes up elsewhere by connecting the motifs of segregation and sacrifice. The young woman is described as being profoundly lazy, incurious, and apathetic: "For the rest, she seemed to limit herself to being there, confined in a static inertia, her face timidly protected from the sun by parasols, milky and vegetative, like the lethargic sovereign of some kingdom of absence where she kept herself" (86). Spending her time taking photographs of a world about to disappear in World War I, she seems to anticipate nothing, to await nothing. Her "artistic" authorship as photographer is here conceived of as being "merely" a task of conservation, mausoleum construction, or the reproduction of a doomed society. Ironically, the technological representation of that world as photographic image both participates in and precipitates its disappearance. It is symptomatic that the narrator refuses to accord her only activity, with its strong anthropological narrativity, any value as act and agency. In what he presents as the mother's profoundly *anarrative* state of inactivity, there occurs instead a massive reversal. Instead of being empowered to enact her life as if it were a teleological narrative of the subject, the mother is shown to be enclosed in—as well as excluded from—a narrative whose movement lies outside her, that is, the narrative of phallocentric culture. The narrator identifies the narrativity of that narrative as that which is waiting *for* her: "as if something were waiting for her which would be a kind of levitation, some apotheosis in which she would figure, transmogrified and swooning, borne on a cloud supported by cherubs and from which she would then be violently hurled into the void" (89). In this extraordinary evocation of the woman as a sort of St. Sulpice Virgin Mary, composed of iconographic and scriptural references, Simon's writing brings into play the whole range of religious and metaphysical narrative figures constituting woman as an anarrative nonsubject.

Another conjuncture of two narrative series, that of amorous quest and military conquest, produces another representation of woman. The encounter between the young woman and the lieutenant from the Jura who will become the narrator's father is described in terms of a siege "of that fortress of prejudice, of indolence, of futility and insolence," in which "passive and consenting, the inaccessible princess" awaits him (92). Referring to his father, the narrator proposes the following juncture of narrative determinations and endings:

> as if, inhabited by a sort of premonition, pressed for time, he had chosen before dying to deposit his seed and to survive in one of those females destined to the reproduction of the species guaranteed by their faculties of inertia, of opulence, and of fecundity: a

need, a necessity, an urgency doubtless confounded, as in that twilight of a world which was going to die along with millions of young men buried under the mud and in which mingled the paradoxical and caricatural images, frozen or jerky, of military parades. (93)

This phantasmatic account shows up the extraordinary narrativity that links the culturally elaborated narratives of biological and social reproduction. It reveals the extent to which these narratives pass through women's supposedly negative capabilities. In a series of oppositions that exemplify Freud's notion of male libido and female receptivity, this passage opposes the necessity and urgency of the male subject's active resistance to death (chosen, survive) to the woman's receptivity (destined, guaranteed by) and her biologically conditioned negative faculty of passivity. The male's foreknowledge and orientation toward the future is opposed to the female's predestination as the means to accomplishing that telos. As readers we recognize in these fictions the cultural (re)production of narratives of gender and history. Significantly, we also read, however, that to these belong also the heroic narratives that bury millions of young people in the twilight of a world. It is a world represented technologically by the jerky cinematic movement that creates parodic effects and caricatural images.

Moreover, Simon's writing brings together the narrative of military and sexual conquest with the narrative of colonialism. First, the narrator's future father travels to the farthest reaches of the colonized world, and later both the narrator's parents travel there, when the father is "posted" as "envoy" to Madagascar. The postcards that remain as traces of their travels and mission attest to the geopolitical enclosure of colonialism, which ensures both military and economic extension of power over distant lands. In the growing rumblings of war the resemblance between the enclosure of the mother and that of the colonized sphere is vividly described. "Perhaps continuing to drift, invulnerable, out of reach, in a sort of lethargy, of lukewarm nirvana, that orgiastic state of vegetal efflorescence, that vaguely fabulous world somehow set apart from the other one, and where the noise of arms, the rumors of war, arrived only muffled, remote, incredible" (107). Simon's writing of details leaves no doubt as to the connection between the immurement of the woman and the conquests of colonies. The two sisters receive postcards from their brother depicting a "succession of smooth feminine faces, the heteroclite booty wrested from barbarous worlds" (59). Material translations of his individual erotic encounters with exotic women in exotic lands, these postcards are also messages concerning the colonizing endeavor as a whole. In 1899 the postcards that the couple send from Madagascar represent it reduced to a backdrop; they are an integral part of the colonizing drive to appropriate people and land. Earlier, on her honeymoon, the young woman sends to her mother a postcard of three skeletal blacks:

> ". . . you wonder if these are human beings like ourselves; [. . .] we are in a café having something cold to drink. Kisses," the postcard representing three blacks, rather three skeletons (or three beanpoles or three scarecrows), three hybrid things, halfway between the human and the vegetal, that is, where it is impossible to distinguish what belonged to one or the other realm, or the place where one realm joined the other, or rather what distinguished the limbs like dry wood from the hanging fibers which half-covered them, revealing the swollen bellies, the conical navels, the protruding ribs (one of them hiding—or holding—his genitals with one hand), each of the three beanpoles surmounted by a shaved skull, with half-closed, oval eyes, enormous pudgy lips, a long wound open over one of the tibias, like a scar in the bark of a tree. (99)

The young woman accepts without question the contiguity between the frozen drinks she consumes and the blacks' starvation evidenced in the photograph; from her ideological position as a white woman, she doubts any common humanity between "them" and "us." Her failure to recognize or to allow any reciprocity between I and thou, a reciprocity that is the foundation of an ethical sense of human community, does not arise ex nihilo, however. The racism implied in her question is already accounted for by the general consent in Europe to colonize the Other. It is, moreover, graphically depicted in Simon's writing of the postcard: the blacks are represented as things, belonging to a hybrid variety in which the vegetal and human realms cannot be distinguished, their members reduced to wooden sticks and fibers. Any reciprocity of feeling, or *Mitfühlung,* for the wound of the black man is violently blocked, because a wound in a tree's bark cannot be felt by anyone. Yet the European woman, who assents to and perpetuates the appalling ideological narrative of racism that the postcard depicts, is herself condemned by a different version of the same narrative because, though not starved and wounded, she is nevertheless similarly spoken of as leading a "vegetal" existence of indifference. Moreover, on losing her husband she becomes a victim of the ideological narrative of segregation/sacrifice that she here fails to acknowledge. Indeed, her own female sex is suggestively figured in the "wound" described on the photograph, and later she herself undergoes massive surgical cutting ("thanks to the scalpels that kept cutting away her body, a sort of living scarecrow" [122]).

The linkage of the two orders, colonialism and the condition of women, occurs in a network of figures establishing repetitions and differential points of contact between them. Their differences, while maintained, come to converge. The differences, for instance, between the narrator and his mother are meaningfully narrowed by the descriptions of a common inertia linking them. In the military train that he believes will lead him to his end, the narrator recalls having been "dragged through an apocalyptic landscape in search of an elusive skeleton" (123). As he remembers his uncomprehending docility then and later during his mother's illness, the narrator thinks of his situation on the train as being analogous to that of his mother in her coffin: "lying as though in a box inside a train compartment" (122). Convinced he will die, he undertakes a process of mourning his past, which he describes as twenty-six years of idleness and

> unconcerned inertia—at best, of anticipatory impulse, of frustrated expectation of something which had never happened . . . , which couldn't have been provoked (or deceived) by any of the disguises successively imposed or attempted, from the stiff uniform with its military cut in which, once the oak box had vanished, they had dressed the boy of twelve, with its collar like a carcan . . . down to the latest one which included as accessories the brushes and palette of a cubist painter, having meanwhile tried the anarchist's belted blouse. (123)

The difference between mother and son is thus reduced but not eliminated. He just barely opposes his own sense of expectation with the lack of it in the young woman who later becomes his mother. For both of them, however, the narrative telos lies not in their actions but in the events that come to awaken the characters, too late, from their indolence and lethargy.

Although the word *docility* is associated first with the nudity of the model who is the narrator's lover, that docility is shown to be shared by all the mobilized soldiers. Simon's narrator detects in the pre–World War I society that the young woman inhabits (public and private, European and colonial) the same elements of blindness, indifference, and docility as in his own society prior to World War II. Except for the MPs, the soldiers once aboard the train are in a state of "gloomy, mute, and docile tumult" (121). Thinking of all the trains simultaneously transporting their "cargo of fear," the narrator lies on his bunk "furiously inert." In the sound of one train he hears innumerable convoys carried into the night, and he imagines people everywhere in a state of "anxious hebetude, the same apathetic terror, the inhabitants of farms scattered through the countryside, of villages, of darkened cities: as if the tears, the faces bathed with tears turning away, abandoning the stations, had flowed back, at first in sad groups, then separating, dividing, ramifying like a river flowing back toward its sources" (126).

Thus, characters and their environment—the woman, the narrator, increasingly larger groups of people, and finally, a "feminized" Europe and a "lethargic universe"—all contribute through their docility and apathy to the inevitability of war. A striking instance of this docility and apathy is found in the scene where the narrator's mother receives the announcement of her husband's death at Verdun. As she reads, her lips begin to move automatically:

> endlessly forming over and over the same phrase, the same mute lacerating howl, with no other echo than the indifferent stir of the branches, the monotonous cry of the same bird, the monotonous scraping of the hoe wielded by one of the lethargic gardeners, as if the whole lethargic universe, the earth which was continuing its slow turning [. . .] were gradually diluting, absorbing, erasing, annihilating the series of words powerless to escape her throat, stam-

mering, disintegrating, returning again, like a litany, a madwoman's mumbled phrase: Thy will be... Thy will be... Thy will ... (212)

In her despair, she experiences a radical loss of will marked by the loss of the ability to bring the sentence to a close.[6]

The reader may believe that nothing could be further removed from the war machine than the apathetic and lethargic young woman who waits, undesiring, for (the narrative of) her female biological destiny to be fulfilled. Figures of immobility and passivity are displaced in Simon's writing, however, shifting from women to other subjects. In making such shifts the writing articulates important relationships between the two prewar periods. The apathy that Simon's narrator describes as being pervasive prior to World War II constitutes a major aspect of the growing militarization and the rise of fascism. In different contexts, the semantic range of the novel shifts from describing the woman's inertia in her assigned role as reproducer of the species to the narrator's own inertia in the years before his mobilization. The young woman's immobility is a prelude to and a condition of her mobilization for reproductive ends. (The notion of reproduction is rendered passive, whereas the woman's capacity to give birth could not so readily be appropriated by the narrative of generation.) The narrator mimes this same "feminized" position: they are both said to have a fondness for disguises; she takes and develops photographs, whereas he is a false artist. Their fundamental phenomenal position of passivity and immobility in the face of disempowerment comes to include, in the general drift toward mobilization, groups of young soldiers, blacks, Jews, mulattoes, and so on. Individuals and entire groups and populations are shown to be powerless in the face of the "order" that mobilizes them and mobilizes forces against them. Proceeding by segregating and then sacrificing individuals and groups to a dying world, this narrative order regenerates itself through the modern technological war machine.

Femininity, then, is not an attribute of women but a condition to be mobilized for reproduction and war. Simon describes the history of mobilization as a process of separation, a sealing off, followed by incorporation and rejection. This history is one of the most powerful narratives of disaster in the modern age. Simon's writing succeeds in elaborating its activity in the figural links it establishes between a "feminized," anarrative position and the experience of being a sacrificial victim. No longer does his narrator have the illusion that his experience of war separates him from women and others. In *La Route des Flandres* Georges's and Blum's stories still constitute woman as Other, as a part of a shimmering peacetime vision. In *Les Géorgiques*, however, the flight of both the expatriate brother, Jean-Marie L.S.M., and the Englishman O., who are hunted like animals, is also described as an experience of feminization. In *L'Acacia* the figuration of women and the pervasiveness of different strategies of "feminization" of the Other finally open onto the more general questions at issue: Does the text manage to avoid reenclosing women? Does its writing replicate the sacrificial narrative? To what extent does it remain complicit with the narratives of the absent father, disaster, and mobilization? I propose that Simon's questioning of the narrativity involved in the prevailing mentality in Europe before both world wars is not motivated by any simplistic illusion of getting beyond ideology. Rather, his work offers an aesthetic and ethical concern with the minute figures of social linkages and historical connections, figures that emerge in his work with unparalleled force and resonance.

From Particular to General Mobilizations

Simon has spoken in interviews of the need to "reprendre les choses en enlevant leurs noms propres" ("take back things by taking away their proper nouns"); that is, to take back things by removing a particular way of using language to impose identities on people, things, places, times, and concepts. Seeking to reduce the power of the proper name, he extends his critique to include the classificatory function of the proper name, which orders things by classes, functions, relationships, positions, races, nations, titles, genders, and genres.[7] The proper name is a particular narrative of naming and "appropriation," whereas the removal or erasure of the proper name builds into reading a different narrativity based on figuration and delayed recognition or identification. Although the removal of the proper name in any definitive or absolute sense may well be illusory, since other series of names will replace the

General and Particular Mobilizations 131

old ones, Simon's desire to "take things back" nevertheless signifies that things and the possibility of perceiving them have been lost to writing because of their appropriation by standardized discourses and ideologies.

The mobilization of language to the ends of modern warfare has not, in Simon's view, ceased. It continues through discourses that simply accept a certain order of representation that is monological, monomythical, and mobilized. Yet Simon does not present mobility and immobility as either opposed terms or dialectical ones. Because his writing links the immobility of individuals, groups, and machines to the generalized figures and forces of "mobilization," it presents instead the conjuncture and encounter of apparent opposites. The relationship between mobility and immobility is rendered more complex in *L'Acacia* because what appears to be restricted to their thematic significance is in fact resituated within a general narrativity of mobilization and demobilization. It is this narrativity that displays the specific conditions of war and peace, annihilation, and the postwar return to writing.

The order to mobilize—"GENERAL MOBILIZATION"—is fully given in the performative headlines (or proper name) of the newspaper from which the syntax has been eliminated.

> for several weeks already—in fact, for several months—in fact, for several years . . . , as if, at the same time as the rules of syntax which assigned them an order of, so to speak, respectable and reassuring immunity, the others (the other words: those by which they were habitually surrounded) had suddenly lost all reason for being, the syntax expelled too, the headlines . . . reduced to the assemblage of two or three nouns isolated and excessively enlarged—the shapes of the letters simplified too: thick, without serifs, simply massive, immense—as though for myopic readers or for idiots. (119)

The order to mobilize comes as a confirmation of previous mass transports. Before the war the narrator and his Mexican friend glimpse, from the train that carries them to Moscow through Berlin, the deportation of Jews before the war: "a growing feeling of discomfort, then (when they saw the several uniformed figures walking among the bundles, the suitcases, and the children, pushing them . . . and finally closing the doors . . .)"

(170). Even before the open "general mobilization," its orders are already being enacted and fulfilled in the referential context of the trains that crisscross Europe, carrying people to their deaths. They transport first segregated Jews and then segregated soldiers into the chaos of the encounter between penetrable human flesh and the (rationalized) technology of death. Simon leaves us in no doubt that the young men's approach to the mobilization center should be read as a form of mass annihilation, a holocaust: "the timid and peaceable beet-growers or the peaceable salesmen who had docilely crowded at the gate of the gas factory with their little valises, like refugees from some disaster, some cosmic cataclysm" (175). In describing this annihilating mobilization, to which the community consents, Simon stresses the act of violent separation performed:

> As if the community which had designated them (as cattle or draft horses are chosen, and according to the same criteria: for their youth and their vigor) had already cut itself off from them, torn them away from itself with horror, excluding them, ostracizing them to its periphery on some extreme fringe of the tribal territory from which populations were driven at their approach.... They could feel at each step their horses took that chasm spreading behind them (or that wall: just as the man with the newspaper had spread between them and himself, like a sentence to signify their banishment, the thin sheet of paper with the monumental letters so to speak mortared in, without cracks or interstices) which henceforth would isolate them from the rest of the civilized world. (186–87)

As this passage suggests, mobilization in Simon is figured as a segregation, a ghettoization that divides and, in dividing, annihilates. The emphasis in mobilization on efficiency, automatism, distance, and control is in fact based on an essential cut, a wall of separation, a division. Simon elaborates the effects of mobilization not only on the individual, figured here by the young brigadier, but on the whole of society, culture, and history. He finds in these general "orders" a segregation that in its violence prefigures the greater violence to come. He writes of mobilization as an order, a performative that divides Europe by segregating

General and Particular Mobilizations 133

and sacrificing its Others. But Simon is not suggesting that such a *partage*, or division, simply occurs after the mobilization order is given. Instead, he shows that such a division is a different version of the other differences that separated the narrator's parents, for instance, whose marriage occurred in the face of insurmountable obstacles. Simon creates links, therefore, between the segregations of the world before World War I, based on sex, race, class, religious, and regional differences. The nineteenth-century world of differences ends, transformed into another, more murderous one modeled in some ways on the old. Simon does not figure a simple split or discontinuity before, during, and after the wars. For the period preceding World War I the question of cultural, sexual, and racial separations is raised in conjunction with the narrative of colonization. (In the scene of the father's departure for World War I, the combined presence of the mulatto woman from the colonies and the narrator's mother provides a reminder of the extent to which colonialism was involved in the war.) Simon's writing suggests as well a logic of continuity between these segregations and those from which stem the destruction and Holocaust of World War II. In conjunction with modern capital, the technological mobilization of people into the war machine sets up other divisions that are more global and, if possible, more devastating as far as particular cultural differences are concerned. One could say that in Simon, the shift to the "general" is itself conceived as a process of "mobilization."

Some of the most remarkable figures of mobilization and their crosstextual narrativity can be located in descriptions of stitching and scarring. In the general mobilization of World War II, for instance, the brigadier's body is incorporated into the military body; it is amputated, rejected, and expelled from the "normal," "civilized" world. By having the narrator borrow his mother's description of the horses being sewn up at the bullfight, which I read as figuring her own suturing in phallic culture, the text proposes an intricate figure of the "stitching" that joins together the sacrificial and mobilizing motifs on a European scale: "in one of those trains which all together, at the same moment, were roaring over bridges, racing through tunnels, crossing rivers, whistling lugubriously, panting across the plains of a continent seamed with scars, somehow or other stitched together again the way they sew up the belly of a horse gored by the bull in order to offer it to the animal once again" (142). The novel contains numerous other figures of "stitching" and "scarring": the mother's ill body, the black man's scar on the postcard, the Soviet flag that the narrator and his Mexican fellow art student smuggle out of Stalinist Russia, and the military patches the narrator receives. A variant of the stitching motif is that of corseting and incarcerating, as in the woman's cultural "corset" of birth, milieu, and education, and the narrator's viselike college uniform. As I have shown to be the case with other figures, the motif of stitching is pervasive, recurring for instance in the idea of defeat or undoing, which in French is the same word, *défaite:*

> then (by one of those disturbing tricks of language which make it impossible to tell if it is based on what it says or the converse) men undone, in every sense of the word, that is, not only because they belonged . . . to a defeated army, but even as individuals: like those bundles, those sacks of which as soon as the cord tying them is undone or cut the contents spread, roll, scatter in all directions, as if the invisible knot which somehow kept together that contradictory magma of passions, desires, constraints, brutality, tenderness, terror, pride, lust, and calculation which constitutes any human creature had suddenly given way. (29–30)

The train is itself the site of a complex figure of stitching, forced immobility, and the headlong rush toward death. As the soldiers' train pulls out of the station, it severs people from one another and reconnects them to the war technology of which it becomes an instrument. The writing adopts a slow-motion technique, tracing the minute details of the train's departure; it describes a woman in red suspended in midair over the platform, at once attached to and detached from a soldier's kiss. The mobilization of space is shown to proceed from a combination of speed and distance. Mobilization effects a cut that is itself both a cutting off and a tying into the war machine. It is the cut of one from another, soldier from civilian, woman from man, Jew from non-Jew, white from nonwhite, a cut that is itself a prelude to and agent of the sacrificial. The train is the site of a mobilization where the young soldiers lie immobile and voiceless. Trains inexorably carry them, together with their anachronistic arms and horses, to their deaths by a superior air power and into a new paradigm of technology and destruction. Trains are themselves part of that paradigm of mobilization.[8]

Whole groups of people such as women, Jews, blacks, and soldiers are mobilized, that is, incorporated and digested by history, that vast war machine figured here as an ogress who devours all to maximize her power. The narrator describes not the death of history (a narrative of origin and end) but rather the devouring and excreting power of an anthropophagic history:

> not the womb but (as if such a thing contained at once its origin and its end) the black corpse of History. Then he thought that it was the contrary, that it was History which was in the process of devouring them, engulfing, alive and pell-mell, horses and riders, not to mention harnesses, saddles, weapons, even spurs, in its impassive and imperforable ostrich stomach where the digestive juices and rust would manage to reduce everything, including the sharp-toothed rowels of the spurs, to a viscous and yellowish magma of the same color as their uniforms, gradually assimilated and finally rejected by its wrinkled anus, like that of some ancient ogress, in the form of excrement. (182)

Paul Virilio has proposed an interesting interpretation of the relation I have been considering between mobilization and its figurations. Writing in 1984, before media's coverage of the Gulf War brought the connection home (literally) to everyone, Virilio argues that the military conquest of space is the conquest of the image. Immediate reality, he argues, has been outflanked by the cinematic paronomasia of the war machine.[9] He quotes a passage from Ernst Jünger's *Steel Storms* (1920): "In this war where fire already attacked space more than men, I felt completely alien to my own person, as if I had been looking at myself through binoculars. . . . I could hear the tiny projectiles whistling past my ear as if they were brushing past an inanimate object. . . . The landscape had the transparency of glass." Virilio comments that "this total transparency affecting object, subject, and surrounding space . . . illustrates the derangement of perception in an environment where military technology is distorting not only the battlefield, but also, especially, the space-time of vision, where the observation machine and the modern war machine are conjoined" (72). The "fateful confusion of eye and weapon," he argues convincingly, leads to "the military use of space whose conquest was ultimately the conquest of the image." Along with the aesthetic of the electronic battlefield, this conquest of the image constitutes an extreme and subliminal form of transparency where technology finally exposes the whole world (88). He points out that "in making attack unreal, industrial warfare ceased to be the huge funeral apparatus denounced by moralists and eventually became the greatest mystification of all, an apparatus of deception, the lure of deterrence strategy. . . . Cinematic derealization now affected the very nature of power, which established itself in a technological Beyond with the space-time not of ordinary mortals but of a single war machine" (79).

Simon has grasped lucidly these and other implications of total mobilization with respect to perception. Thus, where mobilization makes the relationships between subject, object, and space transparent and attack on them unreal, he redirects our perception to their material and linguistic connectedness. His writing about mobilization is essentially a form of "stalling," designed to slow down the speed of the totalitarian tendencies of mobilized representations. He seeks to undo the presumed opposition between mobility and immobility, where mobility would be valorized as a positive dynamic and immobility would be entropic death. His thinking about history passes through the opposed and reversed figures of mobility and immobility, mobilization and demobilization. Thus, mobility for him is inhabited by immobility, and vice versa. For instance, the figure of the widow is in movement, driven by the end she seeks, yet she is immobilized by the end to which she tends. Immobility is that which can be and is mobilized. The work of mobilization and demobilization in Simon is not endlessly reversible however, immobility (passivity) is shown to be recontained by mobilization (the train, the war machine), and mobility (desire) is inhabited by the stillness of mourning and the closure of a crypt. The figures and narrativities of mobility in Simon begin and end, like the branches of the acacia tree or the river's meanders, but they do not become mobilized. Simon's work of writing the detail is one of resistance to totalization, to grand narratives, to the conflicts they perpetuate. To gain a better understanding of Simon's writing, we need to reexamine his aesthetic of the detail with attention to the contexts and the narrativities involved. It is crucial, therefore, not to cut and sever descriptions from their narrative and contextual ties.

Remarks on an Aesthetic of Disaster

The formal properties of Simon's writing must be understood in relation to the notion of mobilization that I have been discussing. The versions of otherness that emerge in his most recent fiction may be related to his aesthetic of the *pas à pas* (step by step), to the figure of blind Orion, who disappears as daylight dawns, and to the figure of Achilles "immobile à grands pas" ("running motionless"). Consider, for instance, the following characterization of description:

> Si la description est impuissante à reproduire les choses et dit toujours d'autres objets que les objets que nous percevons autour de nous, les mots possèdent par contre ce prodigieux pouvoir de rapprocher et de confronter ce qui, sans eux, resterait épars. Parce que ce qui est souvent sans rapports immédiats dans le temps des horloges ou l'espace mesurable peut se trouver rassemblé et ordonné au sein du langage dans une étroite contiguïté.
> [If description is powerless to reproduce things and always speaks of other objects than the objects we perceive about us, words possess on the contrary the prodigious power to bring together and to confront that which, without them, would remain separate. Because what is without immediate relationship in clock time or measurable space may be assembled and ordered within language in a narrow contiguity.][10]

Written some twenty years ago, and read in terms of Simon's privileging of the formal assemblage, or bricolage, of writing, this preface can now be understood in the context of an aesthetic of the detail and the cultural implications of its narrativities. Moreover, this aesthetic serves as an obstacle to mobilization by inventing a kind of writing that cannot immediately be recuperated by ideologies of totality. In sum, Simon's aesthetics of the detail counters betrayal by a traditional narrative order whose legacies of heroism, identity, and telos became massively mobilized for ideological ends.

Simon's writing in *L'Acacia* takes a critical distance from the prewar character whose successive disguises were intended to hide his lack of identity: false revolutionary, false painter, and false soldier. These disguises are presented as fetishistic ways of both revealing and hiding a lack of identity, a lack that could then be mobilized. After his escape from the POW camp, the narrator's turn to writing is a serious attempt to repair the social tie severed by mobilization. Since mobilization appropriated traditional narrative order, Simon refuses in his writing to replicate the same narrative that is complicit with forms of annihilation. This refusal does not mean that the conditions of mobilization can be either ignored or transcended, but they can be displayed in the process of writing and reading. The fury that the narrator experiences after his return to society may be understood as a fury directed at the perversion of the social contract, a perversion that almost managed to kill him. His rage then can be displaced only by the invention of a different writing. Similarly, for Simon the writer the stakes lie in an urgent need that is also a wager: the necessity of inventing a nonsacrificial, nonmobilized, and nonmobilizing writing. Although there is no guarantee that any writing is resistant enough to escape being mobilized by ideology and technology (or techno-ideology), this writer's return to the detail, "to the ground," marks the strong need at least to attempt such a writing and reading.

In *L'Acacia* the conditions of mobilization and their relation to writing involve a series of figurations. In the first of these the novel presents scenes of shock encounters between peace and war within mobilization where visual contact is possible yet actual communication between incommensurate worlds is not: for example, the shock experienced by the narrator and his Mexican friend at the scene of Jewish families being deported at a German train siding (228); the reversal and repetition of this scene that occurs in the link and separation between the family and the newly called up soldiers (236); the strolling German townsfolk so close to, yet so distant from, the narrator and his fellow prisoners of war (317). These scenes of a shock encounter between realities forcibly separated by institutions and laws are not new in Simon's work. They have been present since *Le Sacre du printemps*. What is new is the clarity with which the writing now explores the "how is it possible?" of a situation, the political and historical dimensions of the way a situation is replicated and reversed.

A second series involves the representation and exchange of women's bodies. The novel describes young women whose faces or bodies are appropriated in a number of different contexts, contexts whose linkage is thus affirmed: the postcard depicting "licentious little tarts in panties" (85) that an admirer sends to the indolent young woman; the photographs of non-Western women that the lieutenant sends to his sisters from his colonial peregrinations; a smiling, young blonde woman appearing in a luminous halo on a postcard of an armed cannon flanked by a World War I soldier; young German "women of pink steel" who in 1937 resemble iron flowers in an increasingly mobilized land of steel; the young models at the academy where the narrator and his friend learn to transform "the tender pale nudes sitting or langorously stretched out on the model's platform into steel tubes, cones, and spheres" (134);[11] the pornographic images of childlike women the narrator as prisoner of war draws for the *Feldwebel* in exchange for rations, cigarettes, and at times, dispensation from work.

The precise descriptions of these pornographic drawings are significant: "he repeated the images of the same couple or of the same woman (he had learned to give them a childish face framed by silky hair) in the postures of coitus, of sodomization or fellatio (and at the end—this was the one that was most successful—the same posture: the woman kneeling, her body arched, offering her rump)" (260). After his escape the narrator forgets for a while that he had done these drawings of "tender bodies offered to penetration, the tender swollen vulvas, the childish faces with greedy lips" (262), but his artist's skill was effectively mobilized by the war machine. Bodies, at once ambiguously those of women and children, were appropriated as the vehicle of an exchange between men (victims and oppressors). What is being exchanged, in the context of imprisonment itself, is a replicated image of the child/woman or the woman/child whose reproduction then comes to symbolize a further symbolic realm of oppression within the "espace concentrationnaire." After his escape the narrator adds another to this series of women's bodies by visiting a prostitute who is supposed to be the very opposite of "those breasts, those bellies, those vulvas he had drawn so many times" (280). She, the narrator claims, is a body without falsehood, "something living, moving: hair, membranes, lips, saliva, tongues, eyes, voices, breathing: the flesh without falsehood, credible, docile in his hands, moving, slipping, opening: solitude, death, doubt averted, vanquished" (280). At this point and again soon after, there is a disquieting resonance established by the word *docility* that was used to characterize whole populations that could as a result of their passivity be "mobilized." Simon's writing here reinscribes the problematic sphere of mobilization and its entire figural density. Their reinscription serves as a reminder that docility and the body always continue to remain available for purposes of mobilization, that they can always be sacrificed anew to ideological ends. That the narrator's triumph over his death sentence occurs through the mediation of a young prostitute whose body is here economized, divided, commodified, and separated into its parts is a problematic reminder to the reader that no partitions or *mises à l'écart* are without potentially dangerous consequences. In this sense Simon's aesthetic of the detail is not foreign to the question of woman's integrity as a subject (and not only a partitioned body) and the meaningfulness of the body's narrativization or mobilization. As the narrator proceeds to reintegrate himself into society, first via a woman's body and then by reading, drawing, and finally writing, his return in no way erases the past—that is, the prewar points of linkage between passivity, mobilization, and annihilation. I return at this point to the questions posed: Does the text manage to avoid reenclosing women? Does its writing replicate the sacrificial narrative? Does it remain complicit with the narrative of mobilization?

Unlike the earlier *La Route des Flandres*, where Georges pursues an Oedipal quest through Corinne, in *L'Acacia* the woman's body is not made into either a narrative source or a telos for the war narrative. In the prostitute's body the narrator seeks instead an immediacy or presence that is a flight from the war. It is not certain that his commerce with her, the exchange of sex for money, undermines at all the traditional narrative of the war hero returning to the woman's embrace. Nor, as the language of this encounter shows, is it certain that the narratives of segregation and sacrifice can ever in fact simply be surpassed or transcended once and for all. In any event, the narrator does not linger on the scene. Instead of making the love scenes themselves a matrix of narrative recollection, as in those between Georges and Corinne, Simon has the narrator move on to a separate aesthetic turn, accomplished through drawing, reading, and finally writing.

The narrative legacy in *L'Acacia* becomes radically split between one syntax and its discrediting, one world order and another, one individual self and its others. The novel that begins with the attempt to repossess the father's body and mourn his loss becomes, at the end, a series of attempts by the narrator to repair a severance from and break in the possibility of community. The narrator's sense of becoming the Other is based on the knowledge that the intent was to have him killed—the intent not only of the enemy but of his own army commanders as well.[12] The transition from being an object of sacrifice, a hunted animal rejected and expelled from the human community, to becoming a social and ethical person once more, a subject in a community of subjects, is a difficult one, but becoming Other may be taken as a condition of becoming a subject in an ethical sense, of recognizing a reciprocity between self and Other.

In a postwar perspective Simon's writing provides a particularly thoughtful questioning of what constitutes a reinvention of the social tie or bond. The narrator returns to reading through Rousseau and Balzac's *La Comédie humaine* and to drawing through the details of trees and rocks: "[he] began copying with utmost exactitude the leaves of a branch, a reed, a tuft of grass, pebbles, neglecting no detail, no vein, notch, striation, or crack" (286).[13] Although these drawings display a pure, mimetic realism, they are by no means isolated from the narrator's wartime experience. By comparing them with a description of the narrator's perceptions as he regains consciousness after being struck during an aerial attack, we can see their resemblance: "indeterminate spots that blur, fade out, then reappear, then grow clear: triangles, polygons, pebbles, tiny blades of grass, the stones of the road where he is now on all fours like a dog" (64). The drawings he makes after his second escape (from the war) thus recall, without actually repeating, the details of his minimal awareness during his flight (from aerial attack). The wartime experience of a radical discontinuity and dissociation generates the need for such realist representations of minute detail, but mimetic realism is recognized to be part of a larger order of representation, which is a narrative one. Later, when the narrator attempts to recount what happened, what he calls "these things,"

> he realized that he had fabricated instead of something shapeless, invertebrate, a relation of events that a normal mind . . . might constitute after the fact, according to an established usage of sights and sounds accepted and agreed upon, that is, giving rise to more or less clear and orderly images, distinct from each other, while in truth this had neither definite shapes nor names nor adjectives nor subjects nor complements nor punctuation (in any case no periods), nor exactly temporality, nor meaning, nor consistency if not that—viscous, murky, soft, indeterminate—of what reached him through that more or less transparent glass bell. (216)

The fact that the elementary structure of language and the symbolic order fail him in the face of catastrophe places into question the validity of their narrative orders as well. Yet ultimately Simon's writing does not attempt to remain in the asemiotic and asemantic state of disaster. Whereas his work as a whole does indeed stress the urgency of writing the disaster without distorting it by falling back on mobilized, traditional narrative orders, it nevertheless does not and cannot claim to remain in the state of deprivation of disaster itself. On the narrator's return to the family home, he once again manages to attribute some power to language, to retrieve some interest in telling a story, "in trying with words to make the unspeakable exist" (263). In this sense Simon's work inhabits the space of paradox that haunts the question of literature and the aesthetic today, that of saying the unsayable, of writing the unpresentable.[14]

In the final pages of the novel the narrator returns to a kind of writing that strives to be consistent with such an aesthetic of detail and the movement of writing without mobilization. To help define this aesthetic I take up Roger Dragonetti's and Dällenbach's discussions of Simon's writing. In his discussion of the relation between the general and the particular, Dragonetti links the notion of the General (L.S.M.) to that of

General and Particular Mobilizations 143

generality, "that is, to all that is opposed to the particular: generality being the signifying power that opens the particular to multiple symbolizations." These symbolizations are then held together by a rhythm.[15] The task of generality is to open the individual fact or event to what Dragonetti calls the play of the symbolic (100). He refers to *Les Géorgiques*' writing as the attempt to mobilize letters, as a symbolic putting into form of the particular (102). For Dragonetti (and for Dällenbach) the particular and the elementary are to be overcome, their particularity must be absorbed into generality as the condition of signifying (in general). In his view the particular-destroying power of generality is itself a desire for death (121). He does not question why writing must be fully subordinated to the signifier of generality, however; he detects in Simon's description only a process of fragmentation within symbolization/generality and not, as I have been arguing, the necessity of a specific writing of the particular. When Dragonetti's asymmetrical (but rhythmic) opposition between the general and the particular is situated within other metaphysical oppositions such as order and disorder, presence and absence, presentable and unpresentable, and finality and its lack, his economy of the particular as excess can distinctly be seen to be essentially negative and privative.

Dällenbach refers to modern writing's return to description, which in Simon's case involves privileging the elementary and the primordial, both as theme and source. He identifies examples of an elementary, prehistoric order, "une histoire relevant elle-même d'une non-histoire essentielle" (73; "a history itself dependent on an essential nonhistory").[16] I would argue that a return to the elementary *as such* is not available in Simon. As my readings of narrativity have shown, the primordial and the elementary are already part of ideological narratives of mystification: of woman, nature, Other, hero, origin, and legacy. Dällenbach goes on to note that rather than the return *to* the elementary, in Simon we have the return *of* the elementary, in the sense that the object is essentially lost and to be retrieved. Simon's aim, he claims, is not to remain in the archaic and the primordial but instead to undertake "the search for an order, the invention of a set of relationships" (81, my translation). Dällenbach's conclusion, then, is that the primordial in Simon is not a return to the elementary but on the contrary a way out of it, a way out that is to be thought of as a *"formation, génération* ou *genèse,* la question étant dès lors celle même du *commencement"* (82; *"formation, generation* or *genesis,* the question being henceforth the one of *beginning"*). Simon, he insists, gives us a form in the process of being created (90).

Although I agree with Dällenbach that Simon's aim is the invention of relationships, I argue that even the primordial and the elementary are not invoked in Simon's writing as autonomous raw materials of beginnings, creations, and generations. They never stand alone, and they never occur in Simon's text without their bundles of discursive affiliations, their "ties," their social, cultural, and historical narrativities. In other words, the narrative of the primordial does not elude or escape inclusion in the narrative of mobilization; it is one of the narratives that is most susceptible to being reconnected with the latter's aims.

The myriad connections between figures and their narratives in Simon have yet to be pursued. The privileging of description and detail, exemplified in *La Bataille de Pharsale*'s debate with traditional aesthetics, cannot be read as a celebration of the "present of writing" understood in formalist terms. In the context of this discussion on narrativity, we might recall O.'s reaction to Faure's dismissive judgment on Dürer and German painting of the Renaissance. Interestingly enough, O.'s (elsewhere the first-person narrator's [173–74]) reading of Faure takes place on a train, a situation in which fragments of affects, memories, readings, and descriptions are all in movement:

> "They never take the shortest road to the essential and to the most logical goal. The detail always conceals the whole, their universe is not continuous but consists of juxtaposed fragments. We see them in their pictures giving as much importance to a halbard as to a human face, to an inert stone as to a moving body, constructing a landscape like a geographical map, the decoration lavishing as much care on a cuckoo clock as on the statue of Hope or Faith, treating this statue with the same methods as that clock, and when . . ." O. takes an automatic pencil out of his pocket and writes in the margin: Incurable French stupidity. He looks up and sees sliding by the window. (165)

As I have sought to show, the "dropping of the gaze"[17] marks on Simon's part a resolute break and a turning away from traditional aesthetics' complicity with the narrative of heroism and its economy of sacrifice. In the face of the mobilization of narrative syntax for the ends of annihilation, and the discrediting of its representations, Simon's aesthetic of the detail impairs these profound complicities between writing and violence, literature and arbitrary power. The evocation of the acacia branches at the window, where the narrator continues his apprenticeship through writing, repeats almost word for word the first lines of *Histoire*. On the last page of *L'Acacia* the replication of those lines links up with the vast figures of movement, immobility, and mobilization that have articulated its writing. Neither in the tree's movement nor in its immobility is there any sense of a movement imposed from without, a forced march or mobilization. The branches' description figures its own movement (*mouvement propre*) and its cessation of movement is a "taking back" (*reprenaient*) or retrieval of immobility from its devastating mobilizations:

> remuant par moments comme des aigrettes, comme animées soudain d'un mouvement propre, comme si l'arbre tout entier se réveillait, s'ébrouait, se secouait, après quoi tout s'apaisait et elles reprenaient leur immobilité. (380)
> [occasionally stirring like aigrettes, as though suddenly animated with a movement of their own, as if the whole tree were waking, shaking itself, freeing itself, after which everything subsided and they became motionless again. (289)]

I might note that Simon placed T. S. Eliot's famous verses drawn from *Four Quartets* as the epigraph to his novel:

Time present and time past
Are both perhaps present in time future,
And time future contained in time past.

The mere choice of Eliot may incline critics to find a confirmation of Simon's modernist tendencies. A close reading of the quotation, however, suggests something other than an evocation of temporal order based on the eternal return as repetition of the same. The repetitions marking this quotation at first create a temporality of a cyclical order, a continuity ensured by the presence of the present and confirmed by the progressive and regressive linearity of time. In Eliot faith in time as an agent of coherence seems hardly to be negated by what the poet nevertheless announces as a present that is only hypothetical ("perhaps"). A certain ambiguity persists, moreover, in the last verse, where the word *contained* connotes simultaneously that which is contained in the past as a potential future and that which is retained, enclosed, or encrypted in that same time. The first lines' cumulative, indeed dialectical, movement of time present and past *aufgehoben* in the future is reversed in the last line to propose a different temporal model, the cyclical repetition of the eternal return of the same. In the context of Simon's novels, which I have read in terms of narrative mobilizations and an aesthetics of resistance, the tension in Eliot between two models of time becomes not so much the priority of one transcendental temporal order over another but rather what constitutes the seeds of the past and present in the future and the future in the past. The novelist's response to the poet is that those seeds are already constituted within and by the minute details of the cultural legacies of hegemony and difference, of historical events and catastrophes.

In Simon's writing in general the narratives of details and their tangents do not categorically oppose terms such as origin and end, before and after, war and peace, self and other, man and woman, mobility and immobility, fictionality and referentiality. He shows how the seeds of war are sown in what appears to be peacetime and how an aesthetics of war ("women of pink steel") participates in and programs the disaster itself. Where discourses of authority would impose cuts and *mises à l'écart*, his writing designates stitches between minute cultural details in the rise of totalitarianism, fascism, and colonialism; it detects contradictions and missing links in the discourses of order and legitimation (the disorder of order). His is not, therefore, the type of modernist or formalist aesthetics sustained by a valorization of aesthetic distance and indifference. It is a thoroughgoing critique of forced divisions, segregations, and ghettoizations that are always already mobilized to violent ends. His writing is a practice of points of contact, shock encounters, linkings, and convergences, where the specificity of particular differences is not subordinated to dominant narrative orders. In its work of narrativity, the writing of detail elaborates these links in ways that both reveal and subvert narrative determinations and mobilizations. It attempts, with increasing intensity in Simon's novels, to track the details of sociality and emerging violence without recontaining them in a historical narrative frame, which is identified as itself belonging to that violence.

By revisiting the terms and procedures of master narratives, Simon's writing returns to description its ability to make connections through unprescribed links and tangents. The notion of correspondences that Simon has so frequently used in lectures and interviews can now be seen from another perspective. It refers not to the credibility of formal composition alone but to the very means whereby his writing provokes points of contact between different constructions of persons, things, cultural contexts, institutions, and histories. A different cultural narrativity emerges from a resolutely different practice of the detail that calls on reading to be attentive to its linkages and correspondences. Without proposing a new totalizing narrative scheme, Simon resituates the narratives of legacy and the legacies of narrative with respect to such an aesthetics of the detail. The only way, perhaps, to undo the devastating effects of the general mobilization of people, ideas, and environments to conflictual and paralyzing ends is to return to the story-stuff, to the very bits and pieces and figural details out of which those techno-ideologies are composed and reproduced. In doing just this Simon's writing makes an important contribution to postmodernity by enabling readers to grasp at the same time its minimal and maximal figurations, to unfold some of its most distinct particular and general connections.

Reading the legacies of narrative in their immense diversity enables readers to identify the procedures whereby the most discrete elements of culture attain narrativity and to question and resist their mobilization to ideological ends. At the present time the possibility of reading narrative refigurations and their inventions is one of the most critically enabling undertakings in the overall project of gaining an internally diverse understanding of postmodernity. Such readings not only detect and displace the construction of master narratives but participate fully in discovering and unfolding the discrete, emergent narrativities in palimpsest in contemporary writing. Critical readings in postmodernity are not merely generated as the secondary effects of cultural, technological, and knowledge production. They intervene, by their very practice, in new ways of making cultural sense in the formative narrativities without Narrative of postmodern and other times and places.

Notes

Introduction

1 Representing the former are Ricardou, *Pour une théorie du nouveau roman*; Jenny, "La Stratégie de la forme"; and Dällenbach, *The Mirror in the Text*. The latter include Deguy, "Claude Simon and Representation"; Carroll, *The Subject in Question*; and Britton, *Claude Simon: Writing the Visible*.
2 Jameson, *Postmodernism*. See also Connor, *Postmodernist Culture*, and McHale, *Postmodernist Fiction*.
3 Simon's postmodernism is "the evident emptiness of the subject beyond all phenomenology, its capacity to embrace another style as though it were another world" (Jameson, *Postmodernism*, 133). Hutcheon opposes the modernism of the new novel to the postmodernism of historiographic metafiction in *A Poetics of Postmodernism*.
4 Simon, "La fiction mot à mot," *Nouveau roman*.
5 Simon compares his writing to the links, articulations, and passages referred to in set theory, where the relation of set A to set B is based on qualities common to both and to the mathematical formula of considering "a 'figure' whose 'properties' can be discovered," that is, the power of attraction of images and concepts in establishing relationships between them. In "Roman, description et action" he refers to Tynianov's claim for description's constructive function (85–86). Of two types of *action* (narrative and descriptive), Simon finds that credibility goes to description, which like an octopus projects "tentacles in all directions, selects and calls materials together" (84, my translation). In *Le Discours de Stockholm* he writes that de-

scriptions are no longer limited to stories' beginnings or to presenting characters but mix with narrative action, functioning as a "Trojan horse" by expulsing the fable they were to embody (19–20).

6 DuVerlie, interview with Claude Simon, "The Crossing of the Image."
7 Simon, "A quoi bon inventer?" My translation.
8 Sturgess, *Narrativity*.
9 Sturgess wishes to correct what he sees as a deficiency in existing theories of narrativity by proposing a theory based on the idea of a self-consistent logic of narrativity founded on a higher-level causality. Five of the six principles of narrativity he invokes are intratextual, and the final and only extratextual one is problematic because it is defined as a totalizing "causal logic" of social life that influences the production of the text (289).
10 D. A. Miller, *Narrative and its Discontents*.
11 De Lauretis, *Alice Doesn't*, 105.
12 De Lauretis, "Strategies of Coherence," 108–9.
13 Duffy, "M(i)sreading Claude Simon: A Partial Analysis." On women's structuring and narrative function, see Woodhull, "Reading Claude Simon," and Higgins, "Gender and War Narrative."
14 See Suleiman's critique in *Subversive Intent* of critics who overlooked Robbe-Grillet's sexism.
15 Lyotard, *The Postmodern Condition*.
16 Norris, *The Contest of Faculties*, 22.
17 Althusser defines ideology as "a system (with its own logic and rigour) of representations (images, myths, ideas or concepts, depending on the case) endowed with a historical existence and role within a given society" (*For Marx*, 231).
18 Prince, *Narratology*.
19 Barthes, "Introduction," 79.
20 I discuss narratology's narratives in "A Loosening of Tongues." See Gasché on structure's historicity, "Of Aesthetic and Historical Determination," 139–40.
21 Chambers distinguishes three contextualizing functions in narrative: the text as *language* (a referential system), the text as *discourse* (a communicating practice) and the text as *object of reading* (an interpretive relation) ("'Narrative' and 'Textual' Functions," 28).
22 See Mink, "Narrative Form as a Cognitive Instrument."
23 See Godzich on narratology's complicity in asserting a universal order in his foreword to Coste, *Narrative as Communication*, ix–xvii.
24 Lukács, "Narrate or Describe?"

Notes to Pages xxvi–1   151

25 On description as seriality, montages, and reflexivity, see Sherzer, *Representation*.
26 Hamon, *Introduction à l'analyse du descriptif*, 97–98, 43 (my translation).
27 For Chambers, interpretation, mediating the opposition between description and narration, is crucial for curtailing the hegemony of narrative; see *Meaning and Meaningfulness*, 105. In *Room for Maneuver* he locates shifts in desire producing social change in the distance between narrative and textual functions.
28 Genette, "Boundaries of Fiction."
29 Gelley criticizes Genette and formalism for reducing description to narration, claiming that descriptive cognition is a way of "gaining more immediate access to elements of ideology, of epistemology, of the unconscious" (*Narrative Crossings*, 14).
30 De Man, "Semiology and Rhetoric," in *Allegories of Reading*, and "The Rhetoric of Temporality."
31 J. Hillis Miller, "Ariadne's Thread: Repetition and the Narrative Line," 160.
32 Austin, *How to Do Things with Words*. Performative agency in literary deconstruction is on the side of the text, which is said to claim, argue, affirm, and negate oppositional terms. On the performative, see Paul de Man, *Allegories of Reading*.
33 Rimmon-Kenan, *Narrative Fiction*, 130–31.
34 Derrida, "The Law of Genre," 206.
35 J. Hillis Miller, *The Ethics of Reading*, 5.
36 See Bill Reading's argument in "The Deconstruction of Politics."
37 On the essence of the technological as a transcendental "enframing" see Martin Heidegger, "The Question Concerning Technology."
38 The aesthetic as irreducible particularity opens, Terry Eagleton claims, onto nonalienated cognition, but he subordinates it to ideological totalizations; see *The Ideology of the Aesthetic*.
39 Ricoeur, "Entre temps et récit: concorde/discorde."
40 Ricoeur, *Time and Narrative*. Hayden White praises Ricoeur's synthesis of literary and historical theory and the notion of the narrativistic nature of time itself (*The Content of the Form*, 171).
41 De Lauretis, *Alice Doesn't*, 105.

1   *Like a Narrative*

1   See Lyotard, *The Postmodern Condition*, and White, *The Content of the Form*.

2   Lyotard, *Instructions païennes*, 16 (my translation).
3   Lyotard, 86–87 (my translation). See also *The Postmodern Condition*, chap. 6. On Lyotard's narrative permutations, see Gelley, *Narrative Crossings*, 79–100.
4   See Rorty, *Consequences of Pragmatism*, and Norris, *The Contest of Faculties*.
5   Lyotard, "Preface: Reading Dossier," in *The Différend*, xi–xvi.
6   Roubichou, *Lecture de "L'Herbe,"* 316–21.
7   Burden, *John Fowles—John Hawkes—Claude Simon;* Duffy, "Meaning and Subversion."
8   For Simon "every modern work reflects in its double-sided title the treacherous ambiguity of reality" ("Qu'est-ce que l'avant-garde en 1958?"; my translation).
9   Robbe-Grillet recalls it in *Three Decades of the French New Novel*, ed. Oppenheim, 25.
10 Lévi-Strauss, "The Structural Study of Myth," 94.
11 Vernant writes that fiction reconnects with myth when it personifies time (*Mythe et pensée chez les Grecs*, 98–102).
12 Bakhtin, *Esthétique et théorie du roman*, 157.
13 See Weinrich, "Structures narratives du mythe," and Lacoue-Labarthe, "La Fable (littérature et philosophie)."
14 Valéry, *Oeuvres complètes*, 1:965–66.
15 Lévi-Strauss, *The Savage Mind* and *Mythologiques;* Lacan, *Ecrits*.
16 Lyotard, *The Postmodern Condition*, 27.
17 Ziolkowsky criticizes the Nazi manipulation of myth as antirationality in "Hesse, Myth, and Reason," 135.
18 Barthes, *Mythologies*, 124–26.
19 Bakhtin, *The Dialogic Imagination*, 369.
20 Frye, *Anatomy of Criticism*.
21 Jameson, *The Political Unconscious*.
22 "Repetition has as its function to make the structure of the myth apparent" (Lévi-Strauss, "The Structural Study of Myth," 105).
23 White, *Mythology in the Modern Novel*.
24 Righter, *Myth and Literature;* E. Gould, *Mythical Intentions*.
25 Benveniste, *Problems in General Linguistics*, 208.
26 Sophocles, *Oedipus the King*, ed. Green and Lattimore, 11.
27 Marin, *Utopiques*, 217.
28 Delcourt, *Oedipe ou la légende du conquérant*.
29 Graves, *The Greek Myths*, 13.

30 We find these metaphors describing Oedipus: "the breakers of misfortune swallow him" (Sophocles, *Oedipus the King*, 11) or, translated differently, "behold what a full tide of misfortune swept over his head" (*The Theban Plays*, 68). Montès appears as a drowning man losing his footing in the ocean's backwash and on whom the "liquid mountain" descends.
31 Preface to Simon, *Orion aveugle* (my translation), in which figures prominently Poussin's "Orion aveugle marchant vers le soleil levant." Blind Orion is evoked as well in *La Bataille de Pharsale* and *Les Corps conducteurs*.
32 Jameson, *The Political Unconscious*, 22, 58.
33 Lévi-Strauss, *The Savage Mind*, 18.
34 Simon, "La Fiction mot à mot," 96.
35 Lévi-Strauss, *The Savage Mind*, 19.
36 "La Fiction mol à mot," 74, 81 (my translation).
37 Barthes, *Writing Degree Zero*, 22.
38 Barthes, *Mythologies*, 117.
39 Of the range of mythical elements, the simplest is a limited comparison. In *L'Herbe* Sabine's drunk scene is compared with Dejaneira's wielding of the love potion/poison, while her husband Pierre is likened to a Hercules gone to seed. Aunt Marie's death throes are compared to Vulcan's forge or a hoarse cyclops, and her nurse is described as a mythical character whose body is covered with eyes (that is, Argus Panoptes). Yet the mythical function in Simon exceeds such decorative references.
40 "The emblem of Aphrodite is the shell which on the order of legend recalls birth in the sea and, on the order of symbol, the female organ, the word *kteis* having both meanings" (Delcourt, *Hermaphroditea*, 27).
41 For Sims Corinne is associated with Ariadne, who provided the thread for Theseus to find his way out of the labyrinth ("Myth and History," 74–86).
42 Ricardou, "Un ordre dans la débacle," *Problèmes du nouveau roman*, 45–55.
43 See K. Gould, *Claude Simon's Mythic Muse*. Stressing archetypal features such as the eternal present, repetition, and universality, she argues that Simon's characters "submit to an irrational power over which they have no control" (40). I find, instead, that his narrators vent their fury against the complicity of narrative and mythic forms with the violence, indifference, and dogmatism of representation. On metaphor and archetype, see Makward, "Claude Simon: Earth, Death, and Eros."
44 Lyotard, *Des Dispositifs pulsionnels*, 179–224.
45 Lyotard, *The Postmodern Condition*, 40.

2 Refiguring Narrative and Cultural Legacies

1. Waugh calls the mimetism of "aleatory writing" a response to the multiplicity of styles in everyday culture (*Metafiction*, 12). For Ricoeur antinovelists satisfy the tradition they refuse by imitating "disorderly experiences" (*Time and Narrative*, 1:73).
2. Lyotard calls the narrative apparatus a semiotic or a *théâtrique* in *Des dispositifs pulsionnels* (179–224).
3. Dällenbach, "Le Tissu de mémoire," 303 (my translation).
4. Higgins argues that whereas the war's dehumanization is deplored on a thematic level in *La Route des Flandres*, it is reproduced in the soldiers' discourse on Corinne and when she is in bed with Georges, listening to him relive the war. She is victimized in Simon by the war-narrative genre, which requires her absence to construct a purely masculine fantasy; see Higgins, "Gender and War Narrative."
5. Simon, preface to *Orion aveugle* and "Roman et mémoire."
6. See de Man, *Allegories of Reading*, and Ricoeur, *Oneself as Another*.
7. Simon is quoted as saying "J'ai trouvé dans le *Littré*, parmi d'autres, cette acceptation du mot 'Histoire': Dans le langage familier, se dit d'un objet quelconque qu'on ne peut ou ne veut pas nommer" ("I found in the *Littré*, among others, this meaning of the word '*Histoire*': in familiar usage, it is used to speak of any object that one cannot or will not name"; Chapsal, "Claude Simon: Il n'y a pas d'art réaliste," 5).
8. Rousset writes of the sliding of the descriptive toward the narrative in "*Histoire* de Claude Simon," 131. See Jost on the metaphorization of description, "Claude Simon: Topographies de la description et du texte."
9. See Carroll on portraiture in *The Subject in Question*.
10. Sarkonak, *Claude Simon: Les Carrefours du texte*, 156.
11. Britton, *Claude Simon: Writing the Visible*, 119–24.
12. *Histoire* may be considered an extended attempt to create prosopopeia, which J. Hillis Miller defines as a trope that "ascribes a face, a name, or a voice to the absent, the inanimate, or the dead" (*Versions of Pygmalion*, 3–4).
13. Critics have, of course, compared it to "Combray" in Marcel Proust's *A la recherche du temps perdu*.
14. Vidal describes a fundamental *deixis* in description that takes place "dans l'espace même de renvoi, de l'adresse, de la destination sans véritable cible ou cesse. En prenant des écrits ancestraux comme matière première, Claude Simon joue l'individuel avec le collectif, le particulier avec le général, l'Histoire à l'aune des histoires de famille, le texte au crible effaçant de l'intertex-

tualité" ("in the very space of referral, of address, of destination without a true target or end. By taking ancestral writings as primary material, Claude Simon brings the individual into play with the collectivity, the particular with the general, History by the measure of family stories [histories, affairs], the text by the effacing sieve of intertextuality"; "Les travaux et les jours du déictique").

15   Britton, *Claude Simon: Writing the Visible*, and Dällenbach, "*Les Géorgiques* ou la totalisation accomplie."
16   Charles Baudelaire, "Harmonie du soir," in *Les Fleurs du mal*, 79: "Voici venir les temps où vibrant sur sa tige" ("Now comes the time when swaying on its stem"). In *Baudelaire: Poems*. Transl. Richard Howard. New York: A. Knopf, 1993.
17   Gasché, preface to Warminski, *Readings in Interpretation*.
18   Simon, *La Corde raide*, 174 (my translation).

3   Parody in Postmodernity

1   Rose recalls the epistemological function of parody in Kant's *Anthropology*, where it functions as a form of wit, freeing the mind from preconceptions (*Parody/Metafiction*, 135). See her discussion of Foucault's, "Nietzsche, Genealogy, History" (which appears in *Language, Counter-memory, Practice*). In Foucault, Nietzsche's effective history takes parody as a means to oppose the metaphysical history of origins.
2   Suleiman, "As Is," in *A New History of French Literature*, ed. Hollier, 1016.
3   See Fletcher, *Claude Simon and Fiction Now*, 50, and Hassan, *The Postmodern Turn*, 44.
4   On irony and parody, see Lang, *Irony/Humor*.
5   Barthes, *S/Z*, 140.
6   Barthes, 45 (translation modified).
7   Jameson, *Postmodernism*.
8   See Connor's cogent presentation of Jameson, Lyotard, and Baudrillard in his *Postmodernist Culture*. He argues that all three contract the distance between the social and the cultural, between reality and theory: "In Lyotard's aestheticization of knowledge via the agonistics of language games, in Jameson's anxious awareness of the loss of critical distance between culture and theory, and, at its most extreme, in Baudrillard's adaptive transformation of theory itself into the condition of simulation it theorizes, what began as the attempt to specify the relationship between the fixed and distinct poles of

postmodernity in social and economic life and postmodernism in cultural life ends by dissolving the boundaries between the two realms" (61).

9   See Abastado, "Situation de la parodie," and Golopentia-Eretescu, "Grammaire de la parodie." For Abastado, whereas pastiche is concerned with expression, the author's style or the imitated genre, "parody takes on the ideology of the model and its imaginary universe" (19). Golopentia-Eretescu distinguishes between parody as a "bi-textual synthesis" and the monotextual forms of pastiche based on similarity and metaphor (171).

10 Lyotard, "Apathie dans la théorie," in *Rudiments païens*, 9–31.

11 Lyotard and Thébaud, *Just Gaming*, 12.

12 Derrida, *Spurs: Nietzsche's Styles*, 98 (translation modified).

13 Quoted in Erlich, *Russian Formalism*, 251. In Erlich's view the analyses of the formalists succeed especially when they address themselves to "techniques of quotation" such as parody and stylization.

14 Tynianov, "Destruction, parodie," 67.

15 Abastado, "Situation de la parodie," 15. On the parody of forms, see also Genette, *Palimpsestes*.

16 Abastado, "Situation de la parodie," 14.

17 Hutcheon, *A Theory of Parody*, 11. Parody, according to Hutcheon, is "an exploration of difference and similarity; in metafiction it invites a more literary reading, a recognition of literary codes" (*Narcissistic Narrative*, 25).

18 Hutcheon, *A Poetics of Postmodernism*, 35.

19 Hutcheon, *A Theory of Parody*, 37.

20 Discussing Victor Shklovsky and Mikhail Bakhtin, Martin writes, "parody, irony, and other forms of humor result not from a comparison of words and the world but from the disparity between conflicting sets of words" (*Recent Theories of Narrative*, 50). Such disparity and conflict between sets of words must arise, I argue, from what the "world" determines to be a "set" and from relations of disparity and conflict.

21 Kristeva, *Desire in Language*, 71. See Hutcheon's discussions of Barthes, Kristeva, and Bakhtin in *A Theory of Parody*.

22 Bakhtin, *Problems of Dostoyevsky's Poetics*, 226–27.

23 Bakhtin, *Esthétique et théorie du roman*, 411.

24 "Le mot n'est pas un matériau inerte, objectivé, dans la main de l'artiste qui le manipule" (ibid., 230).

25 Referring to the ironic and parodistic structures of American postmodern writing, Thiher rejects parody in Simon's writing because it "does not so much note a rupture with the past as it strives to retrieve the past out of the presence of multiple forms of representation that compose our daily cul-

ture" (*Words in Reflection*, 215). I disagree with Thiher's conclusion, which rests on his belief that intertextuality is a "logical development of the axiom of language's autonomy" (193) and hence excludes the historical dimensions of narrative.

26 For Schor the detail in modernity is "desacralized, devalorized, and definalized" (*Reading in Detail*, 147).

27 A chapter of Jameson's *Postmodernism*, "Reading and the Division of Labor" (131–53), is devoted to Simon the new novelist, especially *Les Corps conducteurs*.

28 Bakhtin, *Esthétique et théorie du roman*.

29 Lyotard, "Philosophy and Painting in the Age of Their Experimentation," 119.

30 Holter notes the "outraged" voice in the earlier novels, finding it absent from novels such as *Triptyque* ("La Constance difficile," in *Claude Simon: Analyse*, ed. Ricardou, 347).

31 Chapsal, "Entretien: Claude Simon parle," 33.

32 On many occasions, including his Nobel speech, *Le Discours de Stockholm*, Simon has opposed as a form of dogmatism and terrorism Sartre's notion of *engagée* literature.

33 Referring to a study in which *Zitieren* ("to quote") also describes the evocation of ghosts, Rose writes, "the 'exorcizing' function of parody can be described as a form of '*Zitieren*' in which the ghosts of the past are quoted in order to be overcome" (*Parody/Metafiction*, 63).

34 Mortier refers to formal parody in "Discontinu et rupture dans *La Bataille de Pharsale*," c3–c4.

35 Ricardou generates the novel from the epigraph taken from Valéry's "Le Cimetière marin" in "La Bataille de la phrase," and "L'Essence et les sens," in *Pour une théorie du nouveau roman*, 118–58 and 200–210, respectively.

36 "Je fixais avec attention devant mon esprit quelque image qui m'avait forcé à la regarder, un nuage, un triangle, un clocher, une fleur, un caillou, en sentant qu'il y avait sous ces signes quelque chose de tout autre que je devais tâcher de découvrir, une pensée qu'ils traduisaient à la façon de ces caractères hiéroglyphiques qu'on croyait représenter seulement des objets matériels—Marcel Proust" ("I considered closely some image which had compelled my attention, a cloud, a triangle, a steeple, a flower, a pebble, feeling that perhaps beneath these signs was something else I must try to discover, a system of thought they translated in the manner of those hieroglyphs which supposedly represent only material objects—Marcel Proust").

37 O. is occupied successively by the narrator I (the adult as well as the child), the woman who is the narrator's lover, the red-haired painter who is the object of the narrator's jealousy, and the visitor on the studio photograph (who is both "I" and "he," a figure of his uncle).

38 For Jenny *La Bataille*'s intertextual fragments (from the Grand Library's canon) remain within a traditional narrative frame; see "La Stratégie de la forme."

39 "Un outil apparaît endommagé, des matériaux aparaissent inadéquats. . . . C'est dans ce découvrement de l'inutilisable que soudain l'outil s'impose à l'attention. . . . Le système de renvois où s'insèrent les outils ne s'éclaire pas comme un quelque chose qui n'aurait jamais été vu, mais comme un tout qui, d'avance et toujours, s'offrait au regard. Or, avec ce tout, c'est le monde qui s'annonce—Martin Heidegger." ("A tool appears to be damaged, materials appear inadequate. . . . With its unusability thus uncovered, suddenly the tool claims attention. . . . The system of relationships of which tools are a part is illuminated not as something never before seen but as a totality always given beforehand to be seen. With this totality the world announces itself—Martin Heidegger" [my translation]).

40 Benjamin, "The Task of the Translator."

41 See Van Rossum-Guyon, "De Claude Simon à Proust. Un exemple d'intertextualité."

42 Benjamin, quoted in Rose, 156.

43 Ibid., 156–57.

44 Baudrillard, *Simulacres et simulation* and *Selected Writings*.

45 See also Burgin's discussion of Guy Debord's society of the spectacle and Baudrillard's notion of the society of the simulacrum: "There is an incessant sliding of the spectacle over the real in which the referent—re-run, rewound, scrutinised in freeze-frame, run fast-forward—is eaten *live* by the signifier" (*The End of Art Theory*, 170).

46 Baudrillard, *Simulacres et simulation*, 66 (my translation).

47 The re-presentation of the pornographic image in Simon does not therefore reproduce it, as Duffy has argued in "M(i)sreading Claude Simon"; rather, it narrativizes the production of the image and contextualizes its reception.

48 Jameson, *Postmodernism*, 11.

49 Andrews, "Formalist Dogmatisms"; Baehler, "Aspects du personnage simonien."

50 Andrews, "Formalist Dogmatisms," 46.

51 Baehler, "Aspects du personnage simonien," 34.

52 These are among the themes of *Leçon de choses*, which is not treated here. There are also parodies of set "object lessons" in (1) the Flaubertian resonances of the woman's encounter with and betrayal by her lover, with a cow looking on; (2) the soldier's monologue as a parodic response to the deadly disparity between orders from headquarters and the real conditions of soldiers under attack; and (3) a couple of send-ups of *mise en abîme:* the mason's reflecting hard-boiled egg, which he proceeds to eat (136) and a "vache qui rit" (laughing cow) cheese wrapper (159).

53 Pugh, in "From Drawing, to Painting, to Text," suggests that this description in the prologue be read as Simon's parody of "aspects of his own writing . . . subsequent to *Histoire"* (58).

54 Britton, "Diversity of Discourse," 437.

55 Marx, *The Eighteenth Brumaire of Louis Bonaparte,* 9. An intertextual parody of Marx's famous dictum appears as well in *La Route des Flandres:* "Nous y voilà: l'Histoire . . . scintillante et exaltante vision traditionnellement réservée aux coeurs simples et aux esprits forts, bonne conscience du dénonciateur et du philosophe, l'inusable fable—ou farce" (176); "There we are: History . . . a shimmering, exalted vision traditionally reserved to simple hearts and strong minds, the good conscience of the informer and the philosopher, the incorruptible fable—or farce" [139]). Similarly, it is taken up in *Histoire* (352).

56 Derrida, "La Loi du genre."

57 Bakhtin, *Problems of Dostoyevsky's Poetics,* 127.

4 *General and Particular Mobilizations*

1 I use war machine differently from Deleuze, for whom it is a positive term of revolutionary movement, structurally analogous to the notions of rhizome and excess; see his *Mille Plateaux.*

2 Simon, "Et à quoi bon inventer?"

3 Dällenbach speaks of the son's doubling of the father figure; see "Imaginaire parental," in *Claude Simon,* 53–67.

4 Femininity, an aesthetic alibi, collapses when the woman refuses to occupy the place assigned to her in its narrative economy. See my "Claude Simon: The Critical Properties of Painting," 104–9.

5 On docile bodies and the technology of surveillance, see Foucault, *Discipline and Punish.*

6 Answering a representative of the Union of Soviet Writers who asked what he thought the task of writing was, Simon replied: "It consists of trying to

start a sentence, to continue it, and to finish it" (quoted in Lyotard, *Peregrinations*, 4).

7 On the relationship between proper name and title, see Derrida, "Préjugés devant la loi."

8 This reading of mobilization in Simon may be related to what de Certeau identifies as the train's character as a rationalized cell that figures a speculative relation to the world. He also suggests that such a Robinsonnade of the subject, with the beautiful soul intact only because it is separate from the world and surrounded by glass and iron, has now come to an end; see *The Practice of Everyday Life*, chap. 7, 111–114. This end needs to be related to trains' functions as instruments of deportation and holocaust (in, for example, Claude Lanzmann's film *Shoah*) and to shifts in the technologies of mobilization.

9 Virilio, *War and Cinema*.

10 Simon, preface to *Orion aveugle*.

11 The reference in Simon is to the futuristic tendencies in art that coincided with the rise of fascism. Paul Virilio, in *War and Cinema*, comments on the appropriation of the military cinematic image by postwar avant-garde film makers: "It was a final privilege of their art that the First World War showed them military technology in action, and interestingly enough this technological surprise triggered a potent fusion/confusion in 'avant-garde' productions of the immediate post-war period" (20).

12 See Lyotard's discussion in *The Différend* of Auschwitz as the demise of the "we" (the substitutability of I and you) when those who ordain death, the senders, deny any common universe of phrases with those whom they condemn.

13 Joan Miró has been quoted as saying that what he is interested in most of all is "the calligraphy of a tree or a rooftop, leaf by leaf, twig by twig, blade of grass by blade of grass, tile by tile" (*Selected Writings and Interviews*, 54). Simon's work on and with Miró is the text *Femmes*. Simon has also referred to Jean Dubuffet's work, particularly the series called "Roads and Paths." Dubuffet's images were the pictorial equivalent of what he had sought to do with words in scenes where Georges, in *La Route des Flandres*, on all fours after his squadron's ambush, sees beneath him the details of stones and minute plants; see Ricardou, *Claude Simon: Analyse, Théorie*, 410–11. Most of Dubuffet's canvas surfaces in this series are taken up by the pebbles and tiny plants growing in cracks on paved roads. Some titles in series 13 are: *Célébration du sol, Topographies, Texturologies, Récit du sol* (1959), and *Figures*

augures (Celebration of the ground, Texturologies, Narrative of the ground [1959], Figures as augures). See Crouwel, *Dubuffet*.
14 Novelists and theorists whose writing takes place within this postmodern paradox are, for instance, Theodor Adorno, Samuel Beckett, Marguerite Duras, Jean-François Lyotard, Maurice Blanchot, Jacques Derrida, Luce Irigaray, and Jacques Lacan.
15 Dragonetti, "Les Notes du général dans *Les Géorgiques*."
16 Dällenbach, "La Question primordiale."
17 DuVerlie, "The Crossing of the Image," 48, 54.

Bibliography

Books by Claude Simon

Le Tricheur (The cheat). Paris: Sagittaire, 1945.
La Corde raide (The tightrope). Paris: Minuit, 1947.
Gulliver. Paris: Calmann-Lévy, 1952.
Le Sacre du Printemps (The rite of spring). Paris: Calmann-Lévy, 1954.
Le Vent. Tentative de restitution d'un retable baroque. Paris: Minuit, 1957. *The Wind*. Trans. Richard Howard. New York: George Braziller, 1959.
L'Herbe. Paris: Minuit, 1958. *The Grass*. Trans. Richard Howard. New York: George Braziller, 1960.
La Route des Flandres. Paris: Minuit, 1960. *The Flanders Road*. Trans. Richard Howard. London: John Calder, 1985.
Le Palace. Paris: Minuit, 1962. *The Palace*. Trans. Richard Howard. London: John Calder, 1963.
Femmes (sur vingt-trois peintures de Joan Miró) (Women [on twenty-three paintings by Joan Miró]). Paris: Editions Maeght, 1966. Reprint. *La Chevelure de Bérénice* (Bérénice's hair). Paris: Minuit, 1983.
Histoire. Paris: Minuit, 1967. *Histoire*. Trans. Richard Howard. New York: George Braziller, 1968.
La Bataille de Pharsale. Paris: Minuit, 1969. *The Battle of Pharsalus*. Trans. Richard Howard. New York: George Braziller, 1971.
Orion aveugle (Orion blinded) "Les Sentiers de la création," no. 8. Geneva: Skira, 1970.
Les Corps conducteurs. Paris: Minuit, 1971. *Conducting Bodies*. Trans. Helen R. Lane. New York: Grove Press, 1987.

Triptyque. Paris: Minuit, 1973. *Triptych.* Trans. Helen R. Lane. New York, Riverrun, 1986.
Leçon de choses. Paris: Minuit, 1975. *The World about Us.* Trans. Daniel Weissbort. Princeton: Ontario Review, 1983.
Les Géorgiques. Paris: Minuit, 1981. *The Georgics.* Trans. Beryl Fletcher and John Fletcher. London: John Calder, 1989.
Le Discours de Stockholm (Stockholm speech). Paris: Minuit, 1986.
L'Invitation (The invitation). Paris: Minuit, 1987.
Album d'un amateur (An amateur's album). Paris: Editions Rommerskirchen, 1988.
L'Acacia. Paris: Minuit, 1989. *The Acacia.* Trans. Richard Howard. New York: Pantheon, 1991.
Photographies 1937–1970 (Photographs 1937–1970). Paris: Editions Maeght, 1992.

General Bibliography

Abastado, Claude. "Situation de la parodie." *Cahiers du 20ᵉ siècle* 6 (1976): 9–37.
Althusser, Louis. *For Marx.* Trans. Ben Brewster. New York: Vintage, 1970.
Andrews, Mark. "Formalist Dogmatisms, Derridean Questioning, and the Return of Affect: Towards a Distributed Reading of *Triptyque.*" *L'Esprit Créateur* 27 (winter 1987): 37–47.
Attridge, Derek, Robert Young, and Geoff Bennington, eds. *Post-Structuralism and the Question of History.* Cambridge: Cambridge University Press, 1987.
Auerbach, Erich. *Mimesis: The Representation of Reality in Western Literature.* Princeton: Princeton University Press, 1971.
Austin, J. L. *How to Do Things with Words.* London: Oxford University Press, 1962.
Baehler, Aline. "Aspects du personnage simonien: Corinne." *L'Esprit Créateur* 27 (winter 1987): 27–36.
Bakhtin, Mikhail. *The Dialogic Imagination.* Ed. Michael Holquist. Austin: University of Texas Press, 1981.
———. *Esthétique et théorie du roman.* Trans. Daria Olivier. Paris: Gallimard, 1978.
———. *Problems of Dostoyevsky's Poetics.* Ed. and trans. Caryl Emerson. Minneapolis: University of Minnesota Press, 1984.

Barthes, Roland. "Introduction to the Structural Analysis of Narratives." In *Image-Music-Text*. Trans. Stephen Heath. New York: Hill and Wang, 1979.
———. *Mythologies*. Trans. Annette Lavers. New York: Hill and Wang, 1972.
———. *S/Z*. Trans. Richard Miller. New York: Hill and Wang, 1974.
———. *Writing Degree Zero*. Trans. Annette Lavers and Colin Smith. London: Jonathan Cape, 1967.
Baudrillard, Jean. *Selected Writings*. Ed. Mark Poster. Stanford: Stanford University Press, 1988.
———. *Simulacres et simulation*. Paris: Galilée, 1981.
Benjamin, Walter. "The Task of the Translator." In *Illuminations*, ed. Hannah Arendt and trans. H. Zohn, 69–82. New York: Harcourt, Brace, & World, 1968.
Benveniste, Emile. *Problems in General Linguistics*. Trans. Mary E. Meek. Coral Gables: University of Miami Press, 1971.
Bernal, Olga. *Alain Robbe-Grillet: Le roman de l'absence*. Paris: Gallimard, 1964.
Bertrand, Michel. *Langue Romanesque et parole scripturale: Essai sur Claude Simon*. Paris: Presses Universitaires de France, 1987.
Birn, Randi. "From Sign to Saga: Dynamic Description in Two Texts by Claude Simon." *Australian Journal of French Studies* 21 (May/August 1984): 148–60.
Blanchot, Maurice. *L'Espace littéraire*. Paris: Gallimard, 1955.
———. *The Writing of the Disaster*. Trans. Ann Smock. Lincoln: University of Nebraska Press, 1986.
Bonnet, Jean-Claude, and Philippe Roger, eds. *La Légende de la Révolution au XXe siècle: De Gance à Renoir, de Romain Rolland à Claude Simon*. Paris: Flammarion, 1988.
Bourdieu, Pierre. *Outline of a Theory of Practice*. Trans. Richard Nice. Cambridge: Cambridge University Press, 1977.
Brewer, Daniel. *The Discourse of Enlightenment in 18th-Century France: Diderot and the Art of Philosophizing*. Cambridge: Cambridge University Press, 1993.
Brewer, Mária Minich. "Claude Simon: The Critical Properties of Painting." *Review of Contemporary Fiction* 5 (March 1985): 104–9.
———. "An Energetics of Reading: Intertextual in Claude Simon." In *Claude Simon*, ed. Celia Britton, 121–39. New York: Longman, 1993.
———. "A Loosening of Tongues: From Narrative Economy to Women Writing." *Modern Language Notes* 99 (December 1984): 1141–61.

———. "Parodies, répliques, écritures." *La Revue des Sciences Humaines* 220 (1990): 157–71.

———. "Samuel Beckett: Postmodern Narrative and the nuclear *telos*." *Boundary 2* (fall 1986/winter 1987): 153–70.

Britton, Celia. *Claude Simon: Writing the Visible*. Cambridge: Cambridge University Press, 1987.

———. "Diversity of Discourse in Claude Simon's *Les Géorgiques*." *French Studies* 38 (October 1984): 423–42.

———. *The Nouveau Roman: Fiction, Theory, Politics*. New York: St. Martin's, 1992.

Brodsky, Claudia. *The Imposition of Form: Studies in Narrative, Representation, and Knowledge*. Princeton: Princeton University Press, 1987.

Brooks, Peter. *Reading for the Plot: Design and Intention in Narrative*. New York: Knopf, 1984.

Burden, Robert. *John Fowles—John Hawkes—Claude Simon: Problems of Self and Form in the Post-Modernist Novel*. Würzburg: Königshausen und Neumann, 1980.

Burgin, Victor. *The End of Art Theory: Criticism and Postmodernity*. London: Macmillan, 1986.

Carr, David. *Time, Narrative, and History*. Bloomington: Indiana University Press, 1986.

Carroll, David. "Narrative Poetics and the Crisis in Culture: Claude Simon's Return to History." *L'Esprit Créateur* 27 (1987): 48–60.

———. *The Subject in Question: The Languages of Theory and the Strategies of Fiction*. Chicago: University of Chicago Press, 1982.

Chambers, Ross. *Meaning and Meaningfulness: Studies in the Analysis and Interpretation of Texts*. Lexington: French Forum Publications, 1979.

———. "'Narrative' and 'Textual' Functions (with an Example from La Fontaine)." In *Reading Narrative: Form, Ethics, Ideology*, ed. James Phelan, 27–39. Columbus: Ohio State University Press, 1989.

———. *Room for Maneuver: Reading (the) Oppositional (in) Narrative*. Chicago: University of Chicago Press, 1991.

———. *Story and Situation: Narrative, Seduction, and the Power of Fiction*. Minneapolis: University of Minnesota Press, 1984.

Chapsal, Madeleine. "Claude Simon: Il n'y a pas d'art réaliste." Interview of Claude Simon. *La Quinzaine Littéraire*, 15–31 Dec. 1975, 4–5.

———. "Entretien: Claude Simon parle." Interview of Claude Simon. *L'Express*, 5 April 1962, 32–33.

Châtelet, François. "Une vision de l'histoire." *Critique* 414 (November 1981): 1218–25.

Chatman, Seymour. *Story and Discourse: Narrative Structure in Fiction and Film*. Minneapolis: University of Minnesota Press, 1984.

Cixous, Hélène, and Catherine Clément. *Newly Born Woman*. Trans. Betsy Wing. Minneapolis: University of Minnesota Press, 1986.

Connor, Steven. *Postmodernist Culture: An Introduction to Theories of the Contemporary*. Oxford: Basil Blackwell, 1989.

Coste, Didier. *Narrative as Communication*. Minneapolis: University of Minnesota, 1989.

Crouwel, Wim. *Dubuffet*. Amsterdam: Stadsdrokkerij van Amsterdam, 1966.

Dällenbach, Lucien. *Claude Simon*. Paris: Seuil, 1988.

———. "*Les Géorgiques* ou la totalisation accomplie." *Critique* 414 (November 1981): 1226–42.

———. *The Mirror in the Text*. Trans. Jeremy Whitely with Emma Hughes. Chicago: University of Chicago Press, 1989.

———. "La Question primordiale." In Jean Starobinski et al., *Sur Claude Simon*, 63–93. Paris: Minuit, 1987.

———. "Le Tissu de mémoire." Postface to Claude Simon, *La Route des Flandres*, 297–316. Paris: Minuit, 1960.

Danto, Arthur C. *Narration and Knowledge*. New York: Columbia University Press, 1985.

Daprini, Pierre. "Claude Simon, History, and *l'innommable réalité*." In *Literature and War*, ed. David Bevan, 167–78. Amsterdam: Rodopi, 1990.

Davis, Robert Con, ed. *Lacan and Narrative*. Baltimore: Johns Hopkins University Press, 1983.

Debord, Guy. *Society of the Spectacle*. Detroit: Black and Red, 1983.

Debray, Régis. *Eloges*. Paris: Gallimard, 1986.

de Certeau, Michel. *The Practice of Everyday Life*. Trans. Steven F. Rendall. Berkeley: University of California Press, 1984.

———. *The Writing of History*. Trans. Tom Conley. New York: Columbia University Press, 1988.

Deguy, Michel. "Claude Simon and Representation." Trans. Annwyl Williams. In *Claude Simon*, ed. Celia Britton, 59–81. New York: Longman, 1993.

de Lauretis, Teresa. *Alice Doesn't: Feminism, Semiotics, Cinema*. Bloomington: Indiana University Press, 1984.

———. "Strategies of Coherence: Narrative Cinema, Feminist Poetics, and Yvonne Rainer." In *Technologies of Gender: Essays on Theory, Film, and Fiction*, ed. de Lauretis, Bloomington: Indiana University Press, 1987.

Delcourt, Marie. *Hermaphroditea*. Brussels: Latomus, 1966.

———. *Oedipe ou la légende du conquérant*. Paris: Droz, 1944.

Deleuze, Gilles. *Logique du sens*. Paris: Minuit, 1969.

———. *Mille plateaux*. Paris: Minuit, 1980.

de Man, Paul. *Allegories of Reading: Figural Language in Rousseau, Nietzsche, Rilke, and Proust*. New Haven: Yale University Press, 1979.

———. *Blindness and Insight*. 2d. ed. Minneapolis: University of Minnesota Press, 1983.

———. "The Rhetoric of Temporality." In *Interpretation: Theory and Practice*, ed. Charles S. Singleton, 179–209. Baltimore: Johns Hopkins University Press, 1969.

de Romilly, Jacqueline. *Time in Greek Tragedy*. Ithaca: Cornell University Press, 1968.

Derrida, Jacques. "La Loi du genre." *Glyph* 7 (1980): 176–201. "The Law of Genre," trans. Avital Ronell, 202–32.

———. *Of Grammatology*. Trans. Gayatri C. Spivak. Baltimore: Johns Hopkins University Press, 1976.

———. "Préjugés *devant la loi*." In Jacques Derrida et al., *La Faculté de juger*, 87–139. Paris: Minuit, 1985.

———. *Spurs: Nietzsche's Styles/Eperons: Les styles de Nietzsche*. Bilingual edition. Trans. Barbara Harlow. Chicago: University of Chicago Press, 1978.

Descombes, Vincent. *Modern French Philosophy*. Trans. L. Scott-Fox and J. M. Harding. New York: Cambridge University Press, 1980.

Donato, Eugenio. *The Script of Decadence: Essays on the Fictions of Flaubert and the Poetics of Romanticism*. New York: Oxford University Press, 1993.

Doubrovsky, Serge. "Notes on the Genesis of an *Ecriture*." Trans. Annwyl Williams. In *Claude Simon*, ed. Celia Britton, 159–75. New York: Longman, 1993.

Dragonetti, Roger. "Les Notes du général dans *Les Géorgiques*." In Jean Starobinski et al., *Sur Claude Simon*, 95–121. Paris: Minuit, 1987.

Duffy, Jean. "Meaning and Subversion in Claude Simon's *Le Vent*: Some Structural Considerations." *French Studies Bulletin* 15 (summer 1985): 8–10.

———. "M(i)sreading Claude Simon: A Partial Analysis." *Forum for Modern Language Studies* 23 (1987): 228–40.

———. "The Subversion of Historical Representation in Claude Simon." *French Studies* 41 (October 1987): 421–37.

Dugast-Portes, Francine. "Le Spectre de l'ascendance: Fonction tragifiante du personnage de l'ancêtre au fil de l'oeuvre de Claude Simon." *La Revue des Sciences Humaines* 91 (July/September 1989): 201–20.

Duncan, Alastair. "Claude Simon's *Les Géorgiques*: An Intertextual Adventure." *Romance Studies* 2 (summer 1983): 90–107.

DuVerlie, Claud. "The Crossing of the Image." Interview with Claude Simon. *Diacritics* (December 1977): 47–58.

———. "Pictures for Writing: Premises for a Graphopictology." In *Orion Blinded: Essays on Claude Simon*, ed. R. Birn and K. Gould, 200–217. Lewisburg PA: Bucknell University Press, 1981.

Eagleton, Terry. *The Ideology of the Aesthetic*. Oxford: Basil Blackwell, 1990.

———. *Literary Theory: An Introduction*. Minneapolis: University of Minnesota Press, 1983.

Erlich, Victor. *Russian Formalism: History-Doctrine*. The Hague: Mouton, 1980.

Evans, Martha Noel. *Masks of Tradition: Women and the Politics of Writing in Twentieth-Century France*. Ithaca: Cornell University Press, 1987.

Evans, Michael. *Claude Simon and the Transgressions of Modern Art*. London: Macmillan, 1988.

Fitch, Brian T. "Participe présent et procédés narratifs chez Claude Simon." In *Un nouveau roman?* ed. J. H. Matthews, 199–216. Paris: M.J. Minard, 1964.

Fletcher, John. *Claude Simon and Fiction Now*. London: Calder and Boyars, 1975.

Foster, Hal, ed. *The Anti-Aesthetic*. Port Townsend WA: Bay Press, 1985.

Foucault, Michel. *Discipline and Punish: The Birth of the Prison*. Trans. Alan Sheridan. New York: Pantheon, 1977.

———. *Language, Counter-memory, Practice*. Ed. Donald F. Bouchard. Ithaca: Cornell University Press, 1977.

———. *The Order of Things*. New York: Vintage, 1970.

Freud, Sigmund. *Beyond the Pleasure Principle*. Trans. J. Strachey. New York: Norton, 1975.

———. *The Interpretation of Dreams*. Trans. J. Strachey. London: George Allen & Unwin, 1967.

Frye, Northrop. *Anatomy of Criticism*. Princeton: Princeton University Press, 1957.

Garner, Shirley Nelson, Claire Kahane, and Madelon Sprengnether. Eds. *The (M)other Tongue*. Ithaca: Cornell University Press, 1985.

Gasché, Rodolphe. "Of Aesthetic and Historical Determination." In *Post-Structuralism and the Question of History*, ed. Derek Attridge et al. Cambridge: Cambridge University Press, 1987.

———. "Preface." In Andrzej Warminski, *Readings in Interpretation*, ix–xxvi. Minneapolis: University of Minnesota Press, 1987.

Gay-Crosier, R. "*Orion aveugle* ou les configurations de serpent: la palette du verbe." *French Forum* 2 (1977): 168–73.

Gelley, Alexander. *Narrative Crossings: Theory and Pragmatics of Prose Fiction*. Baltimore: Johns Hopkins University Press, 1987.

Genette, Gérard. "Boundaries of Fiction," *New Literary History* 8 (1976–77): 1–13.

———. *Figures*. 3 vols. Paris: Seuil, 1966–75.

———. *Palimpsestes*. Paris: Seuil, 1982.

Goldman, Lucien. *Towards a Sociology of the Novel*. Trans. Alan Sheridan. London: Tavistock, 1975.

Golopentia-Eretescu, Sanda. "Grammaire de la parodie." *Cahiers de linguistique théorique et appliquée* 6 (1969): 167–81.

Gossman, Lionel. "History and Literature: Reproduction and Signification." In *The Writing of History: Literary Form and Historical Understanding*, ed. Robert Canary and Henry Kozicki, 3–39. Madison: University of Wisconsin Press, 1978.

Gould, Eric. *Mythical Intentions in Modern Literature*. Princeton: Princeton University Press, 1981.

Gould, Karen L. *Claude Simon's Mythic Muse*. Columbia SC: French Literature, 1979.

Graves, Robert. *The Greek Myths*. Vol. 2. Baltimore: Penguin, 1960.

Guicharnaud, Jacques. "Remembrance of Things Passing." In *Claude Simon*, ed. Celia Britton, 27–34. New York: Longman, 1993.

Hamon, Philippe. *Introduction à l'analyse du descriptif*. Paris: Hachette, 1981.

Haraway, Donna. *Simians, Cyborgs, and Women: The Reinvention of Nature*. New York: Routledge, 1991.

Hassan, Ihab. *The Postmodern Turn: Essays in Postmodern Theory and Culture*. Columbus: Ohio State University Press, 1987.

Heath, Stephen. *The Nouveau Roman: A Study in the Practice of Writing*. Philadelphia: Temple University Press, 1972.

Heidegger, Martin. "The Question Concerning Technology." In *The Question Concerning Technology and Other Essays*, trans. William Lovitt, 3–35. New York: Harper & Row, 1977.

Higgins, Lynn A. "Gender and War Narrative in *La Route des Flandres*." *L'Esprit Créatur* 27 (1987): 17–26. Reprinted in *Claude Simon*, ed. Celia Britton, 204–13. New York: Longman, 1993.

Hollier, Denis, ed. *A New History of French Literature*. Cambridge: Harvard University Press, 1989.

Hutcheon, Linda. *Narcissistic Narrative: The Metafictional Paradox*. London: Methuen, 1984.

———. *A Poetics of Postmodernism: History, Theory, Fiction*. New York: Routledge, 1988.

———. *A Theory of Parody: The Teachings of Twentieth-Century Art Forms*. London: Methuen, 1985.

Irigaray, Luce. *This Sex Which Is Not One*. Trans. Catherine Porter with Carolyn Burke. Ithaca: Cornell University Press, 1985.

Iser, Wolgang. *The Act of Reading*. Baltimore: Johns Hopkins University Press, 1978.

Jameson, Fredric. *The Political Unconscious: Narrative as a Socially Symbolic Act*. Ithaca: Cornell University Press, 1980.

———. *Postmodernism, or, The Cultural Logic of Late Capitalism*. Durham: Duke University Press, 1991.

Janvier, Ludovic. *Une Parole exigeante: le nouveau roman*. Paris: Minuit, 1964.

Jauss, Hans Robert. *Toward an Aesthetics of Reception*. Trans. Timothy Bahti. Minneapolis: University of Minnesota Press, 1982.

Jefferson, Ann. *The Nouveau Roman and the Poetics of Fiction*. Cambridge: Cambridge University Press, 1980.

Jenny, Laurent. "Enonciations fictives. W. S. Burroughs," *Degrés* 26–27 (spring/summer 1981): j1–j11.

———. "La Stratégie de la forme," *Poétique* 27 (1976): 257–81.

Jost, François. "Claude Simon: Topographies de la description et du texte." *Critique* 330 (November 1974): 1031–40.

Kadish, Doris Y. *Practices of the New Novel in Claude Simon's "L'Herbe" and "La Route des Flandres."* Fredricton NB: York Press, 1979.

Kamuf, Peggy. *Fictions of Feminine Desire*. Lincoln: University of Nebraska Press, 1982.

Kermode, Frank. *The Sense of an Ending: Studies in the Theory of Fiction*. New York: Oxford University Press, 1967.

Kristeva, Julia. *Desire in Language: A Semiotic Approach to Literature and Art*. Ed. Léon S. Roudiez. New York: Columbia University Press, 1980.

Krysinski, W. "La 'Littérature' et le 'paralittéraire.' Fonctionnement de la citation et de l'objet chez John Dos Passos et Claude Simon." In *Carrefours de signes*, 295–311. The Hague: Mouton, 1981.

Lacan, Jacques. *Ecrits*. Paris: Seuil, 1966.

———. *The Four Fundamental Concepts of Psychoanalysis*. Ed. Jacques-Alain Miller and trans. Alan Sheridan. London: Hogarth, 1977.

Lacoue-Labarthe, Philippe. "La Fable (littérature et philosophie)." *Poétique* 1 (1970): 51–63.

Lanceraux, Dominique. "Modalités de la narration dans *La Route des Flandres*." *Poétique* 14 (1973): 235–49.

Lang, Candace D. *Irony/Humor: Critical Paradigms*. Baltimore: Johns Hopkins University Press, 1988.

Lévi-Strauss, Claude. *The Savage Mind*. Chicago: University of Chicago Press, 1966.

———. "The Structural Study of Myth." In *Myth: A Symposium*, ed. Thomas A. Sebeok, 81–106. Bloomington: Indiana University Press, 1974.

Lotringer, Sylvère. "Cryptique." In *Claude Simon: Analyse, théorie*, ed. Jean Ricordau, 313–33. Paris: U.G.E., 1975.

Lukács, Georg. "Narrate or Describe?" In *Writer and Critic and Other Essays*, ed. and tran. Arthur D. Kohn, 110–48. London: Merlin, 1970.

Lyotard, Jean-François. "Apathie dans la théorie." In *Rudiments païens*, 9–31. Paris: U.G.E., 1977.

———. *The Différend: Phrases in Dispute*. Trans. Georges van den Abbeele. Minneapolis: University of Minnesota Press, 1988.

———. *Des Dispositifs pulsionnels*. Paris: U.G.E., 1973.

———. *Instructions païennes*. Paris: Galilée, 1977.

———. *Peregrinations: Law, Form, Event*. New York: Columbia University Press, 1988.

———. "Philosophy and Painting in the Age of Their Experimentation: Contribution to an Idea of Postmodernity." Trans. Daniel Brewer and Mária Minich Brewer. In *The Lyotard Reader*, ed. Andrew Benjamin, 181–85. Oxford: Blackwell, 1989.

———. *The Postmodern Condition: A Report on Knowledge*. Trans. Geoff Bennington and Brian Massumi. Minneapolis: University of Minnesota Press, 1981.

———. and Jean-Loup Thébaud. *Just Gaming*. Trans. Wlad Godzich. Minneapolis: University of Minnesota Press, 1985.

McHale, Brian. *Postmodernist Fiction*. New York: Methuen, 1987.

Makward, Christiane. "Aspects of Bisexuality in Claude Simon's Works." In *Orion Blinded: Essays on Claude Simon,* ed. Randi Birn et al., 219–35. Lewisburg PA: Bucknell University Press, 1981.

———. "Earth, Death, and Eros." *Substance* 8 (winter 1974): 35–43.

Marin, Louis. "Représentation narrative." In *Encyclopedia Universalis.* Suppl. 2:241–43. Paris: Encyclopedia Universalis, 1980.

———. *Utopiques et jeux d'espaces.* Paris: Minuit, 1973.

Martin, Wallace. *Recent Theories of Narrative.* Ithaca: Cornell University Press, 1986.

Marx, Karl. *The Eighteenth Brumaire of Louis Bonaparte.* Trans. Daniel De Leon. Chicago: Charles H. Kerr, 1919.

Mauron, Charles. *Des Métaphores obsédantes au mythe personnel.* Paris: Corti, 1962.

Merleau-Ponty, Maurice. "Five Notes on Claude Simon." Trans. Celia Britton. In *Claude Simon,* ed. Celia Britton, 35–38. New York: Longman, 1993.

Miller, D. A. *Narrative and its Discontents: Problems of Closure in the Traditional Novel.* Princeton: Princeton University Press, 1981.

Miller, J. Hillis. "Ariadne's Thread: Repetition and the Narrative Line." In *Interpretation of Narrative,* ed. Owen J. Miller and Mario J. Valdés. Toronto: University of Toronto Press, 1976.

———. *The Ethics of Reading.* New York: Columbia University Press, 1987.

———. *Versions of Pygmalion.* Cambridge: Harvard University Press, 1990.

Miller, Nancy K., ed. *The Poetics of Gender.* New York: Columbia University Press, 1986.

Mink, Louis O. "Narrative Form as a Cognitive Instrument." In *The Writing of History: Literary Form and Historical Understanding,* ed. Robert H. Canary and Henry Kozicki, 129–49. Madison: University of Wisconsin Press, 1987.

Miró, Joan. *Selected Writings and Interviews,* ed. Margit Rowell and trans. Paul Auster and Patricia Mathews. Boston: G. K. Hall, 1986.

Mitchell, W. J. T., ed. *On Narrative.* Chicago: University of Chicago Press, 1981.

Mortier, Roland. "Discontinu et rupture dans *La Bataille de Pharsale.*" *Degrés* 2 (April 1973): c1–c6.

Mukařovský, Jan. *Aesthetic Function, Norm and Value as Social Facts.* Trans. Mark E. Suino. Ann Arbor: University of Michigan, 1970.

Neefs, Jacques. "Les Formes du temps dans *Les Géorgiques.*" *Littérature* 68 (1987): 119–28.

Neumann, Guy A. "Claude Simon et Michelet: Exemple d'intertextualité génératrice dans *Les Géorgiques*." *Australian Journal of French Studies* 24 (1987): 83–99.

———. *Echos et correspondances dans "Triptyque" et "Leçon de choses" de Claude Simon*. Lausanne: L'Age d'homme, 1983.

Norris, Christopher. *The Contest of Faculties: Philosophy and Theory after Deconstruction*. London: Methuen, 1985.

Oppenheim, Lois, ed. *Three Decades of the French New Novel*. Urbana: University of Illinois Press, 1986.

Paganini, Maria. *Reading Proust: In Search of the Wolf-Fish*. Trans. Karen Litherland. Minneapolis: University of Minnesota Press, 1994.

Pavel, Thomas. *Fictional Worlds*. Cambridge: Harvard University Press, 1986.

Phelan, James, ed. *Reading Narrative: Form, Ethics, Ideology*. Columbus: Ohio State University Press, 1989.

Prince, Gerald. "Introduction à l'étude du narrataire." *Poétique* 14 (1973): 178–96.

———. *Narratology: Form and Functioning in Narrative*. Berlin: Mouton, 1982.

Pugh, A. C. "Facing the Matter of History: *Les Géorgiques*." In *Claude Simon: New Directions*, ed. Alastair Duncan, 113–30. Edinburgh: Scottish Academic Press, 1985.

———. "From Drawing, to Painting, to Text: Claude Simon's Allegory of Representation and Reading in the Prologue to *Les Géorgiques*." *Review of Contemporary Fiction* 5 (spring 1985): 56–71.

———. *"Histoire" by Claude Simon*. London: Grant and Cutler, 1982.

Raillard, Georges. "Trois hautes fenêtres: Le document dans *Les Géorgiques* de Claude Simon." In *Romans d'archives*, ed. Raymonde Debray-Genette and Jacques Neefs, 137–74. Lille: Presses Universitaires de Lille, 1987.

Reading, Bill. "The Deconstruction of Politics." In *Reading de Man Reading*, ed. Lindsay Waters and Wlad Godzich, 223–43. Minneapolis: University of Minnesota Press, 1989.

Reitsma-La Brujeere, Cora. *Passé et présent dans "Les Géorgiques" de Claude Simon*. Amsterdam: Rodopi, 1992.

Ricardou, Jean, ed. *Claude Simon: Analyse, théorie*. Paris: U.G.E., 1975.

———. *Pour une théorie du nouveau roman*. Paris: Seuil, 1971.

———. *Problèmes du nouveau roman*. Paris: Seuil, 1967.

Ricoeur, Paul. "Entre temps et récit: concorde/discorde." In *L'Art des confins*, ed. Anne Casenave and Jean-François Lyotard, 253–63. Paris: Presses Universitaires de France, 1985.

———. *Oneself as Another.* Trans. Katherine Blamey. Chicago: University of Chicago Press, 1992.

———. *Time and Narrative.* 3 vols. Trans. Kathleen McLaughlin and David Pellauer. Chicago: University of Chicago Press, 1984–1988.

Riffaterre. Michael. *Text Production.* Trans. Terese Lyons. New York: Columbia University Press, 1983.

Righter, William. *Myth and Literature.* London: Routledge and Kegan Paul, 1975.

Rimmon-Kenan, Shlomith. *Narrative Fiction: Contemporary Poetics.* London: Methuen, 1983.

Robbe-Grillet, Alain. *Pour un nouveau roman.* Paris: Minuit, 1963.

———. *Le Voyeur.* Paris: Minuit, 1955.

Rorty, Richard. *Consequences of Pragmatism: Essays 1872–80.* Minneapolis: University of Minnesota, 1982.

Rose, Margaret. *Parody/Metafiction: An Analysis of Parody as a Critical Mirror to the Writing and Reception of Fiction.* London: Croom Helm, 1979.

Roubichou, Gérard. *Lecture de "L'Herbe" de Claude Simon.* Lausanne: L'Age d'homme, 1976.

Rousset, Jean. "*Histoire* de Claude Simon: le jeu des cartes postales." *Versants* 1 (1981): 121–33.

Said, Edward W. *Orientalism.* New York: Vintage, 1978.

Sarkonak, Ralph. *Claude Simon: Les Carrefours du texte.* Toronto: Les Editions du Paratexte, 1986.

———. "Un Drôle d'arbre: *L'Acacia* de Claude Simon." *Romanic Review* 82, no. 2 (March 1991): 210–32.

Sarraute, Nathalie. *L'Ere du soupçon.* Paris: Gallimard, 1956.

Sartre, Jean-Paul. *Situations.* Vol. 1. Paris: Gallimard, 1947.

Saussure, Ferdinand de. *Cours de linguistique générale.* Paris: Payot, 1967.

Scholes, Robert. *Semiotics and Interpretation.* New Haven: Yale University Press, 1982.

Schor, Naomi. *Reading in Detail: Aesthetics and the Feminine.* London: Methuen, 1987.

Sebeok, Thomas, ed. *Myth: A Symposium.* Bloomington: Indiana University Press, 1974.

Seylaz, Jean-Luc. "Du *Vent* à *La Route des Flandres*: La conquête d'une forme romanesque." *La Revue des Lettres Modernes* 94–99 (1964): 225–40.

Shapiro, Gary, ed. *After The Future: Postmodern Times and Places.* Albany: State University of New York Press, 1990.

Sherzer, Dina. *Representation in Contemporary French Fiction*. Lincoln: University of Nebraska Press, 1986.

———. "L'Ubiquité de la répétition dans *Les Géorgiques* de Claude Simon." *Neophilologus* 70 (1985): 372–80.

Simon, Claude. "Et à quoi bon inventer?" Trans. Annwyl Williams. In *Claude Simon*, ed. Celia Britton, 51–55. New York: Longman, 1993.

———. "La Fiction mot à mot." In *Nouveau roman: hier, aujourd'hui*, ed. Jean Ricardou, 2:73–97. Paris: U.G.E., 1972. Trans. Barbara Wright. Reprinted in *Claude Simon*, ed. Celia Britton, 41–45. New York: Longman, 1993.

———. "Qu'est ce que l'avant-garde en 1958?" *Les Lettres Françaises* 717 (24–30 April 1958) 1, 5.

———. "Roman, description et action." In *The Feeling for Nature and the Landscape of Man*, ed. Paul Hallberg. Göteborg: University of Göteborg, 1980.

———. "Roman et mémoire." *La Revue des Sciences Humaines* 220 (1990–94): n.p.

Sims, R. L. "Myth and History: Primordial Memory in Claude Simon's *La Route des Flandres*." *Nottingham French Studies* 17 (1979): 74–86.

Sivert, Eileen Boyd. "Permeable Boundaries and the Mother-Function in *L'Asphyxie*." *Tulsa Studies in Women's Literature* 11 (1992): 289–307.

Sophocles. *Oedipus the King*. Vol. 1 of *Sophocles*. Ed. David Green and Richard Lattimore. Chicago: University of Chicago Press, 1960.

———. *The Theban Plays*. Trans. E. F. Watling. Baltimore: Penguin, 1974.

Starobinski, Jean. "La Journée dans *Histoire*." In Jean Starobinski et al., *Sur Claude Simon*, 7–32. Paris: Minuit, 1987.

Sturgess, Philip. *Narrativity: Theory and Practice*. Oxford: Oxford University Press, 1992.

Suleiman, Susan Rubin. *Subversive Intent: Gender, Politics, and the Avant-Garde*. Cambridge: Harvard University Press, 1990.

Sykes, Stuart. *Les Romans de Claude Simon*. Paris: Minuit, 1979.

Thiher, Allen. *Words in Reflection: Modern Language Theory and Postmodern Fiction*. Chicago: University of Chicago Press, 1984.

Tiffeneau, Dorian, ed. *La Narrativité*. Paris: Editions du Centre National de la Recherche Scientifique, 1980.

Todorov, Tzvetan. *Poetics of Prose*. Trans. Richard Howard. Ithaca: Cornell University Press, 1977.

Tynianov, Iouri. "Destruction, parodie." *Change* 2 (1969): 67–76.

Valéry, Paul. *Oeuvres complètes*. Vol. 1. Paris: Gallimard, 1957.

Valette-Fondo, Madeleine. "L'Ordre descriptif dans *Les Corps conducteurs*." In *L'ordre du descriptif*, ed. Jean Bessière, 79–95. Paris: Presses Universitaires de France, 1988.

van Apeldoorn, J. *Pratiques de la description*. Amsterdam: Rodopi, 1982.

Van Buuren, Maarten. "L'Essence des choses: Etude de la description dans l'oeuvre de Claude Simon." *Poétique* 43 (September 1980): 324–33.

Van Rossum-Guyon, Françoise. "De Claude Simon à Proust: Un exemple d'intertextualité." *Les Lettres Nouvelles* 4 (September 1972): 107–37.

Vernant, Jean-Pierre. *Mythe et pensée chez les Grecs*. Vol. 1. Paris: Maspero, 1965.

Vidal, Jean-Pierre. "*Le Palace*, palais des mirages intestins ou l'auberge espagnole?" *Etudes littéraires* 9 (April 1976): 189–214.

———. "Les Travaux et les jours du déictique (*Les Géorgiques* de Claude Simon)." Paper delivered at the Claude Simon conference, Toronto, May 1988.

Virilio, Paul. *War and Cinema: The Logistics of Perception*. Trans. Patrick Camiller. London: Verso, 1989.

Waugh, Patricia. *Metafiction: The Theory and Practice of Self-Conscious Fiction*. London: Methuen, 1984.

Weinrich, Harald. "Structures narratives du mythe." *Poétique* 1 (1970): 25–34.

White, Hayden. *The Content of the Form: Narrative Discourse and Historical Representation*. Baltimore: Johns Hopkins University Press, 1987.

White, John J. *Mythology in the Modern Novel*. Princeton: Princeton University Press, 1971.

Whiteside, Anna, and Michael Issacharoff, eds. *On Referring in Literature*. Bloomington: Indiana University Press, 1987.

Woodhull, Winifred. "Reading Claude Simon: Gender, Ideology, Representation." *L'Esprit Créateur* 27 (winter 1987): 5–16.

Zeraffa, Michel. "Narrativité et textualité dans la fiction." *Revue d'esthétique* 2 (1974): 117–31.

Ziolkowsky, Theodore. "Hesse, Myth, and Reason: Methodological Prolegomena." In *Myth and Reason: A Symposium*, ed. Walter D. Wetzels, 127–55. Austin: University of Texas Press, 1973.

Zizek, Slavoj. *The Sublime Object of Ideology*. London: Verso, 1989.

Index

Abastado, Claude, 78, 156 n.9
L'Acacia, xii, 34, 37–38, 44, 58, 113–48
Adorno, Theodor, xx
Althusser, Louis, 150 n.17
Andrews, Mark, 105
antinarrative, xii, xix, xxiv–xxix, xxxiv
Aphrodite, 22–23
Atreus, 22
Austin, J. L., xxvii, 151 n.32
avant-garde, xix

Baehler, Aline, 105, 158 n.49 n.51
Bakhtin, Mikhail, 8–9, 12, 80–84, 87, 111, 156 n.24
Balzac, Honoré de, xxii, 141
Barthes, Roland, xxi, xxiv, xxxii, 12, 20, 23, 73–74
La Bataille de Pharsale, xii, 21, 23, 83, 92–97, 106, 144, 153 n.31, 158 n.37
Baudelaire, Charles, 155 n.16
Baudrillard, Jean, xxv, 99–101
Beckett, Samuel, xxii, 20
Benjamin, Walter, 95, 99, 100
Benveniste, Emile, 13

Brewer, Mária Minich, 150 n.21, 159 n.4
bricolage, 19–23, 137
Britton, Celia, xii, 53, 62–63, 149 n.1
Burden, Robert, 3
Burgin, Victor, 158 n.45

Carroll, David, 149 n.1, 154 n.9
Chambers, Ross, 150 n.21, 151 n.27
Chapsal, Madeleine, 157 n.31
La Chevelure de Bérénice, xii
Chronos, 6
Cohen, Keith, xv
cold war novel, xx
colonialism, 24, 125–27
Connor, Steven, 149 n.2, 155–56 n.8
La Corde raide, xiii, 2, 71–72
Coré, 23
Les Corps conducteurs, xii, 83, 97–107
cultural narratives, xiii–xix, xxviii–xxix, xxxii–xxxv, 28–29, 32–34, 51–58, 77–82, 84–88, 102–3, 106, 113–48
Cratylian, 53

Dällenbach, Lucien, 40–41, 62–64, 142–44, 149 n. 1, 159 n. 3
Debord, Guy, 73, 158 n. 45
de Certeau, Michel, 160 n. 8
deconstruction and narrative, xi, xxvi–xxix
Deguy, Michel, 149 n. 1
Dejaneira, 22
de Lauretis, Teresa, xv–xvi, xxxi–xxxii
Delcourt, Marie, 152 n. 28, 153 n. 40
de Man, Paul, xv
Derrida, Jacques, xxvi–xxvii, xxxii, 11, 70, 77, 111, 160 n. 7
de Saussure, Ferdinand, xxi
disaster, 66–68, 137–48
Le Discours de Stockholm, 149–50 n. 5, 157 n. 32
Dostoyevski, Fyodor, 8
Dragonetti, Roger, 142–43
Dubuffet, Jean, 44
Duffy, Jean, xvii, 158 n. 47
Duras, Marguerite, xxviii
DuVerlie, Claud, 150 n. 6

Eagleton, Terry, xv
Eliot, T. S., 31, 145–46
epic, xxv
epistemology, xx, xxix
Erlich, Victor, 156 n. 13

fable, xxi
Faulkner, William, 7
Faure, Elie, 96–97, 144
feminist criticism, xviii, xxiii, xxix, 31–32
feminization, 128–30
fiction: "cold-war," xxii; generated by language, xii
fictive, disappearance of the, xiv
Flaubert, Gustave, 74, 84
Fletcher, John, 155 n. 3

Foucault, Michel, xx, xxxiii, 155 n. 1, 159 n. 5
Freud, Sigmund, 51, 95
Frye, Northrop, 152 n. 20

Gasché, Rodolphe, 150 n. 20, 155 n. 17
Gelley, Alexander, 151 n. 29, 152 n. 3
gender, xviii, xxix
general theory, xvii
Genette, Gérard, xxvi
Les Géorgiques, xii, 24, 34, 37–38, 42, 58–71, 85, 94, 106–7, 111, 119, 130, 143
Godzich, Wlad, in Coste, 150 n. 23
Golopentia-Eretescu, Sanda, 156 n. 9
Gould, Eric, 152 n. 24
Gould, Karen L., 153 n. 43
Graves, Robert, 152 n. 29
Greek myths, 16
Greek tragedy, 6, 14, 15
Greene, Graham, 96
Greimas, A. J., xv

Hamon, Philippe, xxvi, 151 n. 26
Hassan, Ihab, 74, 155 n. 3
Heidegger, Martin, 94, 151 n. 37, 158 n. 39
L'Herbe, xvii, 2, 21, 24, 34–35, 38, 84, 89, 107, 119, 153 n. 39
hermeneutics, xv, xix, xxx–xxxi, 2
Higgins, Lynn A., 150 n. 13, 154 n. 4
Histoire, xii, xvii, 21, 23–24, 34, 37–38, 44, 45–58, 83, 90–92, 94, 106–7, 115, 120, 145, 154 n. 12
history, xi–xix, xx–xxi, 20–24, 31–34, 109–11, 135; cyclical, 62–65
Hutcheon, Linda, 79–80, 90, 149 n. 3

ideology, xii–xiv, xvii, xx
interdisciplinarity and narrative, xxx
intertextuality, xxii
Irigaray, Luce, 11

irony, 73–76

Jameson, Fredric, xii, xxv, 19, 73–77, 83–84, 102, 149 n.3, 157 n.27
Jenny, Laurent, 149 n.1, 158 n.38
Jost, François, 154 n.8
Joyce, James, 20

Kristeva, Julia, xxxii, 80

Lacan, Jacques, xxiii, 11
Lacoue-Labarthe, Philippe, 152 n.13
"La fiction mot à mot," 149 n.4 n.5, 153 n.36
Laius, 18
La Jalousie, xviii
Lang, Candace D., 155 n.4
Lanzmann, Claude, *(Shoah)*, 160 n.8
Larousse, 83, 89
Leçon de choses, xii, 83, 97, 106, 159 n.52
Leda, 22
legacy, xviii, xxiv, 31–39, 43–47, 54–58, 65–72, 114–20, 141, 147–48; and law, 69–70; and time, 66–72; and women, 35–37, 47, 61–62, 65–66
Lévi-Strauss, Claude, 5, 12–13, 20
L'Invitation, xii
literature, xi, xii, xvi
Livy, 94
Louis XVI (Louis Hugues), 69–70
Lucan, 94
Lukács, Georg, xxv, 150 n.24
Lyotard, Jean-François, xxxii, xxxiii, 1–2, 26, 28, 74, 76, 87, 154 n.2, 159–60 n.6, 160 n.12

Macherey, Pierre, xv
Makward, Christiane, 153 n.43
Mallarmé, Stephane, 20
Marin, Louis, 15, 152 n.27

Márquez, Gabriel García, 75
Mars, 22
Martin, Wallace, 156 n.20
Marx, Karl, xv, 110, 159 n.55
master narratives, xvii, xviii, 109, 113; denaturalization of, xx; waning of, xxxiii, 1, 31
McHale, Brian, 149 n.2
"Medusa's Head, The," 95
memory traces, 21
Mercury, 18
metafiction, xvi; reflexive, xxii
metanarrative, xxiv
metaphor, xvi, xvii
metaphorical nature of language, xiii
metonymy, xxvi
micronarratives, xxxiv
microtextual, xiii, xv
Miller, D. A., xv
Miller, J. Hillis, xv, xxviii, 154 n.12
mimetic representation, xix
Mink, Louis O., 150 n.22
Miró, Joan, 160 n.13
mise en abîme, 25, 85
mobilization, xvii, xiii, xxix, 113–48
modernist, xi–xii, 28, 145–46
Mortier, Roland, 157 n.34
myth, xiv, 2, 10–25; narrativity of, 23–25; and parody, 22–24; and woman, 22–23
mythological discourse, xxiv

narrativity, xii–xix, xxii–xxx, xxxii–xxxv, 56–58, 87, 114, 121, 124–27, 133–34, 144, 146–48; and time, 61, 66–72; without narrative, xi–xix, xxviii, xxxv, 56–58, 102–7
narratology, xx, xxi, xxvi
Nietzsche, Friedrich, 45, 155 n.1
nonnarrative, xix, xxiv, xxvii
Norris, Christopher, 150 n.16

Oedipus, 16–18, 41, 43–44, 52–53, 78, 116, 140
Oedipus At Colonus, 16
Oedipus Rex, 14, 16, 153 n.30
Ollier, Claude, xxiii
Orestes, 18
Orion, 17
Orion aveugle, xii, 137, 153 n.31
Orwell, George, 61

Le Palace, 37, 44, 89–90, 107, 110
parody, xiv, xix, 73–111; and formalism, 78; and myth, 22–24; and postmodernity, 73–80
Pasternak, Boris, 35
pastiche, xii, 75, 102
performative, xxvii, xxviii
permutations of narrative, xxiii, 42–44, 76–77, 87–88
phallogocentrism, xvii, xxviii
phenomenology, xvii, xi
Pinget, Robert, xxiii
Pleynet, Marcellin, 74
Plutarch, 94
pornography, xvii, xviii, 139–40
postmodern, xi–xvi, xviii, xx, xxiii–xxiv, xxix, xxxiii, 25–29, 146–48; crises of the, xix; fiction, xi, xxii, xxvi, xxv, xxix, 31–32; rejection of narrative, xix, xxiv
poststructural, xviii
Prince, Gerald, xv, 150 n.18
Proust, Marcel, 20, 96, 154 n.13, 157 n.36
psychoanalytic, xvii, xviii
Pugh, A. C., 159 n.53
Pynchon, Thomas, xi, 75

Reading, Bill, 151 n.36
reference, referentiality, xvi, xxii, xxiv
reflexive turn, xxvi

replication, 77, 83–92, 108–11
revolution, 52–57, 88–90, 110–11
Ricardou, Jean, xii, 23, 83, 149 n.1, 157 n.35
Ricoeur, Paul, xxiii, xxx–xxxi, 154 n.1
Righter, William, 152 n.24
Rimmon-Kenan, Shlomith, xv, xxvii
Robbe-Grillet, Alain, xviii, 8, 152 n.9
Rorty, Richard, 152 n.4
Rose, Margaret, 155 n.1, 157 n.33
Roubichou, Gérard, 2
Rousseau, Jean-Jacques, 107–8
Rousset, Jean, 154 n.8
La Route des Flandres, 22–24, 34, 37–45, 86–88, 107, 114–17, 130, 140
Russian formalist, 78

Le Sacre du printemps, 114
Sarkonak, Ralph, 52
Sarraute, Nathalie, xx
Scholes, Robert, xv
Schor, Naomi, 82, 157 n.26
self-reflexivity, xxii
Shakespeare, William, 7
Sherzer, Dina, 151 n.25
sign, arbitrary nature of the, xxi
Sims, R. L., 153 n.41
simulacrum, xvii–xviii, xxiv, xxv, xxix, 54, 70, 77, 83, 98–104
Sophocles, 14, 16, 153 n.30
Spanish Revolution, 28, 54–57
Sphinx, 17, 91
structuralism, xiv, xx–xxi, xxvii
Sturgess, Philip, xv, 150 n.9
subjectivity, xvi, xix, xx, xxi
Suleiman, Susan Rubin, 74, 150 n.14

technology, xi, xiv, xxiv, xxix–xxx, 32, 113–14, 122, 125, 135–36, 147–48
temporality, xix, xxi, 6
textuality, xii, xvi

Thébaud, Jean-Loup, 76
Thiher, Allen, 156–57 n.25
Tiresias, 18
Tournier, Michel, xxiii
Le Tricheur, 47
Triptyque, xii, 83, 97, 101, 104–6
truth, xix, 11–13
Tynianov, Iouri, 78
Typhon, 6

universal: subject, xix; narrative order, xi, xiv, xx, xxiv

Valéry, Paul, 4–5, 11–12
Van Rossum-Guyon, Françoise, 158 n.41
Le Vent, xii, 2–29, 32–33, 83–86, 114
Venus-Aphrodite, 22
Vernant, Jean-Pierre, 152 n.11
Vidal, Jean-Pierre, 154–55 n.14
Virilio, Paul, 135–36, 160 n.11

Le Voyeur, xviii, 8

war, xiii–xiv, xviii, xx, 38–43, 62–65, 114–48
Waugh, Patricia, 154 n.1
Weinrich, Harald, 152 n.13
White, Hayden, xv, xxx, 151 n.40
White, John J., 152 n.23
women: and agency, xvii, 61–62, 65–66; cultural figuration of, xviii; and ideological mobilization, 119–30, 139; and legacy, 43–44, 47–54, 57; and mobilization, 119–30; and myth, 22–23; and parody, 84–86, 102–6; and war, 43–44
Woodhull, Winifred, 150 n.13
World War I, 48, 113, 115, 124, 128, 133
World War II, xiii, xx, 28, 114, 129, 133

Ziolkowsky, Theodore, 152 n.17